Praise for the Pedestriennes...

"...spellbinding...."

Dick Beardsley, motivational speaker, 2:08 marathoner, co-author of "Staying the Course, a Runner's Toughest Race," activist for Dick Beardsley Foundation

"That women were front and center of such a grueling sport at a time when they couldn't even vote makes for a fascinating story."

Kara Thom, author, "Becoming an Ironman: First Encounters of the Ultimate Endurance Event."

"...an absorbing account of the redoubtable women walkers..."

Edward S. Sears, author of "Running Through the Ages"

"Harry Hall has done a remarkable job writing a complete history of this forgotten part of American history. Each page is inspirational and fascinating."

Francie Larrieu Smith, five-time Olympian, Head Men's and Women's Cross-Country and Track and Field Coach, Southwestern University

"Harry Hall has struck gold with this story of a nearly forgotten sport. It's written with a fine sense of putting readers in the arena..."

John Darrouzet, co-writer and producer of "The Contract," starring Morgan Freeman and John Cusack.

The foreward is written by Ben Montgomery, enterprise writer for the *Tampa Bay Times*. Montgomery is a Pulitzer Prize finalist, winner of the Dart Award and Casey Medal, and author of "Grandma Gatewood's Walk: The Inspiring Story of the Woman who Saved the Appalachian Trail."

Capt. Bobbie Willis

The Pedestriennes
America's Forgotten Superstars

Congratulations on a
Tremondous career &
Life

Harry Hall

Harry
Hall

Photo Cover credits:
Upper left Exilda LaChapelle
Upper right Fannie Edwards
Both courtesy of Bancroft Library Univ. CA Berkeley

First published by Dog Ear Publishing
4010 W. 86th Street, Ste H
Indianapolis, IN 46268
www.dogearpublishing.net

dog ear
PUBLISHING

ISBN: 978-1-4575-3429-4

Library of Congress Control Number: has been applied for

This book is printed on acid-free paper.

Printed in the United States of America

For Gerry and Charlotte Curtis

Acknowledgments

I used to read author acknowledgments and wonder, "How can so many be involved in writing a book?"

Now I know. Because writing a book can take years requiring dozens of mentors, teachers, and encouragers.

I probably would have never pursued this project if not for my decades-long passion for distance running, which has taught me many lessons about discipline, myself and life; goal setting and bouncing back from disappointment.

Running led me to writing. In the late '80s, I wanted to break into journalism. So I approached Kathleen Stockmier, then editor of *The Las Colinas People*, about covering   health/fitness and amateur athletics for them. Many times, my only pay was Kathleen critiquing my work and giving me pointers on how to improve.

In many ways, those lessons proved far more valuable than any monetary reward.

Writing for *LCP* proved a remarkable experience. In those days, Las Colinas hosted all forms of high-profile professional and amateur athletic contests. I covered the *Byron Nelson Golf Tournament* and numerous charity tennis events. During those years, I met and interviewed several top-named athletes, including Nick Price, Pete Sampras, Jim Courier and Martina Navratilova.

I spent the next few years building my resume at publications such as *SportsPulse*, *The Burb*, *Runner-Triathlete News*, *DFW Suburban Newspapers*, and *The Wylie News*, where I worked for and learned from: Kirby Warnock, Marie Raym, and Chad Engbrock. Since 1990, I've written for various renditions of Texas Runner-Triathlete News, reporting to Lance Phegley, who has become more of a friend than an editor.

In 2004, I began freelancing at *The Dallas Morning News*.

There, mostly through editors Hector Cantu and Jennifer Okamoto, I wrote longer pieces, including features on people such as Chuck Norris and Robin Roberts.

Like many writers who have worked at their craft for years, I longed to write a book. I spent months looking and researching and finally decided to do one on the history of American women distance runners. Wanting to discover the real roots of women's competitive distance running, I found a book at SMU called, *Runners and Walkers: a 19ᵗʰ Century Sports Chronicle*. About halfway down page 102, author John Cumming, in an almost throwaway line, mentioned how in 1879, a "Madame Anderson" walked 2,700 quarter miles in 2,700 hours (it was actually quarter-hours). He then mentioned a half-dozen or so other "pedestriennes" with similar and sometimes even greater accomplishments.

I was hooked.

I took some notes, logged on the internet, punched in "pedestriennes," and predictably, found little.

But I did run across a 1999 research piece by Dahn Shaulis titled, "Pedestriennes: Newsworthy but Controversial Women in Sporting Entertainment." At the end, he acknowledged the assistance of: Ed Sears, David Blaikie, Peter Lovesey, and Cumming. Shaulis followed that with more than 100 citations, mostly newspaper clippings. I read the 17 page document over and over, trying to grasp the tenor.

In August, 2003, I made my first of five trips to the Library of Congress which was only a few miles from my brother's home in Virginia. I stayed with him and his wife each time. Without the hospitality of Monte and Beth Hall, this book would have been a much bigger challenge.

During my second visit I found a *Washington Post* article, titled, "Attempt to Burn Women's Home," which told of attempts to destroy the home of playwright Emma Howard Wight and one-time pedestrienne turned painter, Bertha von Hillern. The two most significant elements to the story were 1). The date, October 24, 1910 was the most recent I'd found on any researched pedestriennes by 20 years and 2). The incident took place in Winchester, VA, only about 70 miles from where I stood. The next day, I took what little info I had to the *Winchester Star* newspaper, where reporter FC Lowe wrote a story titled, "Author Chases Ghosts."

A week later, I received an e-mail from Charlotte Curtis, great-granddaughter of pedestrienne May Marshall (whose real name was Tryphena Curtis). She told me she and her sister Gerry, had a scrapbook chronicling their great-grandmother's accomplishments. We met several months later in Winchester and traded information. Virtually none of it duplicated. I had all the big publications from Washington, New York, Philadelphia and Chicago. The scrapbook was comprised almost totally of New Bedford, Lowell, and Taunton (MA). They also had a couple of faded photographs, a copy of a program, and other artifacts I wouldn't have found any other way.

Romance novelist LaRee Bryant walked me through the early stages with the book. From there I joined the Tejas Writers Group and later, DFW Writers Workshop, where I got dozens of weekly critiques from capable writers, most notably Daryle McGinnis, who must have heard and read this book, or at least a version of it a dozen times. Additionally, Del Cain probably still has a wet shoulder from me crying on it as I made which was for me, the painful struggle to morph from newspaper reporter and feature writer to storyteller.

Though my work improved, agents said time and again, "We like the story, but your writing is lacking."

Marissa Alanis put me in touch with George Getschow, writer-in-residence at the University of North Texas. More than 10 years ago, George founded the "Mayborn Literary Nonfiction Conference" and with his vision and passion, turned it into the largest non-fiction writer's conference in the country. With his encouragement, I took some grad j-school classes at UNT, and my skills improved. Those teachers and classmates pushed me to yet another level. Most notable was an eight-day excursion to Archer City, Texas, where classmates and I experienced the thrill of interviewing literary legend Larry McMurty and learning from master storyteller Bill Marvel. Another class required me to fly to Atlanta and spend two days with *Sports Illustrated* senior writer Tom Lake, who showed me how to dig for details. The list of those who helped is only getting started. Special thanks to Winchester, VA librarian Rebecca Ebert. Joy Holland of the Brooklyn Library, who introduced me to Cezar Del Valle, who shared his immense knowledge of the history of the Brooklyn theatre. To Mary Leb of the Fond du Lac Library for finding valuable background info on Exilda La Chapelle. For the encouragement of my brother Mitch and Debbie Hall. For writing a fine foreward, Ben Montgomery. And thanks to Barbara Henry, who gave me insights into the life of her great-grandfather, sports promoter Mike Henry.

And so many others contributed in various ways.

The late Steve Orthwein, Fred Campos, Theresa Smart, Cindy Dawn McCallum, Mitch Haynes, Heather Whiteside, Bob Ganley, the good folks at Dog Ear Publishing, Tony and Karen Chu, the members of Irving Toastmasters, some of whom spent years listening to speeches on the pedestriennes; Mike McGee, researchers Janice Todd and Paul DeLoca; Dick Beardsley, Francie Larrieu Smith, Tess Klimm, Tracy Sundlin, Kara Thom, Dr. Randy Miller, Janell Stadler Ridenour, Kristin Breckenridge, John Darrouzet, Dave Kelly at the Library of Congress; the Librarians at Texas

Women's University, my training partners from the MetroPlex, specifically Clyde and Beca DeLoach, Ted Melton, Clayton Duff, and Mike Snow, members of the Dallas Press Club, my classmates at UNT. And thanks to the Men's Bible Study at Pkymouth Park Baptist Church for their prayers and encouragement.

Most of all, thanks to my wife Susie and my son Zane, who put up with my frustrations and sacrificed more than I can imagine while I spent more than 10 years pursuing this dream. You are the best.

Foreword

I'm glad you're holding this book.

I'm glad because there are a million ways it could've never happened.

In my experience, there are two ways in which books come to be, and neither of them are pretty. The first and most common book-birthing process goes like this: An established writer goes fishing for an idea, lands on something meaty and has an agent shop it around to publishing houses. Then, if one bites, if the story is good enough and the audience is predictable, it's off to the races.

Far less common is Harry Hall's experience: A good idea finds a man, latches its tentacles around that man's mind and doesn't let him go. This man must learn to write, learn to report, learn to dig up dusty documents. He goes back to school late in life to hone his skill. He faces down discouragement, loses artistic sensitivity, turns criticism into fire.

And in the end, he puts down on paper one word at a time until the idea that captured him is ready to share. He invests his own money to make it a reality. All of this takes twelve years.

Twelve. Think about that.

I met Harry at a journalism conference in Texas, and I could see his excitement for this project from the start. He has found a heretofore untold story about a group of women who were the most celebrated athletes of their day. The Pedestriennes.

Long before football, before even baseball, Americans enjoyed watching people walk. Really.

You can't imagine that? That thousands would pack stadiums to the rafters, would pay hard-earned money for tickets, to spend hours watching men and women saunter in circles?

It happened, short-lived though it was. "Pedestrian Fever," the *New York Times* called it.

And thanks to Harry, we now know the untold story of the women who made fame and money out walking. It doesn't sound like much, but these were great displays of determination and human endurance — complete with blisters and twitchy legs and utter exhaustion — and they captured the attention of a nation on the verge of massive and rapid change in how people got from Point A to Point B.

Anthropologists estimate that man relied primarily on bipedal locomotion for six millions years, and that early man walked some 20 miles a day. Mental and physical benefits were attributed to walking as far back as ancient times. A prominent Greek writer named Pliny the Elder (23-79 A.D.) described walking as one of the "Medicines of the Will." Hippocrates, the Greek physician, called walking "man's best medicine" and prescribed walks to treat emotional problems, hallucinations and digestive disorders. Aristotle lectured while strolling.

Through the centuries, the best thinkers, writers and poets extolled the virtues of walking. Leonardo da Vinci designed elevated streets to protect walkers from cart traffic. Johann Sebastian Bach walked 200 miles to hear a master play the organ.

William Wordsworth was said to have walked 180,000 miles in his lifetime. Charles Dickens captured the ecstasy of near-madness and insomnia in *Night Walks* and once said, "The sum of the whole is this: Walk and be happy; Walk and be healthy." Robert Louis Stevenson wrote of "the great fellowship of the Open Road" and the "brief but priceless meetings which only trampers know." Friedrich Wilhelm Nietzsche said, "Only those thoughts that come by walking have any value."

But by the 1870s, things were changing — and fast. Americans would soon overwhelmingly choose to sit and ride rather than walk. The automobile was born in 1880s. As the celebrated pedestriennes walked circles in sawdust, men were busting their knuckles building the Benz Patent-Motorwagen and the Daimler Stahlradwagen, the crude predecessors of the iconic Ford Model T (circa 1908) which would reshape the country and usher in decades of roads-building.

Few saw it coming. Henry David Thoreau was one of them.

In June 1862 *Atlantic Monthly* published one of Thoreau's most famous essays, "Walking," in which he preached the virtues of communing with Nature on foot. His goal was sauntering, a word derived from the wanderers who roamed in the Middle Ages, living off charity under the pretense of going *a la sainte terre*, to the Holy Land.

Thoreau's essay reads like prophecy.

At present, in this vicinity, the best part of the land is not private property; the landscape is not owned, and the walker enjoys comparative freedom. But possibly the day will come when it will be partitioned off into so-called pleasure-grounds, in which a few will take a narrow and exclusive pleasure only, when fences shall be multiplied, and man-traps and other engines invented to confine men to the public road, and walking over the surface of

God's earth shall be construed to mean trespassing on some gentleman's grounds. To enjoy a thing exclusively is commonly to exclude yourself from the true enjoyment of it. Let us improve our opportunities, then, before the evil days are upon us.

Thoreau's man-traps would soon be ubiquitous. In that light, the achievements of the pedestriennes — and the frenzy they incited — seems like one last, fitting hurrah to the art, dignity and triumph of walking. That's worth remembering. Celebrating, even.

— Ben Montgomery, Tampa, Fla., June 16, 2014

Introduction

"Why hasn't more been written about the pedestriennes?"

I'm frequently asked that question, and over the last several years, I've given it a lot of thought. After all, for more than 125 years, with the exception of a handful of research papers, an occasional article, or mention in a book, the pedestriennes' story has gone pretty much untold.

Pedestrienne anonymity comes down to many factors, far more than could be listed here, but I've come up with three major ones.

One, the early 1880s public soured on the athletes. Major papers chronicled their failures, which left even die-hard fans shocked. The early successes of May Marshall, Bertha von Hillern and Madame Anderson gave many mostly immigrant women false hope about their own chances for success. The professional pedestriennes employed capable support staffs, got constant medical attention, and most importantly, were trained as athletes. The desperate amateur hopefuls, stepped onto tracks just thinking they were out for a stroll, then quickly discovered the overwhelming strains of their tasks. After just a few days, or even hours, the exhaustion, overtaxed muscles, dehydration, blisters, and loneliness all became their constant companions. They had neither the mental or physical training to live the brutal life of a professional athlete.

Two, the pedestriennes' faddish popularity only lasted a few years. The first race took place in Chicago in 1876, a six-day contest between May Marshall and Bertha von Hillern. While the sport's demise is a bit harder to define, a case could be made that it ended in San Francisco in 1881, giving only five years as a frame of reference. It would have required far more time to build a big and enduring following or develop a nostalgic background for a fan base that was already losing interest in it.

Three, the sport lacks detailed written accounts of the athletes' accomplishments. Writing gives credibility and permanency. When the pedestriennes' names faded from the headlines, so did many of their stories. The "inside information" that could have revealed insights into their personalities and what drove them wasn't popularized and is now gone forever.

On a personal note, that presented a slight problem for me as an author. Although the era's newspaper writing exhibited a flashier style than today's "facts only" reporting, they still often omitted details that add color necessary for scene creation. In rare moments, I had to do some "literary painting" to add life to an otherwise flat moment.

Unlike the women the men, especially Daniel O'Leary and Edward Payson Weston enjoyed decades of celebrity. Therefore, a handful of writers recorded their successes and struggles. It wasn't much, but we do have details of their lives on paper. However, because of the times, the women lacked the staying power of the men. With only limited written records, the significance of the women's achievements was destined to fall into obscurity.

But the time has come for recognition of the pedestriennes and their fledgling steps toward modern society.

And that was my intention in this book, to tell the complete story of the pedestriennes.

CHAPTER 1

Madame Anderson's Grand Appearance

At precisely 7:45 p.m. December 16, 1878, "Captain" Alexander Samuells led "Madame" Ada Anderson into Brooklyn's Mozart Garden and across the tan-bark covered oval track. An 18-inch high railing circled the outer edge. Several hundred chairs filled the infield. Since opening the previous August, Mozart Garden had proven a financial success, becoming one of the big attractions in Brooklyn's vibrant Fulton St. entertainment district. AR, as Samuells was called, had ensured that his next event would keep it that way. Newly installed gas lamps illuminated the arena, their smoke rising to the ceiling, which was designed to resemble the sky. Madame tried to ignore the upgrades. She'd only performed indoors once before, and it had resulted in failure and humiliation, nearly ending her career. She vowed to never perform indoors again. But circumstances forced her to renege on that plan.

She averted her eyes and quickly refocused to the painted landscape adorning the stage, located on the Garden's wide east wall where a brass band awaited the cue that would begin a four-hour concert.

At 7:50 they began playing a medley of popular numbers, "Pretty as a Picture," "Way Down Upon the Sewanee River," and an almost comical selection in light of the evening's headlining act, "Don't Get Weary."

The music brought the moment home, uplifting her spirits. Her heart pounded. Thrilled by all the attention, she almost basked in the moment. She had embraced the stage even before she left home at age 16 to pursue an acting career. But nearly 20 years later she had enjoyed little more than marginal success. She had to travel across the Atlantic Ocean to hopefully achieve her lifelong goal, the one she had fantasized about since growing up in Lambeth, England.

Now she faced her big moment.

Performing on stage in America.

It didn't seem possible.

1

At 7:55, Madame and AR took the stage near the band. Two minutes later a warning bell would sound, signaling that she had three minutes before commencing her quest.

The arena was half-filled with 400 or so patrons consisting of local politicians, theatrical luminaries, followers of pedestrianism, a handful of "sporting men," who, sensing a potentially big payday, gave favorable odds to most anyone who would take a bet against her.

AR could feel the excitement, too. While Mozart Garden often featured headliners, it had fallen short of his high expectations. AR didn't build the structure merely to dominate Brooklyn's nightlife. He'd set his sights on challenging the popularity of the theatre-rich area of New York. He specifically stated in the *Brooklyn Daily Eagle* that Mozart would challenge the open air of Gilmore's Garden. In late 1877, Gilmore's completed a remarkable run of six weeks with PT Barnum's Greatest Show on Earth. In no way could Mozart compete with such a spectacle, but AR would hear nothing of it. He believed in Brooklyn, in his arena, and most of all, in himself. He had a marvelous eye for talent, but headlining an unknown, unproven female attraction could sink him and his new arena. His motives went beyond a potentially big payday. He saw this as an opportunity to finally top William Vanderbilt, the owner of Gilmore's. Vanderbilt turned down Anderson's request to perform there. Vanderbilt, by virtue of being the oldest son of transportation magnate Commodore Cornelius Vanderbilt, inherited virtually all of his father's incredible fortune of more than $100 million. He had more money than many governments, but he, like AR, felt an attraction to the glamorous world of show business. AR's wealth had peaked at $250,000, with most earnings coming from an oyster bar and popular billiards hall. No matter how great his success, however, he could never approach his rival in money or name recognition.

He hoped that Madame Anderson could at least temporarily narrow the financial and popularity chasm between the two.

She smiled at the large number of women seated throughout Mozart Garden. Brooklyn residents were seeing this woman for the first time. So much had been written and discussed about her since she and her entourage arrived on the steamship *Ethiopia* the previous October. To some she was a curiosity, to others a fraud. For the hardcore aficionados, she represented a hope of reinvigorating a sport that was clearly dying.

Madame Anderson was a pedestrienne, a professional female endurance walker.

She stood but five-foot-one, with grayish-blue eyes, a short nose, and a low forehead with straight eyebrows. But her most striking characteristic was her muscular build, a "chiseled physique" of about 140 pounds. One paper commented, "She should have been born a man."

She had heard that criticism during her entire 20-year acting career in her native Britain, so she did her best to project a softer, more feminine image. She wore a red and white striped tunic, and pink tights. A blue and scarlet cap trimmed with white lace and a dainty feather covered her dark hair, which cascaded down her back in a braid. She held a riding crop in her hand, a typical accessory for the era's female walkers. She hoped colorful outfits and frequent costume changes would keep women talking and coming to see her perform. Her efforts seemed to be working. The *New York Herald* would report, "There is nothing unwomanly about her appearance."

The only exception to her feminine persona was a stout pair of boot-like laced walking shoes she had worn for the many European endurance walking exploits.

AR announced some of her walking feats to the attentive crowd: one-thousand half-miles walked in 1,000 half hours at Cymbrian Gardens, an accomplishment that took just under three weeks to finish; 1,008 miles in 672 hours, a full four-week trek. That walk beat the performance of endurance walking standard-bearer Captain Barclay Allardice at Newmarket in 1809. It put Madame Anderson among the top walkers of any generation, male or female.

But it also proved a brutal physical ordeal. Afterward, her feet were so swollen attendants bathed them in turpentine and wrapped them in raw beef.

AR said completing the task was less about remuneration and more about the promotion and encouragement of physical health among women and children. The advancements of the Industrial Revolution, which had provided an improved lifestyle and conveniences for millions, had a downside: The more convenient and sedentary lifestyle was devastating Americans' health.

He further stated that for the month to come, she would subsist only on "rare beefsteak, roast beef and mutton, a little beef tea, and port wine and champagne, and would take no pork or veal."

After finishing his introduction, AR made a formal proclamation about her goal at Mozart Garden: to walk 2,700 quarter miles in 2,700 quarter hours around the track that measured 188.57 feet. She would need seven laps to the quarter mile. If successful, she would total 18,900 laps, 37,800 turns, 675 miles, approximately the distance between Chicago and Baltimore. She would finish at 11:00 p.m., January 14, 1879, 28 days, three hours from now.

The Brooklyn surveyor's certification was critical to the event's success.

Both men's and women's pedestrian tournaments were fraught with frauds, con artists and unprofessional behavior. In lesser contests, track distances were estimated or allowances made for unusual circumstances. One promoter, upon "discovering" post-event that his square-shaped track measured short, justified the discrepancy by claiming the athlete received lap credits for "having to negotiate so many ninety degree turns."

A 12 x 28 foot tent stood 28 feet outside the track (which could be used for official distance, if needed) would be her temporary home for the next four weeks.

Along the way she would be monitored by doctors, nurses and other assistants, most notably a woman named Elizabeth Sparrow, who helped Madame with most of her successful walks in Europe.

AR had enlisted Mike Henry, Brooklyn's highly respected sports promoter, to maintain order. Henry had a strong athletic background, especially in baseball and boxing. His name and presence brought much needed credibility to the event. No legitimate sporting event in Brooklyn happened without his blessing. His six-foot, four-inch frame commanded respect, which served him well when he worked as a jailer. AR and J. W. Webb, Madame Anderson's agent, were listed as meet co-directors. Architect and race starter Fred Coles would act as supervisor to timekeepers Charles "C.B." Hazelton and George W. Force. Judges would record distances and verify every quarter mile with each signing his own log book.

As independent insurance of what she called her "honest work," reporters from the *New York Times, Brooklyn Daily Eagle* and the *New York Herald* would each take an eight-hour shift, recording times and distances until she finished or couldn't continue.

*   *   *

AR drew wild cheers as he concluded with his prediction that Madame Anderson would complete her journey.

After the applause died down, AR stepped back and motioned with a sweep of his arm. On cue, the pedestrienne stepped forward, smiling confidently.

In her English accent, she promised that for the next four weeks she would give all her strength and "nervous force" to complete her task. But she warned that her brain, heart or circulatory system could break down because of physical strain due to stress or lack of sleep.

Fans of pedestrianism were aware of the suffering. Papers often reported in graphic detail about the last stages of a grueling six-day "go as you please" format, in which the women managed their own walking, sleeping and breaks for nearly a week. Late in those contests they often doubled over with stomach cramps, experienced strange dreams, and had trouble keeping down even the most agreeable types of food. Opiates were often administered to calm them. They frequently dragged themselves around the track to complete a few extra laps.

The reports attracted both critics and followers to the sport. And while everyone knew about the hardships, this was probably the first time a pedestrienne had been so specific and public about her upcoming physical trials.

Hoping to create a family atmosphere, Anderson encouraged gentlemen to bring their wives, mothers, sisters and daughters to see her at any time of the day or night, and to lend their moral support.

AR had taken it a step further, establishing separate entries—a more accessible door on Smith Street reserved for families, and one on Fulton Street, near the alley, for gamblers and prostitutes. He hoped the latter would stay outside to solicit business.

Concluding her speech, Madame implored the audience to withhold their applause until they saw whether she deserved it at the finish.

"If I fall helpless, or may be dead on the track," she added, "then I shall lose my money."

She was already winning converts. She captivated Brooklynites with her pluck. They admired her confidence and her show business persona.

The feeling, or at least the hope, was that she would make history.

At 8:00 p.m., Coles, the starter, checked the timers for an OK, then turned to the pedestrienne and shouted, "Go!" To generous applause, she was off. For the next four weeks, including Christmas and New Year's Day, the Mozart Garden track would be her world, the privacy tent her only refuge.

Along the way she would battle fatigue, cold, hunger, thirst, blisters, and crude but somewhat effective methods of medical treatment. Arnica, an herb and a member of the sunflower family, would reduce inflammation in swollen, stiff joints; opiates would calm her nerves; whiskey poured in her shoes would soften toughened feet; the application of leeches "cured" bruises and a variety of other ailments. She would fight the choking fumes emitted by the inefficient gas lamps that illuminated the building, made worse by the many male patrons who ignored the 'No Smoking' signs scattered throughout Mozart Garden.

But her most predictable and consistent enemy would be long hours of late-night monotony, when the bands didn't play and the venue sat virtually empty and silent, and the pedestrienne had to battle loneliness with only a handful of spectators and the weary officials, and the endless crunch, crunch, crunch of her tiny feet on the tan-bark track to keep her company.

The resulting "sleepy spells" that many predicted would doom Madame Anderson could strike with little notice. They might last for hours, causing her to shuffle like an old arthritic woman, kicking up dust and wearing out her shoes as she dragged her feet. Or, she would stagger around the track, eyes locked shut, trapped in a stupor, standing for several seconds as if gathering all her mental and physical strength before the next agonizing, hobbling step.

"Sleepy spells" were the six-day walker's number one nemesis.

For the next four weeks, she wouldn't get more than 10 minutes' continuous rest.

If she survived.

"Even babies don't break up their sleep in such small increments," the *New York Times* reported on December 18. "Such tests are alike useless and unattractive."

No one in America, not the great pedestrienne rivals May Marshall or Bertha von Hillern, nor the still undefeated Daniel O'Leary, had ever attempted such an endurance contest.

And gamblers were offering one-hundred-to-one odds that Madame Anderson wouldn't either.

CHAPTER 2

Captain Barclay

Endurance walking and running charmed and entranced Europeans since the late 17th century.

In those days, endurance walking generated great excitement. In a world without vehicles, or much in the way of organized athletics, a good endurance walking contest proved a welcome distraction from a life focused on little more than the grind of daily survival.

Church socials and county fairs held competitions for men, who earned prizes for catching a greased pig or climbing a greasy pole for a flitch of bacon. Other contests included wrestling, cudgeling, sack hops and donkey races.

Women's activities included races of about a half mile, with fields limited to two or three younger competitors, at a time when society considered 35 as old. The women struggled to run in the long, heavy and sleeved dresses, but more comfortable clothing would have offended the Puritan social protocol. Even minimal liberties drew cries of indecency.

Winners earned a leg of mutton, aprons for younger competitors, or a pound of tea for older women.

But the most popular competitions were called 'smock races.' Before the race, the smock, homemade and taking days or weeks to sew, would be placed on a high tree branch or post for all to see.

Men's and women's cricket matches played host to more lascivious and infrequently held occasional races. They attracted a less sophisticated crowd. Many featured competition among 'gypsy women.' At least one cricket match invited women to run "in drawers only."

By the early 19th century, races could last for several hours and competitors' ages ranged from eight to 70. Formats included solo efforts against the clock, each other, and occasionally against men. One woman reportedly walked 50 miles in eight-and-a-half hours. Another, who worked as a door-to-door bookseller, attempted 50 miles a day for

20 consecutive days, but quit after just seven. Some had big money waged on them, as much as 50-100 pounds, and gamblers would attempt to sabotage the walker to win a bet.

Locals took up a small collection, as most long-distance walkers barely had enough to eat. By the 1820s, the county fairs, long a host for many contests, had pretty much died out. Due to its increasing association with immoral behavior, both real and imagined, women's endurance walking lost respectability with the public. Contests were either not held or conducted outside the public's consciousness.

While the women fell into disfavor, the men, long-engaged in more grueling activities, found someone who made the genteel sport more attractive to them. Over the next few years he would, with style, persona and charisma, essentially create the sport of professional pedestrianism. For decades men and at least one woman tried to equal his accomplishments. If not for him, it's unlikely pedestrianism would have achieved international fame.

His name was Robert Barclay Allardice, popularly known as Captain Barclay.

Born in 1777 to an ancient Scottish family distantly related to the Barclay banking empire, the Allardice family earned renown for performing remarkable feats of strength–uprooting trees with their bare hands, wrestling bulls, and carrying large sacks of flour with their teeth. As a teen Robert won a 100-guinea wager when he walked six miles inside an hour. By the age of 20, he won bets by lifting a 250-pound man with one hand.

But he would earn his greatest fame as an endurance walker.

Thanks to him, pedestrianism grew in popularity in Great Britain through the 19th century, with top athletes earning significant money by walking hundreds of miles in just a few days. Local newspapers sometimes covered their exploits. Even then, sports provided a form of escapism for the average worker, who could fantasize about a lifestyle that included money and fame.

In 1813, Walter Thom wrote in his book *Pedestrianism*, that Captain Barclay didn't adhere to any specific training regimen, and he had a reputation for robust eating and drinking. But his training methods, which included purging, sweating and eating meat, proved popular with pedestrians throughout much of the century. Thom credited Barclay's strength to his walking style that included bending the body forward, thereby throwing the weight on his knees, and taking short efficient steps where the feet barely broke contact with the ground.

Captain Barclay knew how to capitalize on gambler's greed, occasionally engaging in what would later be called "gamesmanship."

In 1801, he wagered 1,000 guineas he could walk 90 miles in 21 hours, but lost when he claimed to have caught a cold. He doubled the bet, and lost again. He won only after raising the stakes to 5,000 guineas. Over the next several years, he amazed locals and fattened his wallet with remarkable achievements in pedestrianism. In 1802, he walked 64 miles in 10 hours; three years later, he covered 72 miles in less than a day. In 1808, starting at 5:00 a.m., he walked 30 miles for grouse hunting, 60 miles home in 11 hours, then dined and hiked 16 miles to a ball. He returned home by 7:00 a.m. and spent the next day shooting, having traveled 130 miles and going without sleep for two days.

Rejecting traditional walking garb, he frequently wore a top hat, cravat, woolen suit, lambs' wool socks and thick-soled shoes.

But Captain Barclay elevated pedestrianism and his own legacy in 1809 with a trek almost everyone thought impossible. From June 1 to July 12, in Newmarket Heath, a town located about 100 miles north of London, Captain Barclay started a journey of 1,000 miles in 1,000 hours, or one mile every hour for six weeks.

He marked off a ½-mile smooth stretch on Norwich Road. Gas lamps, a new technology, were set up 100 yards apart on either side of the path. The illumination not only helped him see, but also offered him protection from gamblers intent on sabotaging him at night. He also carried pistols in his belt, and he hired a former boxer as a bodyguard.

Captain Barclay's times slowed from 15 minutes in the walk's early days to 21 minutes as he neared the end. Before mile 607, he stood while sleeping. To wake him, an assistant took a cane and beat him around the head and shoulders. In addition to rousing him, the whipping resulted in the captain letting loose with a torrid of cursing. His exhaustion nearly incapacitated him as he neared the finish, so officials fired pistols near his ears to keep him awake.

On the last day, thousands jammed into Newmarket, Cambridge, and every other nearby town and village, to see the finish. The crowd included farmers, tinkers, maids and pickpockets, the latter of whom enjoyed such well-attended events. Throughout the vicinity, all beds were filled, and no horse or other form of transportation could be had. As Captain Barclay completed his last mile, his bodyguard led the crowd of more than 10,000 in wild cheers.

Newmarket church bells rang, and reporters sent detailed accounts to their papers. Barclay had become a national hero, setting a record that would become the standard for long-distance walkers.

He had invented the sport of professional pedestrianism.

At a time when a farmer took home 50 guineas a year, Captain Barclay reportedly earned 16,000. Rumors circulated that aggregate bets totaled 100,000 pounds, the equivalent to 5 million pounds and $8 million in modern US dollars.

Although a successful athlete, he still wanted to expand his sphere of influence.

He sponsored boxer Tom Cribb, the bare-knuckles champion of the World in 1807 and 1809. Captain Barclay also earned fame as an excellent marksman and successful gambler. In his 50s, he started the "Defence" stagecoach line, one of the most efficient and reliable that Scotland had ever seen. He occasionally drove the London mail coach to Aberdeen single-handed, requiring him to drive for nearly three days and nights.

A horse kick killed Captain Barclay Allardice, and on May 8, 1854, he died of paralysis. But he saw his pedestrian accomplishments influence Britain and the athletic world for generations. Because of him, people constantly tested the physical and mental limits of human endurance.

*   *   *

In 1815, six years after Captain Barclay's celebrated walk, a reporter for Swansea's *Cambrian* newspaper wrote, "A whole race of 50-mile-a-day men has emerged, and soon every county will have to boast of its own pedestrian champion. What was before the disease of an individual has become an epidemic; and where it will end I know not."

By then, top walkers made small fortunes. Some prize money came from fanatics (the source of the term fan) who paid to see the athletes. Others earned money from sponsors, who would put up substantial sums as part of an athletic prize for the prestige of having their names associated with a big-time performer.

But not all walkers enjoyed positive relationships with the public.

Due to his job, pedestrian George Wilson found it necessary to make the journey from Newcastle on Tyne to London and back about six times a year, a total of 550 miles round trip. He experienced less success in business. While in debtors' prison in 1813, he staked his watch against the 61 shillings he owed that he could walk 50 miles inside of 12 hours in the prison yard, a space measuring 33 feet by 25.5 feet. He covered the 10,300 circuits with five minutes to spare. On another occasion, police arrested him for walking on Sunday. Still, he proved a successful pedestrian putting on exhibitions in Chelsea, Norwich, Manchester, and other towns. In 1819, at the age of 53, he covered 1,000 miles in 18 days.

A Wilson contemporary, Josiah Eaton, between Boxing Day 1815 and December 5, 1816, twice beat Captain Barclay's record when he

walked 1,100 miles in 1,100 hours, the second with the added require-
ment that he limit his rest time by commencing each mile within twenty
minutes after each hour. By contrast, Barclay would walk two miles in
succession, starting one near the end of one hour, then immediately begin
the next one. His strategy gave him longer breaks, while still meeting the
parameters of both time and distance.

In 1817, at the age of 47, Eaton took on a man for a walk of 2,000
miles in 42 days on west London's Wormwood Scrubs, an open area used
as cavalry training. Eaton trailed early, but eventually he prevailed. Later
that year, he walked 51 miles from Colchester to London each day for 20
straight days, totaling 1,020 miles.

In 1838, a pedestrian named Harriss, in front of a crowd estimated at
between five and six thousand, completed a walk of 1,750 miles in 1,000
hours. The *London Times* reported on December 4, 1838, that "His feet
were badly blistered, and he has at intervals suffered considerable pain in
his limbs . . ." Afterward, the pedestrian said he looked forward to six or
seven days off, because he learned from 14 years' experience that after any
pedestrian undertaking, the rest time resulted in more excruciating pain
than during the actual performance.

He made 200 sovereigns for his efforts.

By mid-century, even a few women had taken up pedestrianism.

In 1851, hoping to get a glimpse at "the world," an 84-year-old Cor-
nish fishwoman, Mary Callinack, attracted the attention of Queen Victoria when she walked the 300 miles from Penzance to London's Hyde Park
to see the Great Exhibition, the precursor to the World's Fair.

On September 17, 1864, 31-year-old Emma Sharp of Laisterdyke,
wearing men's clothes described by the *Bradford Observer* as "a red and
black checked coat and inexpressibles [presumably a more acceptable
term than the sexually explicit "trousers"], and completing her ensemble
with a straw hat adorned with a white feather," covered 1,000 miles in
1,000 hours, walking two miles at a time, then recovering for 90 minutes
in the nearby Quarry Gap Hotel. She followed that schedule until October 29, when the *Observer* said she completed her task to the "accompaniment of a grand gala, a brass band, a fireworks display, a cannon firing,
and roasting of a sheep." She finished with armed escorts and carrying a
pistol after someone, probably a person who had a significant wager on
her failing, threw hot cinders on her path.

John, her husband, reportedly spent much of the time in a pub
because, "he didn't like fact she had drawn so much attention to herself."

He also might have objected to the outfits she wore, or to the harass-
ment he might have gotten from friends and co-workers for the money
she made, likely around 1,000 guineas.

CHAPTER 3

Ada Nymand

*A*pproximately 150 miles east of its genesis near Kemble, England, the River Thames flows past south London, curving into an upside down L as it forms the northwest and north border of the borough of Lambeth. In the middle of the 19th century, one could see nearly a half-dozen theatres along that three-quarter mile stretch of Lambeth Beach. A handful more were scattered about a half-mile inland. Within that narrow area, residents of North Lambeth and surrounding boroughs could, for not much money, enjoy a variety of evening and weekend entertainment from Shakespeare to pantomimes to low comedy.

That must have proved an exciting world for Ada Nymand.

Born on February 10, 1843, she developed a strong work ethic and adventurous spirit; Ada dared to dream. She had excellent timing. Queen Victoria had been crowned in 1837. During her 60-year reign, England enjoyed marvelous growth thanks in large part to the Industrial Revolution and many of Her Majesty's reforms. Consequently, the lifestyle of most Brits rose dramatically.

Most of Ada's life in Britain remains a mystery. Her mother was a British-born homemaker. Her German-Jewish father, Gustavus Nymand, worked as a milliner, a job that paid 28-30 shillings a week. In 1851, farm workers earned half that. Officials of the era calculated poverty at 18 shillings a week.

Without elaborating, Ada would later say, "I inherited courage from one parent and insensibility from the other."

Many Brits wore hats in Victorian England. Hats indicated status. Boys and working men wore cloth caps. Artists preferred floppy hats. Beachgoers donned straw hats. Society conscious women wore hats at social gatherings.

Although her father earned a comfortable living, the Nymands' daughter didn't fully embrace the middle-class lifestyle that appealed to so many in the mid-1850s.

Despite society's then stigma against actors, Ada dreamed of headlining a major play. Each day as she left her home on Blackfriar's Road and walked past popular night spots such as Astley's Amphitheatre and the Surrey Theatre, she would look up at the featured players and ask, "What shall I do to get my name up there?"

She sought a bigger stage than Lambeth, one dominated by famous actresses who wooed packed houses and demonstrated power and grace. Ada wanted to see the audience's eyes follow her as she sashayed across the stage, the object of desire like such performers as Laura Keene and Madame Vestras.

By her mid-teens the restless teen could no longer remain in the confines of Lambeth.

Ada Nymand left home to pursue the stage.

She joined the many others who sought fame. Most found it elusive. Only a handful would reach the London stage, and precious few of those would reach their goals. Getting there meant facing years of hardship. Sir Henry Irving, the first actor to be knighted, toiled for 15 years before finally establishing himself as a star in 1871.

Ada not only battled long odds in achieving stardom, but also the Victorian contempt for the acting profession.

Newspapers often interchanged the terms 'actress' and 'prostitute.'

A performer in the play, "Through the Stage Door" said, "Women who can't advertise any other way go on stage."

In the 1838 production of "Prostitutes of London," this exchange took place: "Is not a theatre a brothel?"

"The two," came the response, "are linked together by mutual interests and mutual pursuits; their morals are identically the same."

Toward that end Ada, like so many in her situation, probably took a stage name, which prevented bringing shame upon their families.

But Ada soon found battling the public's opinion of acting couldn't compare to the struggles from within.

Those political wars and posturing for positions and choice roles must have disappointed and alienated star-struck Ada, who, like the other naïve aspirants, found the profession more brutal and unforgiving than they could have imagined. Too many hopefuls and a shortage of parts meant an overflow of actresses, almost all lacking experience, but still hoping for the chance to perform and get their names on the marquees. Only a few, such as Ellen Terry and Laura Keene, survived the intense competition. Terry became one of the world's most renowned actresses, frequently playing Shakespeare during a career that extended into silent movies. Keane went international, becoming one of the first women theatrical managers in history. She achieved her greatest fame on April 14,

1865, when performing "Our American Cousin" at Ford's Theatre in Washington, DC. That night she managed to work her way into President Lincoln's private box, and rested the dying president's bloody head on her lap.

But they represented a minority. Irene Vanbrugh described the plight of actresses as, "one long fight ... there are others, many others, in the field if she stops fighting for one single moment. She will be tramped under foot, 'for every actress life is a lone battle ....'"

Another said, "The life of a Victorian actress is, 'a state of war without bloodshed.'"

Even making it big didn't guarantee long-term success in the unstable world. Despite writing melodramas for several theatres, including Surrey, Adelphi and Olympic, Charles Somerset found himself producing two-act dramas for the miserly rate of 25 shillings. Later, he stood in front of the Mansion House (the official residence of the Lord Mayor of London) with a label round his neck declaring, "Ladies and gentlemen, I am starving."

But one could minimize the agonizing years of trials through connections. Both Terry and Keene had relatives in show business. Unfortunately, Ada had no such advantage. She would rely on work ethic, which was probably her greatest asset. Even as a child she reportedly could physically accomplish in a few hours what grown men needed two days to do. A young Ada believed she could "pull the house down and put it back up again."

Ada likely spent the years after leaving Lambeth traveling through small towns in low-rung theatrical companies, such as penny gaffs or 'box theatres,' where the troupe set up a makeshift stage wherever they found space and a small audience. The group's productions were spontaneous, haphazard and unscripted, the latter not usually a big issue, since many of the actors couldn't read. Audiences, out of frustration with their own lives or poor quality of the productions, often responded by throwing rotten vegetables at the performers.

On top of a typical 16-hour workday, actors rehearsed for no pay. If they missed a performance, if the play failed to make money, or if an unscrupulous manager ran off with the meager profits, they were left with nothing.

However, they did get numerous opportunities to develop a variety of skills that hopefully would take them to the London theatres, especially the hallowed West End.

Ada appeared to have made it to a major stage, but she likely didn't stay long, or ever headline or land a major part. In all of her British newspaper interviews, no mention was ever made of her having a theatrical background. It seemed she remained an unknown hopeful, one of the scores whose name never graced a marquee. She mostly traveled and performed with provincial shows, and while a step up from the box theatres, the constant traveling and endless days hardly fulfilled her dream.

For 15 years Ada Nymand battled to "make a name." She likely fought ostracism from her parents and a public that, especially when she started, identified her with being a prostitute. With no connections and limited talent, she still thought it possible to overcome those liabilities with enormous focus and strong will.

But she suffered from one other shortcoming, and that alone probably doomed her career even before it started.

In addition to connections and talent, Keene, Terry and the other top actresses could lay claim to another asset, one that no amount of work or training could teach or develop. The headliners made strong first impressions with high cheekbones, thin, well-defined faces, flowing hair, tantalizing smiles, and figures that almost created a scandal when they wore form-fitting designer dresses.

Despite a slow growing respectability of actresses, couch politics could still make or break their careers, and success meant possessing the tools that attracted men. One actress said that on two occasions she lost a part to a manager's mistress.

Unfortunately, Ada's features included a stocky body, square jaw and wide nose that seemed to set her eyes too far apart. No one in the press gave Ada Nymand credit for even possessing moderate good looks.

As Ada passed 30, she not only battled more with the attractive actresses, but younger ones, some by a decade or more.

The stage no longer held her future. It represented failed dreams, and in some ways a shattered life. Her ability to outwork most of her fellow performers might mask a lack of star-quality talent, but it couldn't overcome the awkward way she filled out a dress.

She would never star on a stage, never feel the audience following her every move, never bring down the house with a stunning scene, never experience the glow of a standing ovation. Those magic moments of connecting with a crowd would forever be reserved for some other actress. So, around 1875, Ada left the stage. She married for the first time, to a man named Anderson, and the couple began their lives as a theatrical management team.

Now she dealt with the boring side of books, fighting with managers, working with temperamental performers, and innumerable other tedious behind-the-scenes tasks that rarely elicited a 'thank you' much less a public's acknowledgment.

She and her husband managed a theatre in Cardiff. For the next year, they learned the skills necessary to run a successful theatre. By virtually all accounts, the couple made a go of it.

Then tragedy struck. The next year, Ada's husband died. In her mid-30s, she found herself alone. Within months she'd be nearly bankrupt.

CHAPTER 4

O'Leary vs. Weston Sets Standard

*A*bout the time Ada Nymand retired from acting, a 29-year-old Irish immigrant, Daniel O'Leary, lived the life Ada had sought as a child. After years of struggling through a series of jobs, O'Leary enjoyed stardom in Chicago as probably the most renowned athlete in America, if not the world.

Born in Ireland in 1846, he survived the potato famine that wiped out the primary food source for one-third to one-half of the country. During the next seven years an estimated one million Irish left the country for England, Australia and America. Another million who stayed died from starvation and related afflictions, such as cholera, scurvy, measles, diarrheal diseases and tuberculosis. The population declined by 20-25%. With hundreds of thousands thrown out of their homes, overcrowded work houses, where many displaced Irish turned for survival, proved an ideal environment for typhoid.

O'Leary arrived in America in 1866 with no money or prospects. He settled in Chicago, working at a lumber yard and eventually earning $13.50 a week, well above the average annual income. Fearing the oncoming winter, he headed south and took on a job at a cotton plantation. In 1868, he returned to Chicago, where he found employment as a book canvasser, an exhausting, futureless job that paid little and required a spirit that thrived on rejection.

Three years later, tragedy struck. The Great Fire of 1871, falsely attributed to Irish immigrant Catherine O'Leary, whose cow allegedly knocked over a lantern (the Chicago City Council absolved her of any blame in 1997). The fire burned for 30 hours from October 8-10, killing 300, leaving 90,000 homeless, destroying more than 17,000 buildings, and causing $200,000,000 in damages.

Many of Daniel O'Leary's customers, some of whom owed him hundreds of dollars, vanished. He lost inventory and sales records. The shattered city had no appetite for buying books.

*   *   *

17

Now desperate for a future, O'Leary began following the pedestrian exploits of Edward Payson Weston, a Rhode Island native whose long-distance walking accomplishments and promotional skills earned him the nickname, "The Father of Modern Pedestrianism."

Weston first caught America's attention in 1861 when he made a bet that he could walk from the Boston statehouse for a 450-mile-trek to Washington, DC in 10 days, arriving on March 4, in time for President Lincoln's inauguration. A large crowd waited to see him off, and adoring women kissed him, requesting he relay their affection to the new president. He never promised to complete the exchange.

He took off at 12:48 p.m. Along the way he hit snow, mud and injured his ankle fleeing a dog. In Worcester, MA he talked an officer out of arresting him for non-payment of a previous debt. He managed to maintain his pace until he hit a snowstorm in Baltimore, and he missed his goal by about three hours. That didn't stop the nation from admiring his efforts. He accepted the new president's invitation for a White House visit. Weston's turned down Mr. Lincoln's offer to pay his train fare home, the disappointed yet determined pedestrian preferring to partially redeem himself by walking back to Boston.

Weston turned pro and six years later collected on a $10,000 wager when he walked from Portland, Maine to Chicago (1,326 miles) in 26 days. During his hike he encountered one attacker and received numerous death threats from gamblers who had bet against him.

Later, Weston set American and world records at 24-hour and six-day contests.

He often carried a riding crop as a symbol of strength. That image would influence walkers for years to come.

In spite of Weston's achievements, O'Leary believed he could beat the American.

O'Leary began his athletic career on July 14, 1874, when he completed 100 miles in 23:17. He quickly followed that with a century walk in 22:19, breaking the world record. Wanting to claim the title, "Champion Pedestrian of the World," he joined Weston as the only pedestrians to walk more than 500 miles in six days, earning $1,000 and taking home a gold watch. This earned him the right to challenge Weston for the crown.

After failing at several scheduling attempts, the two agreed to a six-day walk on November 15, 1875, in Chicago's Exposition Building. Each athlete would walk on his own track. Weston held the inside that measured 1/7 of a mile, with O'Leary's outer oval measuring 1/6. The upstart O'Leary dominated throughout. At the end he completed 503 miles to Weston's 451.

The win earned Daniel O'Leary the undisputed title, "Champion Pedestrian of the World."

His athletic successes and Horatio Alger story made him an instant national star. For the next several years newspapers across the country trumpeted his victories. The national magazine *Harper's Weekly* wrote a feature on him. His dark hair and mustache gave him a photogenic Edgar Allen Poe look, a perfect attraction for the Chicago stores that sold his picture. Everywhere he went rabid followers clamored for his autograph.

In addition to his athletic winnings, he earned thousands more through personal appearances.

In fewer than 10 years, Daniel O'Leary had risen from poverty and obscurity to become the best-known athlete in America. His determination, growth and resolve mirrored that of Chicago.

In less than a decade, many images and characteristics of what would define Chicago for generations were in its infancy. The city's rebound after the horrific 1871 fire displayed to the nation Chicago's strength. Architects Burnham and Root, who would be instrumental in bringing the 1893 World's Fair to the city, were beginning a nearly two-decade partnership. George Pullman's Pullman Palace Car Company would famously use the slogan, "Travel and Sleep in Safety and Comfort." Meat packer Gustavus Swift developed the refrigerated car, which saved money by eliminating the need of shipping live cattle via rail. Marshall Fields, already a fixture in Chicago's retail district, expanded in 1875.

Of greater interest to O'Leary, the city shined under the spotlight of professional sports, especially baseball. In February 1876, one of the Chicago White Stockings' (renamed the Cubs) best players, Albert Spalding, would start his own sporting goods company. Later that year he and teammate, and fellow future Hall of Famer, Cap Anson, would lead the White Stockings to the inaugural National League pennant.

Although baseball fascinated Chicagoans, no one, not even Spaulding or Anson could match the popularity or income of O'Leary. With economic growth in a vibrant city all around him, O'Leary, with his marvelous sense of timing and risk-taking, believed he could expand the sport of pedestrianism.

His rivalry with Weston had turned endurance walking into a national obsession. Using that same formula, why couldn't women participate as well?

* * *

Sometime in 1875, a German teen named Bertha von Hillern defeated a woman in a small endurance walk in Peoria, Illinois. The victory attracted O'Leary's attention. Something about her appealed to him. Von Hillern possessed intelligence, charisma and athletic ability. However, she spoke only broken English and had come to America only a few months earlier.

Born August 4, 1857 to a military family in Freiberg, Germany, Bertha displayed athletic gifts as a child, often beating boys in physical education contests. Her paternal grandfather fought at Waterloo, and her father served as an aide to Von Moltke in the Franco-Prussian War.

In the early 1870s, Germany fell into the throes of a major depression as companies went bankrupt and the free market policies of Otto Von Bismarck, which helped propel Germany's economy for almost 10 years, failed to keep up with the rest of the world. The Von Bergs suffered through what Von Hillern later described as "financial ruin." Sensing greater opportunities abroad, the adventurous teen left her family and came with friends to America, where she eventually settled in Chicago.

Her father, probably leaning on a strong sense of nationalism due to his military experience, rode out the depression with his wife, and life in Germany improved greatly during the 1880s.

She stood barely five feet tall with blondish hair and blue eyes. One paper described her as having "pleasant features." Her low-key personality and demeanor more closely resembled a nun than a jezebel, but not overly so. She took life and pedestrianism seriously. Von Hillern's athletic background, walking success and personality made her O'Leary's ideal choice to become a professional female endurance walker.

Unofficially, America had its first pedestrienne.

But Von Hillern couldn't start or carry the new sport alone. Successful athletic contests thrive on rivalries. Rivalries generate interest. Competition inspires athletes to elevate their performance. The public takes sides. Co-workers argue the merits of each athlete. Neighbors lay down friendly wagers. Local papers have more interesting angles for stories. Athletes' strengths and weaknesses are assessed and argued. O'Leary owed much of his athletic success to beating Weston. When that happened, the world noticed.

Finding her a competitor, even in Chicago would be tough. O'Leary needed a talented athlete, preferably an American, as two unknown foreigners would not likely draw great interest. Any opponent would have to challenge Von Hillern's ability, tenacity and mentality of a professional athlete, and still have some personality and appeal to mainstream Chicagoans. She also needed confidence, and preferably living a life of desperation. If the potential rival lived too comfortably, if she saw the endurance contest as something she could back out of when she grew physically exhausted or emotionally stressed, or if she clung to the idea of returning to her own stable world, she would probably not make a good candidate.

Both O'Leary and Von Hillern came to America looking to fulfill their dreams, leaving behind an otherwise unspectacular, if not dreary existence, and a bleak future. They probably saw escaping poverty as a motivator to success. That internal desire would propel the prospective athletes after exhausting all their physical resources. That "failure is not an option" mentality would prove a driving force in separating winners from losers.

Even if a rival met all those qualifications, she still might fall short, as the patrons would have high expectations.

The walkers had to put on a good show. Many of the attendees would have a deep understanding of the sport. They knew O'Leary and thousands of Chicagoans were thrilled by his victories. Paying customers had to get their money's worth to feel the excitement, to be a part of the frenzied atmosphere that became the trademark of the men's races.

If in the inaugural women's race one, or both, failed to finish, or if one routed the other, professional women's walking would shut down before it started. And the failure would weigh heavily on O'Leary. The women could go back to an anonymous existence, their names quickly forgotten, their lives unchanged. Whether successful or an embarrassment, people would come because of O'Leary's name and reputation.

Dream or nightmare, O'Leary would own it.

However, O'Leary trusted his instincts and they rarely betrayed him. His owed his remarkable success and fame to winning most of his long-shot plays.

He obviously believed the pedestriennes would be worth the risk, so he issued a challenge: Bertha von Hillern would take on any woman in the State of Illinois to a multi-day race.

*　　*　　*

About the same time Bertha Von Hillern found a new home in Chicago, 500 miles to the east in Dunkirk, Pennsylvania, a desperate 34-year-old Tryphena Lipsey sought a better life.

The birthplace of Tryphena Curtis, the oldest of Northrup and Elizabeth Smith Curtis' seven children, remains a mystery. Sources list it as either: New Hampshire; Delta, Michigan; or "English-speaking Canada." The Curtis family did own a farm in eastern Canada, and that is where family sources say she gave birth to Allen, her only surviving child, perhaps born in the same home as his mother. Another son, James, died young. Tryphena married Canadian Thomas Lipsey in 1862. Sometime, probably after the Civil War, Tryphena's parents and younger children moved the family to the Erie-Dunkirk, Pennsylvania area, where Northrup found success in the steel business, probably working for Andrew Carnegie. However, railroad production slowed in the 1870s, causing many steel producers to shut down or cut back on workers, so the Curtis family moved to Chicago, which was still rebuilding after the Great Fire in October 1871.

Due to Thomas' abuse and alcoholism, he and Tryphena had a rocky and short marriage. He died in the mid-1870s, leaving Tryphena to fend for herself with baby Allen.

Tryphena moved to Chicago and, leaving Allen with her mother during the day, and began selling books door-to-door. Like O'Leary, who had only recently left the profession, the long hours and little pay made for a meager existence and a bleak future. She had almost no prospects for a better life.

Like virtually all pedestriennes, she possessed three qualities a successful walker must have: drive, focus and desperation. Either of her own initiation or prompting from O'Leary, who might have found her through bookselling connections, she accepted Bertha's challenge.

On the surface it looked like another huge mistake in her life. The walk offered no guarantees. Women didn't walk in public alone, as that's where the term "streetwalkers" originated, so she risked further damaging her reputation. Few understood the concept of getting paid for participating in an athletic contest that, like show business, wasn't considered a respectable profession. But widowed and raising a child alone, this opportunity was her best, and maybe last, opportunity to improve her life. She had to take the longshot. She made another decision before diving into the profession. Maybe to protect her family or herself should she fail, she opted to hide her identity.

She would walk under the stage name of May Marshall.

CHAPTER 5

Training the New Pedestriennes

O'Leary relied on his own perceptions in believing in the women's athletic abilities. Neither one had ever engaged in such a physical challenge.

Reports vary on O'Leary's role in preparing the new pedestriennes for their match. No mention is ever made of him specifically assisting Von Hillern. Regarding Marshall, one newspaper stated that he helped her train for a month leading up to that first walk. Since O'Leary was the event's high profile personality, and he needed the match to succeed, he probably wouldn't have risked failure by leaving their preparation to chance or hurt his reputation by training one without the other. Without his help the walkers would have been too ill-prepared mentally or physically to take on such a task, and the walk would have been little more than a chaotic scramble with each athlete quitting early, leaving patrons angry and confused.

He had a lot riding on these unproven athletic hopefuls.

The duo had just a few weeks for transformation from amateur walkers to professional athletes. They had to make dramatic changes in their lives and learn about proper training, nutrition, dealing with the public, clothes, shoes, treating injuries, maximizing rest periods, and a myriad of other details beyond the scope of their imaginations. To help them focus on training, O'Leary might have even financially supported them.

While the specifics of the women's training isn't known, the typical athlete's routine then had them in bed every night by 11:00, up at 6:00 for a quick pre-morning walk, then breakfast of a well-beaten egg in a cup of tea, or a small glass of sherry and a slice of currant bread or toast. In case of bad weather, athletes commonly worked indoors incorporating the use of dumb bells and rope skipping. Following the early workout, they consumed 8-10 ounces of broiled mutton chop or veal cutlet with one-day-old bread or toast, without butter, and three eggs boiled three minutes with some watercress. They would wash that down with a half-pint of tea. The walker would rest for an hour before joining the trainer for another walk of an hour or two.

At noon the athlete would eat dinner, considered the most important meal of the day, and usually consisting of roast beef or mutton, or occasionally rabbit or fowl, with stale bread and maybe a potato or other vegetable. All could be taken with a pint of ale, sherry or water, with an occasional dessert of tapioca pudding. Supper consisted of a light meal with lean mutton or fowl, or a broiled chop with a cup of (black) tea. The athlete then took an easy walk to help aid digestion. All nutritional advice was predicated on the walker's personal preferences.

The athletes also worked on their form. While each walker perfected his or her own style, most kept an erect torso with shoulders back and elbows at right angles swinging back and forth with thumbs just crossing the breastbone. Trainers emphasized relaxation of the lower body and the importance of heel landing first, propelling the body forward, then transferring the weight to the ball of the foot. The action took place quickly, or else the knee would buckle, putting undue stress on the big toe. Landing on the ball or toe of the foot resulted in an action called 'lifting,' which would cause the walker to break into an unintentional trot, an act punishable by forfeiting a lap.

To record miles walked, the pedestrienne hopefuls likely carried an "American Pedometer" in their pocket which could be adjusted to measure any stride length from 23-35 inches. While crude, it gave the women an idea of the mileage they were logging.

Proper "pedestrian" or balmoral canvas shoes could be bought for $3.50. Welcher's made a walking shoe with a steel spring shank, therefore probably too stiff for long-distance performances, for $8. Another model had the added feature of allowing the insertion of spikes, which could be removed and, according to one ad, "The shoes could be worn in the streets without injury." That shoe seemed a bargain at $3.25. Its high tops sacrificed comfort, but the shoes wore longer. They also gave its wearer another advantage, one that must have shocked the novice walkers. The hard-soles offered protection against potential sabotage.

Gamblers, professional and amateur, frequently hung out at pedestrian matches. With so much fraud in the business and high frequency of failure, "sporting men" often enjoyed good days in spite of giving favorable odds. If some of the more unscrupulous betters suspected big losses they could, presumably during the late-night dead times when only judges and a few sleepy patrons were on hand, scatter sharp rocks and tacks on the track, hoping to cripple a performer. Walkers in hard leather shoes provided stability, but those who opted for the softer and more comfortable kid soles would find that such shrapnel could shred the shoe, leaving the injured foot mutilated and vulnerable to infection.

The women were also warned about accepting seemingly gratuitous food from "friends," as it could be poisoned. Flowers laced with chloroform also served as another potential avenue for subversive attacks.

To guard against the crimes, police often watched the track, with race officials acting as a "back-up." The mere presence of police would often discourage all but the most corrupt and desperate acts. Ultimately, the athletes themselves had to watch for any potential saboteur, but doing that while trying to concentrate on such a physically demanding task only added to their stress.

Injuries were treated in the most primitive ways. Leeches were applied to bunions every other day for a week, and then brushed with iodine every third day. Blisters were punctured with a needle, compressing the sac to squeeze out all the fluid. Broken blisters required collodion (a mixture of pyroxylin, alcohol and ether that not only healed wounds, but also aided in processing photographs). Other treatments included powdered Gum Arabic, and bathing in strong salt water with powdered alum and vinegar. Corns were treated with iodine and then soaked in warm salt water. When dry, the afflicted area got rubbed with sandpaper or pumice.

Even after weeks of preparation, determining true athletic ability couldn't be assessed until they experienced competition. Only then could an athlete's heart be measured.

While it's true that athletes must "want to win," that attitude can't be turned on for a competition. It has to be cultivated every day in training so that they push beyond previous unreachable boundaries. They struggle mentally with the next workout, often battling themselves to get out of bed in the morning. Even with that level of discipline, nothing is guaranteed; it only increases the chance of success.

The walkers undoubtedly struggled daily with fatigue, dehydration, stiffness and sore muscles. They also suffered from mental stress. After seeing the preparation it took to become a professional athlete, they had to wonder if they were up to the grueling task of walking 250-300 miles in six days. Just doing the math, figuring daily totals of 45-50 miles, had to make them shake their heads and wonder how such a feat could be accomplished.

They also needed a strategy that would not only maximize the benefit of their walk-rest periods, but also satisfy the most number of spectators. The pedestriennes stayed on the track during the day and throughout the evening times so they would get encouragement from the fans. Besides, if spectators only saw one walker for very long, they'd feel they weren't getting their money's worth, and the familiar one would become the crowd favorite, diminishing the desired rivalry effect.

Athletes typically rested between midnight and 5:00 a.m., when the band left and only a handful of customers and officials remained. During those hours the athletes' bodies would be screaming for a long break, and even whispers reverberated throughout the arena.

Because of their high profile, the women were opening themselves up to verbal and physical abuse, and risking developing wanton reputations. O'Leary surely warned them to stay away from men interested in excessive flirting, "come-ons," threats of physical violence, and even offers of money as if the women were prostitutes. His advice about avoiding gamblers had an insidious undertone. The women wouldn't be subject to the temptation of "fixing" a race, or purposely losing the contest while getting a cut from a dishonest better.

The women also learned the "finer points" of walking strategy, and exciting patrons. Eating while walking not only saved time, it delighted the crowd. "Making an entrance" with some new outfit could "wow" the females in the audience, and at the same time elevate a tired walker's sagging morale. They would need costume changes for both style and function. Most 1870's venues lacked effective heating, so warm coverings such as gloves and a shawl helped battle inclement weather.

All of those details were covered, and the women's confidence grew. But while O'Leary advised them based on his vast experience, they knew nothing.

What if O'Leary missed his own calculation? What if women couldn't perform well enough to suit the tough Chicago populous? Success meant not simply good performances; they needed clean competition. If one or both walkers failed to go the entire six days, or if they struggled so much that they quit after only a few miles, O'Leary's experiment would fail.

He could prepare his young charges, but until they raced, when their training, preparation and their souls were tested in front of hundreds or thousands of screaming spectators, no one knew if they were truly professional endurance walkers

While no women had gone through such a trial, men's challenges were well known. Late in the six-day races, eating proved a necessary evil for the hungry walker. During the roughest times, even favorite foods were turned down by some walkers, whose empty stomachs were knotted, making sustenance either unpleasant or impossible. Sleep would become not much more than a series of restless tossing and turning episodes that did little in providing much-needed rejuvenation. Twitching and flip-flopping would eventually turn into almost writhing due to excessive exhaustion, hunger and dehydration. When the athlete arose, he would sometimes find himself in a fit of confusion and/or anger, maybe worse off than when he went to bed four of five hours earlier. Overly fatigued pedestrians suffered from cramps, and some would arise in the middle of a "sleep," thinking they should walk. In severe cases he might fight an attendant about whether or not he should return to the track. Also challenging were the late-night segments when the walkers' psyche was smothered by silence. With few on hand to cheer them on, the walkers heard little more than the "crunch, crunch, crunch" of their own footsteps. Each minute seemed like an hour; a lap felt like a mile. The time dragged slower than their exhausted feet that struggled to cover the next lap, but another seemingly endless rotation awaited them.

O'Leary could do little but try and prepare the women for what lay ahead. But even the best advice proved inadequate. It was like childbirth or climbing a snow-capped mountain: You can teach people about handling the obstacles, but you can't train them on what to expect. And with each woman doing her first six-day walk, an endless list of unforeseen circumstances could spell failure.

But O'Leary had overcome so much, surviving the potato famine as a boy, suffering on a long, arduous trip from Ireland to America, then defying all logic and odds in becoming the most famous athlete in the New World. How could anyone think he would fail now?

CHAPTER 6

Pedestriennes Invade Chicago

*B*y early 1876, all of Chicago buzzed about hosting the first professional women's walking match. The *Chicago Times* said, "…it was much talked about." The *Chicago Tribune* reported, "Considerable interest is being manifested in the coming walking match between the two female pedestrians."

To host the event, O'Leary sought a venue with affordable rent, but still convenient to downtown Chicago. He picked the Second Regiment Armory. Armories served as military storage facilities and office space, recreation and training areas.

The Second Regiment Armory would become one of the most famous structures in America. The 1877-78 Chicago City Directory listed the Second Regiment Armory's address as on Canal, NW corner of Jackson. In 1891, the publication listed the armory's location as Washington and Curtis, its same address in 1988 when Oprah Winfrey purchased it and after renovations, turned it into the home of Harpo Productions.

O'Leary had the armory reconfigured with a 10-laps-to-the-mile track and seating for 3,000, with each patron paying an admittance fee of twenty-five cents. He decorated the armory in American colors—the red, white and blue—and German colors of black, gold and red. Each walker would start wearing outfits featuring their native colors, and the newspapers would routinely refer to the contest as "American Girl" vs. "Fraulein."

The typical six-day races commenced just past midnight on Monday morning, as most cities banned Sunday athletic competition. For some reason, O'Leary scheduled this one to begin late Monday morning and close Saturday night, February 5. That meant the pedestriennes would walk 132 hours instead of the typical 144. Few, if any, took issue with the discrepancy, and still called it a six-day race.

Since the O'Leary and Weston rivalry had popularized this format, the public had grown comfortable with it. It sent the significant message that O'Leary believed women could compete on the same level as men. By arranging for a Saturday night finish, he could take advantage of the profitable two weekend evenings while avoiding the controversial and likely suicidal, act of walking on Sunday.

By 10:00 a.m. on Monday morning, January 31, 1876, a large crowd began filling the armory. At 10:40, Von Hillern and Marshall stepped to the start line. Standing on the inside lane, the German wore a red, black and yellow skirt with trimmings, a black velvet basque with a yellow shield on her breast, and white kid gloves covering her dainty hands.

On the outside the slightly taller Marshall was outfitted in a red skirt with blue and white trimming and a blue basque with white stars, and a blue and white shield on her breast. A black hat with a red feather topped her blonde hair, and red and white stockings clung to her legs. She held a fan in her kid-gloved hands.

Both athletes wore boots with low heels and broad soles.

They would discard the bulky but stylish outfits after a few laps, but they added to the nationalism tone.

The judge stood near the women, raising his arm to silence the crowd while he read the rules for all to hear. Confident that both walkers understood, he motioned for O'Leary to begin. Standing just off the track, at 10:46 a.m., O'Leary shouted, "Go!" Simultaneously, the judges' watches clicked and the women were off to sudden cheers.

They started briskly, speed walking shoulder to shoulder. Marshall's inexperience showed as she stayed to the outside, forcing her to walk a bit farther each lap. She left the track for two minutes due to a broken shoelace, and Von Hillern led by three minutes after one mile.

"American Girl" Marshall walked in a more relaxed manner, eyes focused forward, legs swinging freely. It contrasted sharply to Bertha's shorter stride, erect posture, chin held high. Marshall's strategy involved taking more frequent breaks while Von Hillern planned to wear down her faster opponent with a plodding, steady pace.

Just hours into the race, the pedestriennes faced their first problem. Men, ignoring the "No Smoking" signs, created a smothering, choking cloud that enveloped the armory. The pollution forced the German off the track. The next day, the *Chicago Tribune* would write, "Mr. O'Leary, who has charge of such matters, should stop that at once." Offenders were encouraged to use the "smoking room" set up in the building's west side. The problem is never mentioned again.

Throughout the week, Chicago papers rated "American Girl's" speed and strength superior to "Fraulein's" plodding. The press might have been playing favorites. The heavy pro-American crowd cheered every emergence from her tent each time she lapped the teen. The crowd included an over-whelming number of gamblers who'd put big money on Marshall.

All of the public support must have given Marshall a huge psycho-logical boost. On day three, a reporter from the *Chicago Evening Journal* entered Marshall's privacy tent and asked her about the probable out-come. Marshall said, "There is no probable about it. I will win the prize just as sure as you have a nose on your face."

She continued, "For I must do it, and I will certainly unless some now unforeseen misfortune befalls me. Miss von Hillern is an excellent walker, but I don't think she is possessed of the requisite endurance, and another thing that is in my favor is that I am now more than six miles ahead of her."

She suggested that the German might catch her in the evening, but she added with a cunning nod and wry grin, "I will be resting and fresh in the morning, and will walk away from her."

Stories about *Fraulein* lacked the positive spark that Marshall enjoyed. One of the few insights focused on how, after two days, Von Hillern already suffered from exhaustion. While in a half-asleep stupor, she dreamed of seeing herself rising above an astonished May Marshall with a wooden sword in one hand and a purse of $1,000 in the other.

At the end of day three, Von Hillern picked up the pace for 20 min-utes before heading for bed. Marshall retired five minutes later. Von Hillern turned to an attendant. "Please wake me at four am," she said, entering her tent.

Overhearing the order, Marshall whispered to her colored attendant, "Then wake me at 3:30."

At that point Marshall led 117-112, but both suffered from exhaus-tion. Their slowing pace and shuffling gait inspired one newspaper to write, "They were like a free lunch before a posse of hungry beer guzzlers."

But Marshall's problems extended beyond exhaustion. Her qualifi-cation of winning "unless some unforeseen misfortune befalls me" might be truer than she believed.

Unlike her rival, her feet were already swelling.

*　　*　　*

Both walkers hit the track at 3:45 a.m. on February 3, day four. They walked together for seven miles, but Marshall lost a mile when she rested for 15 minutes to remove sand and sawdust from her shoes. She took longer and more frequent breaks due to her painful feet, which had grown to twice their normal size. She tried bigger shoes, but her pace slowed to 20-minute mile pace.

Momentum had clearly swung in Von Hillern's favor.

A reporter visited Marshall's tent. Chicago newspapers, all reporting accounts of her walk, scattered the floor. She sat on a couch, her mangled-looking feet elevated on a chair. She told the reporter she would be "used up" at the end, but she wasn't disheartened.

The newspaper reports, the close race, and the insights from the interviews with Marshall all contributed to increasing excitement as the conclusion drew near. During prime hours the armory was filled with cheering fans.

At times police walked with the athletes for several laps, attempting to keep the track clear of frenzied spectators, but their efforts accomplished little. Around the track's perimeter, people constantly pressed against each other, desperately reaching and screaming to touch, to get a closer look, hoping to become a small part of America's newest sport.

The city had clearly embraced the women. "Our citizens are seized with walking mania," reported the *Chicago Tribune*. "Through the entire forenoon and evening, the hall was filled with people, many of whom traveled as much as five miles to witness the exhibition . . ."

Much of the excitement could have been attributable to the race. Going into day five on February 4, May Marshall's once dominant, six-mile lead had dwindled to just three laps.

With only two days remaining, O'Leary's gamble looked like a success. Chicagoans were filling the armory; the walkers were exhausted, but they both looked fit enough to finish.

But one would face many struggles.

*   *   *

As they started day five at 4:15 a.m., they approached the judges' stand to confirm correct mile totals.

Marshall said, "Good morning, *Fraulein*, how do you feel?"

"Mine anklez are stiff, and mine feet blitzered," replied the German, who apparently cared nothing for an early morning conversation.

"I'm still one mile ahead," said Marshall of her three-lap lead.

"That's okay, you vot be by 10 o'clock tomorrow night," said *Fraulein* as she shot past her rival. For the next five hours she pressed the pace against American Girl. By 10:00 a.m. she had built a three-mile lead.

Maintaining her optimistic facade, Marshall said during a break that she would overtake her rival before six that evening, and by noon the next day would be four miles ahead. However, her prediction seemed unlikely. The *Chicago Inter-Ocean* reported that her feet were covered with "galled spots." She had grown pale and nervous, and had lost her ability to speak.

She suffered from cold, stiff joints and abdominal pain. Now her feet were so swollen she could no longer wear shoes. The paper also speculated she had done herself permanent harm.

Still, she forced a smile and said she would win the race or "die in my tracks."

Dr. William Dunne was called to address Marshall's multiple ailments. He dressed her swollen feet with arnica, a flower-based liquid treatment for blisters, and she soon returned to the track. The foot wraps offered some relief, but she only made good time when an officer accompanied her. She limped badly and, unable to fit into any of the five pairs of her own shoes, was forced to wear a pair of O'Leary's. The boisterous, pro-Marshall crowd continually cheered for her, and somehow she held her own. At 6:00 p.m. she still trailed by three miles.

By contrast, Von Hillern showed few signs of fatigue, although she refused breakfast due to abdominal pain. Her step remained graceful; her head erect. The *Inter-Ocean* said, "She looks well. Her dress is neat and her hair is combed as if she is on stage." She ignored the lone blister on her foot.

Her main complaint was lack of support from German citizenry.

Her entire time on the track, she rarely heard encouragement in her native tongue.

"If mine vriends would only come and talk wit me on der drack, I would win,"reported the *Inter-Ocean* in her broken English, "but they not come to me at all, and I was left alone."

In spite of her solitude, most believed that barring a dramatic turn of events, Von Hillern, would win. There's also widespread hope American Girl's day would end mercifully and she could return to selling books.

But Marshall continued her improbable push. Late in the day, Von Hillern increased her lead to five miles. However, citing the German's strength and Marshall's obvious pain and exhaustion, the papers predicted a *Fraulein* win: "Her (von Hillern) victory is almost a sure thing," wrote the *Chicago Inter-Ocean*; "[Von Hillern] gives evidence of an ability to hold out the longest," said the *Chicago Daily News*; "[Marshall] seems pretty much exhausted ... [Von Hillern] expresses herself confident of being able to defeat her opponent," reported the *Evening Journal*.

Exactly what happened at the Armory on day six, February 5, 1876, will always remain a question.

By all accounts, Marshall rose sometime between 9:00-10:00 a.m. Her throbbing feet kept her awake all night. They were so swollen she struggled to wear the pair borrowed from O'Leary. She asked two policemen to help her walk around the track. She finally dismissed them, then took off her shoes and continued walking in stockings so saturated with blood they squished when she walked.

In a sharp contrast, Von Hillern emerged from her tent about the same time, carrying a whip and a white feather on her head.

A full house of 3,000 had assembled by 10:00 a.m., eager to witness the finish 12 and a-half-hours later. The exhausted athletes walked for several hours before taking a break in their tents.

No one could explain what happened next.

Marshall shocked everyone as she bolted from her tent rejuvenated, and somehow walking at a pace not seen in days. With the packed house cheering louder with every completed lap, Marshall made up ground on her rival at a stunning rate. The German seemed oblivious to her antagonist's charge, maintaining the consistent plodding that had resulted in a small but significant lead. As race time dwindled from hours to minutes, a handful of gamblers gradually and almost imperceptibly made their way to the judges' stand near the finish. They jammed the area and created confusion, keeping officials from conferring with each other about the correct number of completed laps. Unable to maintain an accurate count on the tote board, they resorted to tallying on personal notepads. Gamblers "corrected" both real and perceived discrepancies. Frustrated people yelled, threatened, pointed and stuck fingers in "miscalculated" totals on the pages. In just a few minutes the crowd that had teetered on madness for two days had morphed into a mob.

Meanwhile, the walkers carried on, ignoring the chaos that now engulfed the armory and suddenly threatened the race's integrity. With only seconds remaining, May passed Bertha one more time before finishing to the deafening yells of the crowd that filled every chair, aisle and even packed the infield. But that did little to quell the confusion at the finish.

A delirious Marshall collapsed in the arms of a waiting Dr. Dunne, who immediately carried the semi-conscious pedestrienne into her privacy tent where he administered laudanum.

At the officials' stand, hundreds of spectators continued pointing and gesturing wildly, painting a picture of something going wrong. Marshall had made several laps on Von Hillern during the last three hours, and Von Hillern also had lost some of her five-mile lead from the night before, but did Marshall in 24 hours cover the 50 extra laps necessary to overtake the *Fraulein?*

No one knew.

The now overflowing and out of control crowd rose and clogged so thick around the scorer's stand that the judges could no longer consult each other for verification. Police fought to keep patrons off the track and maintain a semblance of order. Officials' concerns turned from the race results to worry about their safety. While some placed wagers on the German, the crowd overwhelmingly favored the American.

While enthusiastic responses to men's pedestrian matches were the norm, no one had ever witnessed such a terrifying scene.

O'Leary's plan to increase interest with the nationalism theme might have worked too well. If they declared the "wrong" walker the winner, the mob might destroy the armory.

With pandemonium breaking all around them, panicked judges apparently reached an unspoken consensus.

By 9:30, their records showed Marshall up by one and-a-half miles. At 10:30, judges declared Marshall the winner, 233.9 miles to 231.5.

The crowd cheered. The judges breathed a sigh of relief and scrambled for the exits.

Inside Marshall's privacy room, Dr. Dunne calmed the delirious Marshall with opiates. The *Times* said her feet, "looked like raw beef." They predicted she would need weeks, if not months, to recover. The *Chicago Daily News* had a mixed analysis of the champion, saying, "May Marshall's fame, if she survives the fearful ordeal, is set for life."

Confusion even surrounded the condition of the German.

The *Inter-Ocean* said, "Bertha Von Hillern left the track suddenly Saturday and is lying seriously ill due to the exertion. Her mouth is forced open to get her food. She is being attended to by Dr. Dunne, who is doing all he can for her."

Another version said that Von Hillern, realizing the smothering crowds kept the scorekeepers from properly marking totals, convinced her she'd been cheated out of several laps and ultimately, victory. She left a message for her rival: "I'll take you on anywhere, any time, but not in Chicago."

Many questions arose. How did Marshall, who'd suffered from so many maladies for almost three days, suddenly explode from her tent with renewed energy? How did she overcome the pain that kept her up all night? The swollen, bloodied feet? What medical secret did Dr. Dunne administer?

Von Hillern's biggest obstacles might have been isolation. All week the crowd overwhelmingly favored the American. But Von Hillern, who built a late lead, looked to have the strength to hold off the American for just a few more hours. Or did a language barrier prevent her from understanding correct lap totals?

Some questioned the race's integrity. A fix seemed unlikely, since O'Leary put his professional reputation on the line. He couldn't afford even an appearance of scandal. Plus, as one paper pointed out, nobody would put themselves through so much torture for a hippodrome (fixed race).

Many papers condemned the event. The *Times* said, "There is talk of a match of other women, but the hope is that it will fall through." The *Inter-Ocean* ran an editorial titled, "Women Can't Walk." The *New York Times* later said only that the Chicago results were "unsatisfactory." Organizers couldn't have been happy with the result. While crowds were large and enthusiastic, and the walk proved profitable for O'Leary, the disputed finish overrode everything. Papers targeted May's post-walk condition as reason enough to do away with any similar events. A frustrated Von Hillern soon went to New York and never competed in Chicago again. Marshall picked up the $1,000, and didn't walk professionally again for more than 10 months.

Chicago wouldn't host another major women's walking event for nearly three years. O'Leary wouldn't manage another women's race for almost four years.

Another women's contest wouldn't be held for months. After one race the pedestriennes' future looked murky at best.

CHAPTER 7

Von Hillern Goes It Alone

O n November 6, 1876, 10 months after their controversial contest in Chicago, May Marshall and Bertha von Hillern met in New York's Central Park Garden. Unlike the first one, which ran a half-day short, the second race covered a full six days.

The two battled for three days, but Marshall again suffered from blisters and a swollen leg and *Fraulein* pulled away the last half, with her rival sitting out much of the last 36 hours. She humiliated Marshall, 323 miles to 281. Afterward, officials carried away both women to safety to avoid the crush of spectators.

Marshall, again badly damaged both physically and now emotionally, (and probably financially) wanted to quickly make up for her loss, and get her career back on track.

She found an unlikely foe.

Philadelphia professional sprint walker Peter van Ness, in New York for business, accepted Marshall's challenge to a walk. They agreed to three consecutive nights of 20-milers on the same 22-laps-to-the-mile track where Marshall had just met defeat.

Under those circumstances, not many gave the pedestrienne a chance.

They commenced at 7:04 pm on November 16, just five days after a still-hurting Marshall lost to her German rival.

Still hampered by swollen and blistered feet, the pedestrienne's only hope would be maintaining a steady plodding pace versus Van Ness' speed. He took the early lead in first race, but frequent breaks cost him. He soon fell behind, and never caught up. The second night, Van Ness again set the pace, and this time, he held off Marshall for the victory. Van Ness covered the 20 miles in 3:15, nearly two hours faster than Marshall's winning time from the night before. Most observers believed he would win the third contest. Marshall had no chance of matching his speed.

Thinking he had found a winning strategy, patrons bet on him heavily in race three. He took off again, and at 10 miles he enjoyed a two and a quarter mile lead. However, he lost it during a 45-minute rest period. He returned and they battled for two more miles before taking another costly break. Marshall continued pressing and she finished as he began his last mile. Her time was 5:09.

In just three days, May Marshall redeemed herself, gave further credibility to the still fledgling sport, challenged traditional thought concerning the roles and capabilities of women, captured the admiration of thousands of New Yorkers and took home $500. She received wide acclaim in the New York papers. Most commended the pedestrienne for showing courage and pluck.

The excitement created by the best-two-of–three format could have, should have generated enough pressure to get the top two pedestriennes into a huge third race, with the winner earning thousands along with the title, "Champion Long-Distance Walker of the World."

Marshall even posted requests in the December 30, 1876 *New York Graphic*, issuing a public challenge to Bertha von Hillern to a third match, for $500 a side.

The public pressure should have forced another contest between the two.

But it didn't.

Von Hillern, either didn't want to risk losing another potentially controversial race, as she had in Chicago; didn't care about a title; was convinced of her athletic superiority and ability to draw a crowd; enjoyed publicly jabbing her rival, or a combination of any and all those possible reasons.

Von Hillern committed to perform only solo efforts.

Each walker went her own way, and stayed busy building their respective names and increasing the sport's visibility.

After her victory over Van Ness, Marshall took some time off, presumably to give her battered feet time to recover and possibly spend some time with her son, who was staying with her mother in Chicago.

When she returned in the spring of 1877, she spent April to July putting on at least 10 performances throughout New England. She twice followed Von Hillern 50 mile and 100 mile performances in Boston, besting her time on both occasions. On April 11, Marshall completed a remarkable tramp at Horticultural Hall, maybe the best of any pedestrienne to date. She promised to beat Von Hillern's 100 miles in under 28 hours by walking the same in less than 27 hours. Since Von Hillern wouldn't walk against her, she believed that completing such a task would permit her undisputed claim to the title of Champion Pedestrienne of the

World. The next evening, in front of a packed house adoring her every move, she covered 100 miles in 26:47.48. She was presented with dozens of floral bouquets and many gifts, plus a gold medal that said, "Mrs. Marshall, Champion of America, presented by her friends."

She again had trouble with her feet, and walked the last 17 miles without shoes. She avoided serious potential injury when officials found rocks and sharp tacks on the track, probably put there by a person or persons who had bets on her failing.

Not all of her walks went well, however. On May 30, she failed to finish 50 miles in 12 hours in Providence, and one month later in New Bedford's Pirian Hall, she took longer than the announced 28 hours to cover 100 miles. She blamed the latter failure not only on her sore feet, she couldn't walk on her own afterwards, but on the neglect of her hired coach, professional pedestrian George Avery. Avery was supposed to walk with Marshall, but she often found herself alone. Without Avery's presence, spectators overwhelmed the track, forcing her to weave and lose time and increase distance on every lap. In spite of the spirited crowd's response to the pedestrienne, she only logged 98 miles in the time frame. Avery's whereabouts were soon revealed. He had become enamored with teen pedestrienne Bertie LeFranc, who walked 25 miles as an undercard, and whom papers mentioned as Mrs. Marshall's pupil. During the walk, the couple disappeared for hours. When the carriage arrived to escort the pedestriennes back to their hotel, Avery and LeFranc got in, leaving an exhausted and furious Mrs. Marshall to fend for herself.

Marshall returned the next week in New Bedford. With the help of her companion professional pedestrian William Brown, she accomplished her goal. Locals hosted a banquet for her, and she accepted a prize of just over $600, giving $50 to Brown.

She wrapped up her season with a successful 50 miles inside of 12 hours in Taunton.

She then likely took her winnings and spent the next few months buying and setting up up a house in Chicago.

While Marshall made some good money and garnered considerable headlines, she couldn't keep up with her younger German rival, either on the track or in the newspapers.

*   *   *

Unlike Marshall, Von Hillern stuck to the track.

She also enhanced her persona by hiring a manager, David S. Thomas.

For three years, he worked as publicity man for showman P.T. Barnum. From all accounts the well-liked Thomas knew his job. He got his client publicity in local papers, but much more than just race results and a quote or two. Through Thomas' guidance, Von Hillern made herself available for long revealing interviews, in which the masses found out about her background, diet, daily routines, upbringing and her strict Roman Catholic faith. Dozens of small and large papers around the country ran results and snippets of the pedestrienne. The public couldn't get enough of the inspirational German. The papers' editorials began questioning when the little marvel might visit their towns.

In what might have been a first for a professional female athlete, her name appeared in ads for at least two restorative products, "Chiropodin," for "strong feet," and Giles' Liniment Iodide Ammonia which, "...gives her strength and endurance. She is never without a supply of the liniment."

Just before Christmas in 1876, in Boston's Music Hall, she finished 350 miles in six days in front of 4,000 people. Afterward, a writer for the *Women's Journal* said, "...the hall being filled with fashionable men and women, who almost buried the tired girl with flowers and compliments."

The February 15, 1877 issue of the *Boston Journal* reported that a 'bold and adventurous fan' put the letters Bertha von Hillern on the highest access of the Equitable Insurance Building.

In May, 1877, the *Worcester Gazette* told of Von Hillern's afternoon visit to an insane asylum and attending a play that evening. She dropped by the local jail and later in the week attended two church services.

The next week, she walked 16 miles in four hours, and received an ovation from many townspeople when she passed through Clinton. During a professional walk in Providence, city bulletin boards posted hourly progress reports. She encouraged women to walk for health, resulting in the formation of several women's walking clubs. She gave lectures and walking demonstrations in many cities where she appeared.

She was probably most admired in Worcester, MA and Boston, her new home. During her first walk in Worcester, the local paper promoted her as, "The Little Wonder!" On May 16, 1877 the *Worcester Evening Gazette*, reported of the crowd's response to her nearing the end of her 100 mile/28 hour performance in Mechanics' Hall, "...the now large crowd followed her every motion with eager eyes, the patter of ladies' hands and fans, and the waving of handkerchiefs preceding and following her like a wave around the hall." Wheaton's ran an ad announcing the arrival of the new "Von Hillern hats," calling them the "latest out and very stylish."

But she was not above some public scrutiny. The *New Orleans Times Picayune* occasionally took snarky cheap shots at her, questioning the purpose in her accomplishments, and even questioning her femininity. In Philadelphia, the *Inquirer* ran an ad announcing a new "Burlesque Fizzical Kulture (the term physical culture equated to today's physical fitness) in which Miss Birdie Von Kill-em will accomplish the wonderful feet of walk 2,800 miles in 11 or 8 minutes." It's hard to say if the play was parody or ridicule.

But these criticisms were rare.

Other pedestriennes appeared, such as LeFranc and Millie Rose, each of whom earned some fame. Rose actually acted as an undercard and failed in her quest to walk 50 miles in 13 hours during the first Marshall-Von Hillern match in Chicago. While some newcomers enjoyed success, none had the talent and name recognition of the top two stars.

And one of them was about to make a career change.

CHAPTER 8

William Gale Comeback

While managing a theatre in Cardiff in the summer of 1877, Ada Anderson attended an event that would redefine her life. She had spent almost 20 years and moved up to a provincial-level performer and later a manager. She had seen standing ovations reward a powerful performance, when excited patrons almost demanded a popular actor make multiple curtain calls. She had marveled at audiences aching with laughter one minute, then overwhelmed with tension at an unexpected dramatic moment.

She had seen it all.

Or so she thought.

In her decades in show business, she had never witnessed a performer like William Gale.

Gale drew big crowds. His name headlined the papers, everyone knew him, and the money he earned drew gasps from even the highest-paid theatrical stars.

Despite all his glory he lacked the charisma of even a bit player. Most entertainers spent years developing the right look and public persona to woo an audience and develop a following. Then they constantly worked to maintain a strong bond with the public. Lose that and a performer might not ever get it back. Gale apparently made no effort to develop any kind of charm or panache.

The *New York Herald* later wrote of him, ". . . his thoughts were entirely on the great feat in which he was engaged, and not on the applause of the public..." and that he was a "quiet, inoffensive person . . ." and "...a bad caterer of public approval."

Anderson possessed far more star quality than the five-foot-three, 116-pound Gale. She had better ownership of a stage, more ability to work a crowd, and a greater persona. She outshined him in virtually any area of performing.

Gale didn't act, sing or dance. The *Herald* noted, "Of circus tricks and advertising advantages, he is totally ignorant; he played no cornet and gave no orations. . ."

But his one talent made up for all other shortcomings.

Gale had made his name as an athlete, a rare accomplishment in mid-19th century Great Britain. He had excelled in the tradition of Captain Barclay and a succession of professional pedestrians. He may have been the best of them all. His performances had dazzled and amazed Brits for years.

And his mastery of that singular skill attracted crowds that exceeded those of a favorite actor or singer. Men celebrated his achievements by standing and stomping their feet; women waved handkerchiefs. The papers almost universally gave him glowing reviews.

He lived the life Anderson had fantasized about since her childhood.

But the stage where Gale performed bore little resemblance to the one Anderson pursued. In theatre, the actor's delivery set the tone and carried the emotion. People came for the journey, not the outcome. Did the performer make patrons "feel" the moment? Did he bring the crowd with him? Did he capture those key scenes? Could he pull off a big finish?

When Gale performed, the drama rested in the unknown regarding his success or failure. The mystery of what would happen next. With little warning, a debilitating muscle cramp could cripple him, ending his quest. Or he might succumb to dehydration in a slow, deliberate manner, as though he'd contracted a disease. With the seemingly never-ending repetitive nature of his task, many wondered how he avoided delving into madness.

Success meant spectators possibly witnessing history. When they read or talked about him, they could smile and say, "I cheered for him. I helped make that happen."

Unlike the theatre, where people applauded for a job well done, they cheered Gale to help him achieve a remarkable and improbable feat. Who couldn't get excited about that?

Anderson watched and felt his power, and had seen the command he possessed. She wondered, "Is this my calling?"

*　　*　　*

Gale walked in the tradition of Captain Barclay.

He carried on a great British tradition, and did it better than anyone else. He even trumped his famous predecessor.

A one-time bookbinder, Gale began his pedestrian career as a 19-year-old in 1850. Within three years he had rewritten England's ideas of athletic excellence, equaling Captain Barclay's record of 1,000 miles in 1,000 hours.

He followed that record with 1,000 miles in 500 hours in Birkenhead on the Wirral Peninsula near Liverpool. Then on the Walton Highway, again near Liverpool, he destroyed Barclay's longstanding record, topping the Captain with 1,500 miles in 1,000 hours at Lillibridge, a performance not seen in 40 years. The walk cemented his place as the top pedestrian of all-time. The newspapers dubbed him, "The Flying Eagle," and said he possessed "iron bone and steel wire veins."

For 17 years Gale dominated the pedestrian landscape, putting on solo performances that amazed even longtime followers of the sport and frustrating potential rivals, who almost always fell short even of his most modest achievements.

In September 1870, he capped his 20-year career by completing a three-week-long walk of 2,000 quarter miles in 2,000 quarter hours at the Canton Recreation Grounds in Cardiff. He earned 50 pounds for the victory. Local dignitaries honored him with a dinner, several toasts, and at least two purses of what newspapers called "substantial sums."

Then he retired.

By the late 1860s pedestrian headlines shifted to Weston, then O'Leary. Their rivalry created professional pedestrianism in America and expanded. In late 1876-1877, they came to Great Britain for a series of pedestrian contests and exhibitions, and wowed the locals with their pedestrian talents.

The duo trounced the English, winning the admiration of public and press, and possibly raising the ire of William Gale.

No one knows why William Gale came out of a seven-year retirement to return to professional walking. Maybe he got bored or he needed the money. A likely guess is that Americans' success at beating Britain's top walkers upset his sense of nationalism, and he wanted to prove England, home of the sport, still produced the best pedestrians. In 1877, at the age of 44, Gale returned to the track.

Dispirited followers of pedestrianism undoubtedly welcomed the announcement, but his proposed debut performance must have shocked the country. From June 28 until July 25, 1877, William Gale would return to Cardiff's Canton Recreation Grounds, the site of his last professional walk. He vowed to walk a quarter mile, or two laps, around a 220-yard dirt track every 10 minutes, 24 hours a day. He would total 4,000 quarter miles in 4,000 quarter hours, 8,000 laps or 1,000 miles. For the entire month sleeping would consist of a maximum of six-minute mini-naps. He would never take an unscheduled break or time out to nurse the inevitable muscle strain or upset stomach. To deviate from the announced goal would violate his professional agreement, and Gale would go home disgraced and without pay. Worse, his failure meant British pedestrian pride taking another crushing blow.

Completing a walk of such physical stress, especially by an aging athlete who had been out of the game for years, seemed impossible. Along the way he would fight cold, rain, heat, hunger, cramps, muscle soreness, spasms, and any professional pedestrian's constant companions, fatigue and loneliness. He had battled all those foes before, and he triumphed. But could he still do it?

The day of his return, a wooden apartment sat on the track's infield. There he would clean up, eat, rest, and enjoy frequent but brief respites. His attendants would expertly handle a variety of tasks. They would wake him at the appropriate times, prepare his food, tend to his medical needs, clean his clothes, and ready his makeshift shower. They also monitored the use of scents, washes, liniments, oils, and various other preparations and treatments needed for his well-being.

Judges working in shifts would record each completed lap. Gamblers, some of whom staked hundreds on his failing, would stand watch and keep their own tallies. Exhaustion, injury, boredom, or any other problems meant a big payday for the sporting men. Not many believed he would succeed.

The *Cardiff Western Mail* reported on his solitary start, which began at 1:00 a.m. under a "pale moonlight" and "a keen wind stirred the branches of the sturdy trees that line the Canton Grounds." Most of the few souls on hand that night were assistants to the slightly-built man, with short-cropped hair, with a woolen wrapped around his neck.

He finished the first of his planned 4,000 quarter miles in 2:45.

That first night, officials followed him via the hissing light of the oil lamp he carried and the glow from the cigarette he occasionally smoked as he walked. Even with that, his silhouette was barely discernible under the faint glow of the moon.

He continued for three weeks, suffering though the usual pedestrian battles. Confidence grew that he was defying age.

But with only days remaining, Gale collapsed three times in one week. Doctors, who frequently checked the athlete, attributed the first to delirium, the second to physical weakness, the third to mental and physical stress. But somehow each time he lifted himself within one minute (any physical assistance would have negated the effort), completed the requisite quarter mile, and recovered during his brief respite. Long stretches of solitude were replaced with hours of excitement; empty grounds with throngs of crowds; and silence with the melodies of a band that, as the pedestrian neared the finish, played "Conquering Hero."

As he neared the finish four weeks after he started, Canton Grounds filled with frenzied spectators. Women, with tears streaming down their cheeks, waved their handkerchiefs and strained their necks to catch a glimpse each time he passed. Men raced across the infield yelling encouragement that seemed louder with each completed lap. Children, many oblivious to the event's significance, played on the infield, some mimicking the walker's actions.

Gale started his final quarter-mile at 7:30 p.m. on July 25. The immense crowd's cheering and yelling grew with every step. When he finished number 4,000 in 4:30, the packed grounds let out a shout that drowned out the band.

The thousands who witnessed what the *Mail* called "the greatest feat of pedestrianism on record" mobbed the walker. Just as he had done almost a quarter-century earlier, William Gale had elevated the sport and British pride.

The triumph meant more than personal achievement to Gale. His pedestrian resume had remained unchanged for seven years. He returned not for personal glory. He had already secured his spot in pedestrian history. He came back to help inspire his countrymen.

The mob carried him around the track and the masses couldn't get enough. Some leapt in his direction, reaching for a quick hand clasp or at least a brush with an arm or leg. Others hoped for eye contact, or just to see him so they could make a stronger connection with the moment. They had witnessed a miracle. With the success of one event, he had restored national pride to a sport that the British practically invented almost 70 years earlier when Captain Barclay set the standard for all subsequent pedestrians.

The Americans, Daniel O'Leary and Edward Payson Weston, had had their day. Their 100-mile and six-day races seemed like a warm-up compared to Gale's accomplishment. Gale had set a new standard for pedestrian excellence for the century; maybe for the ages.

The Brits could reclaim ownership of their sport.

The *Western Mail* authenticated that William Gale had commenced his task at 1:00 a.m., Thursday morning on June 28, 1877, and had walked one quarter mile every 10 minutes, finishing 1,000 miles in 1,000 hours at 7:34.30 p.m. on July 25, 1877. The paper affirmed that officials and judges were on hand and had certified that the performance had been carried out "in strict compliance with the conditions laid down, and that the editor of the *Mail* was in possession of every quarter-mile time."

The paper also listed the names of almost three dozen men who had agreed to sponsor a subscription to honor Mr. Gale the following Wednesday evening at 7:30 p.m.

Anderson witnessed the event from afar. She had experienced more than just the excitement of seeing of Gale's victory. She felt it and wanted that for herself, the cheering crowds, the adulation. Most of all she wanted to feel the sense of accomplishment, actually doing something that seemed impossible. In athletics she didn't need a relative to influence others. She wouldn't have to play politics. And her plain looks wouldn't break her career. Endurance walking played to her greatest strength, her work ethic.

She wanted to enter that exciting world, performing in front of large crowds, all cheering for her, pulling for her to succeed. After so many years of frustration she had found her calling. She knew she only had a limited time to "make a name," and that professional pedestrianism might be her last chance.

She knew nothing of the sport, but she could get to know William Gale.

She would ask him for help.

CHAPTER 9

Making a Name

*L*ittle is known about the relationship between Ada Anderson and William Gale. However, we do know of Gale's no-nonsense temperament. He possessed a direct manner with people and had no pretenses and a strong sense of nationalism. Anderson could claim many of those same qualities, but unlike Gale, her years of learning how to perform either brought out or refined her outgoing personality.

He likely admired her determination, and could identify with many of her qualities and goals. She probably saw him as her final opportunity to help her "make a name."

As a walker she would take the formal name "Madame" over Ada, and keep her married name "Anderson." From now on most professional references would call her "Madame Anderson."

Gale had much to teach his new charge. Her transformation into a professional endurance walker only started with training. And even though she appeared to possess all the qualities necessary to succeed as a pedestrienne, like O'Leary with his charges, they wouldn't know her ability to compete until she raced.

After only about six weeks of training, he believed she was ready.

She would debut on September 1877, in Newport Wales and walk 1,000 half-miles in 1,000 half-hours, a trek that would take three weeks to complete.

At no point would she get more than 20 minutes' continuous rest.

In those days, the dangers of sleep deprivation were virtually unknown.

Intense physical activity forestalls sleepiness for a while. Its first symptoms are loss of fine motor skills, which play little part in endurance walking, further masking early signs of fatigue.

For nearly a month, Madame Anderson would alternate between walking and what would later be called "Phase One" sleep, which lasts about five minutes or so. At this stage the muscles relax, heart rate and breathing slow, and body temperature drops. Brain activity shifts from transmitting rapid beta waves to slower alpha waves to theta waves, whose appearance signals that phase one sleep has been reached. For the first few days, brief but effective 10- to 15-minute "micro-naps," as they would be called, would keep Madame Anderson functioning at a respectable level.

She would first experience some loss of cognitive process and mental focus. If she spoke only occasionally and in short stints, the symptoms could be temporarily hidden. Also, training for such a schedule would help keep her awake. However, after five days with only frequent breaks allowing for micro-napping, Madame Anderson, in addition to other problems, would start experiencing and exhibiting some symptoms of serious sleep deprivation, including loss of gross motor skills and decreased motivation.

Gale, as Madame Anderson's coach, would have trained her for all the physical, mental and emotional battles that she would face, but training has its limitations.

They quickly found out about her mental toughness.

Although she fought through several days of rain and at one point carried an umbrella in one hand and a lamp in another, she completed her journey.

The press at least did not initially greet her in the warmest fashion. Under the heading, "A woman styling herself Madame Anderson," still another asked, "Who is the Champion Female Pedestrian?" Even her limited physical attractiveness entered into the dialogue, as an announcement/ad in the stage magazine *Era* referred to her as, "The Lady (not so-called, but actually)." One wonders if anyone at that publication knew Madame Anderson as an actress, and if so they apparently kept it to themselves. She didn't let on either.

For most, however, Madame Anderson's first effort proved a significant step in the embryonic world of women's walking.

Her next attempt would prove a setback.

The following month in Exeter, Madame Anderson was scheduled to walk 1,250 half miles in 1,000 half hours, another three-week trek. She failed when a storm blew in, forcing her from the grounds for several hours.

The next walk was critical. If she failed again, many of her growing following would likely leave her, convinced that women, or at least she, couldn't make it as a professional athlete.

But instead of backing off their plans, she and Gale accelerated, scheduling a task that seemed ridiculous, especially in light of her recent failure.

They moved on to Plymouth, England, where in November, 1877, she and Gale scheduled the impossible: 1,250 miles in 1,000 hours, or 1.25 miles every hour for six weeks. Accomplishing that would put her, only three races into her career, into an elite class by beating Captain Barclay's long-standing benchmark by 250 miles, and leave her trailing only Gale's Lillibridge mark of 1,500 miles in 1,000 hours. And like Gale, she wouldn't "game" the system as Captain Barclay had done when he started a mile at the end of one hour, then immediately launching into the next mile at the top of the following hour.

When she completed that task, many considered her the greatest walker ever, male or female. Now the British could lay claim to the top man and woman professional walkers. In four months, William Gale and Madame Anderson had not just restored British pedestrian pride, they elevated it.

Newspapers such as *Era* that just weeks before almost poked fun at her, questioning her identity and even her sexuality, now referred to her as, "Champion Lady Walker," and "lady champion walker of the world."

In a just a few weeks, Madame Anderson put nearly two decades of theatrical stagnation behind her. She had moved beyond the tragedy of the untimely death of her husband. She had gone from the obscurity of theatre management to achieving the lofty perch of professional excellence that had been her dream since her days growing up in Lambeth, and had eluded her for two decades on the stage.

Madame Anderson earned the right to call herself a professional athlete.

But many lessons lay before her.

*   *   *

With two long, successful performances under her belt, the next one, a 100-mile, 28-hour walk again in Plymouth, England differed in many ways. This would be much shorter, and for the first time she would walk indoors. The loops were smaller—inside a circus ring—but she would avoid battling the uncomfortable and often unpredictable European climate.

An indoor facility created a more intimate and controlled atmosphere. Patrons could monitor her progress, and cheer whenever she completed a critical mile.

However, the loops became monotonous, and the tent held in pollution from men's cigar smoke and gas lamps, causing her severe coughing and respiratory problems. She fell at 60 miles, then again at 87 miles. After struggling for nine more miles, she collapsed into unconsciousness just four miles from the finish.

Another setback, but Madame Anderson went to the press and vowed to never take on another task she couldn't finish.

Returning to the track in mid-January 1878 at Plymouth, she completed a two-week trek of 1,344 quarter-miles in a similar number of quarter hours.

*   *   *

Just days after the Plymouth triumph, she planned a month-long walk of 1,008 miles in 672 hours, or 1.5 miles an hour for 28 days at the Corn Exchange in Boston (Lincolnshire), England.

Local magistrates told her they didn't approve of such exhibitions, believing they contributed to corrupted morals, and many objected to walking on Sundays. However, the local mayor claimed that Boston was "more moral than Plymouth, where Madame Anderson last indulged in the sin of walking on Sunday."

On February 13, she began one-and-a-half miles an hour for 28 days. On March 3, the *Era* reported, "This feat is causing the greatest sensation in Boston, hundreds being turned away hourly." Upon completing the task, management and police united to keep the masses from "storming the place."

Madame Anderson and her assistants were moved by the show of affection.

"The whole town turned out," said Elizabeth Sparrow, her most trusted attendant, then said later, "and the parish bells rang when she was finishing."

"My heart seemed to come up in my throat and nearly choked me for a while," said the pedestrienne, "it was the proudest moment of my life."

The emotion extended beyond walking success or peoples' adoration. After years of frustration, Ada Anderson had experienced her dream. She had attracted the attention that had eluded her since childhood. For the first time large numbers of people cheered for her. She finally felt part of the entertainment world.

However, in addition to the emotional high, she took a physical beating, and only alert and skilled attendants, who applied turpentine and raw beef to her bloodied feet and got her walking again.

On April 8 at the Olympian Grounds in Leeds, she sought to tie Gale's record of 1,500 miles in 1,000 hours. She finished on May 20, and afterwards, continued walking a quarter mile every quarter hour. Almost single-handedly, she created a competitive industry for females in England. From now on, all pedestrians, male and female, would be compared to her. Her standards, like those of her predecessors, Barclay, and now Gale, would become the benchmark for all professional endurance walkers.

Madame Anderson might have just completed a record-breaking performance, but Ada Anderson had one more important item of business in Leeds.

On May 22, just two days after finishing her walk, she went to the Parish Church where she married a theatre man named William Paley.

*   *   *

In the summer she completed three more walks in Skegness, King's Lynn and Peterborough.

From September 1877 to August 1878, her first year as a professional athlete, Madame Anderson recorded a remarkable eight successful, multi-week walks in England. She had become an industry, owning the title champion pedestrienne. She built an audience and proved that women could perform as professional athletes.

In England, at least, she owned the sport.

And that domination became a problem. She already beaten Captain Barclay's record and tied Gale's. What else could she do?

She needed a rival. After all, Weston and O'Leary didn't popularize pedestrianism; Weston vs. O'Leary did that.

Gale knew the public would tire of watching a solo act. Domination invites boredom. Without a rival, Madame Anderson would morph into a novelty, and novelties wear quickly. Before long the excitement would vanish (her popularity might have already peaked) and she would be done. Without a rival she could only take the sport and her aging body so far.

Besides, the pedestrienne needed motivation, too.

Athletic competition is about athlete vs. athlete, not athlete vs. the clock. Sport thrives on your best vs. my best; your will vs. my will. Exciting comebacks and spectacular finishes; cheering for and betting on a favorite personality or the hometown hero. Losing today but promising to return victorious. Sometimes, the races put national pride on the line. Weston and O'Leary vs. the Brits. *Fraulein* vs. American Girl.

Gale had seen Madame Anderson top the accomplishments of almost anyone, man or woman. Neither Von Hillern nor Marshall had put on any performance close to that of Madame Anderson. But while the American duo had been accepted and drew big crowds, headlines and lavish paydays, a British interloper might not play well.

But, she had to walk in America. And she had to do it quickly.

At age 35, Ada wouldn't have time to build an audience. She must make an immediate impact in the New World. So she must do something unimaginable. She had one chance to put on a spectacle Americans had never seen.

America had shown great interest, if not a fascination with professional walkers, including women. A performance familiar to everyone would not draw big crowds to Madame Anderson, an aging immigrant with no following. Shysters and scam artists represented "pedestrians" who claimed great accomplishments, but failed on the track. Madame Anderson would again have to prove herself to a skeptical public.

A walk that took days or even weeks to complete would also allow her to showcase not just her athletic ability, but other stage talents. While people gladly paid anywhere from twenty-five cents to one dollar to watch the established male and female athletes, any other entertainment fell to the band that often played during the more popular hours of attendance.

Madame Anderson could offer more.

While never a beauty or headlining act, she could sing, play practical jokes, make speeches, and banter with the press and the public. She would sell herself, her personality, her persona. And while some big-name and lesser-known pedestriennes often made such positive public relations gestures, no one could do it with the panache of a 20-year stage veteran.

She would go to America, but without Gale. Due to obligations, he would stay in England for several weeks.

On October 13, 1878, Madame Anderson, William Paley, her manager J. H. Webb, and long-time assistant Elizabeth Sparrow all boarded the steamship *Ethiopia* for America.

CHAPTER 10

A Pedestrienne Retires

eginning in late 1877, Bertha von Hillern again made the rounds, this time to bigger cities, all first-time stops.

She developed a routine. She walked twice each in Baltimore, Washington, Pittsburgh, Cincinnati, and Louisville. At each stop, she covered 89 miles in 26 hours, then a few days later, followed that with 100 miles in 28 hours. Each time, the result was the same. She enjoyed unrivaled success. Houses were packed, the throngs cheered. She talked with the press.

When she finished her 100-miler in Louisville on April 13, the *Louisville Courier* ran a summary of the crowds that watched her complete, "the house rang with raptures of applause...Ladies waved their handkerchiefs and the men clapped their hands and hurrahed until the noise was deafening."

The paper then ran her pulse, temperature, and respiration rate at four key spots in the race, and David Thomas had affidavits sworn to that the track was accurate and the Miss Von Hillern had walked 100 miles between 7:00 p.m. April 11 and 11:00 p.m. April 12.

The Courier closed out by saying, "This is the last exhibition Miss Von Hillern until the cold weather sets in."

In just a little over two years, Bertha von Hillern had gone from being an unknown German teen who barely spoke English into one of the most famous and richest women in America. She had inspired hundreds, if not thousands of women to begin a fitness walking program. Her rivalry with May Marshall had actually started professional women's pedestrianism in America. Von Hillern had challenged the traditional roles of women in America and redefined about the capabilities of the "fairer sex." Her presence had been requested at cities all over America. Her name had been used in advertisements. While in Washington in January, she had called on President Rutherford B. Hayes. Papers reported that First Lady Mrs. Lucy Hayes expressed a request to see her perform.

Starting with her defeat of Marshall in Central Park Garden in November, 1876, she had walked a total of 32 times in 16 cities. She'd only experienced two defeats, June 5, 1877 in Worcester and the following August 29 in Lowell. Both times she failed to complete 50 miles in 12 hours. The first she attributed to breaking from her routine when she spent the evening entertaining a lady friend instead of getting her usual pre-race rest. In Lowell she succumbed to the heat.

But those setbacks did little to dampen the public's enthusiasm for "The Little Wonder."

She had won the adoration of hundreds of thousands, if not millions of women throughout her new homeland. And they would form the foundation of her fans in a new discipline.

On April 13, 1878, what the *Louisville Courier* didn't know, nor maybe even Thomas or Von Hillern herself was that she wouldn't return to the track.

In subsequent weeks rumors would abound that she was paralyzed, that the excessive walking had destroyed her young body. Sure she had achieved fame, glory and riches, but at what price?

None of the rumors was true, and one wonders where and how they got started? If Thomas was the source, why? Was he trying to elicit sympathy for his client? Did the two of them hope to diffuse criticism or disappointment from fans who couldn't understand why she would leave the sport after accomplishing so much?

If the source wasn't Thomas and Von Hillern, then where? And what was their motive?

It didn't really matter. Bertha von Hillern was already planning for the next stage of her young life.

Probably during one of her Boston walks, Von Hillern met painter Maria Beckett (aka Maria A'Becket). The two became close friends, and Beckett often accompanied Von Hillern to some of her races, once even walking 20 miles with her. Beckett might have influenced Von Hillern to pursue a career in landscape painting. They became two of the few women who studied under famed artist and teacher, Boston-based William Morris Hunt. They eventually opened a studio in Boston, and participated in exhibits in Boston and Pennsylvania.

To the chagrin of many and the delight of others, Bertha von Hillern left endurance walking at the age of 21. She made a fortune, and garnered even more admiration when she sent $9,000 home to her parents in Germany, who probably hadn't seen their daughter since she left the homeland circa 1875.

She successfully made the transition from the tan bark track to the canvas, but her absence left a huge hole in women's endurance walking. Barely two years old, the sport lost one of its stars.

And it only had two.

May Marshall could now lay claim to the world's to pedestrienne.

Although she lacked Von Hillern's promotional skills, she was the top draw.

Now the question arose, could she carry the sport?

* * *

While Ada Anderson was in England learning the craft from William Gale, May Marshall set out to prove she was worthy of the title "Champion Pedestrienne of the World."

But without the challenge of a rival, which elevated the game of both athletes, her performances faltered.

First, Marshall lost a 27-hour "go-as-you-please" walk in Marysville, Ohio. In June, in she quit in the middle of a poorly attended 50 mile in 12 hour tramp in Toledo, leaving her manager in arrearages.

Looking to expand the sport, she scheduled a first-ever tour of the south in the summer of 1878, where she walked in Arkansas and Texas, but ran into serious trouble in Memphis, which was in the early throes of a yellow fever epidemic.

Memphis, due to its proximity to swamplands and lack of sanitation, frequently saw yellow fever outbreaks. Of the six yellow fever episodes that would hit Memphis between 1828 and 1879, number five, in 1878 would prove the worst. Beginning in July, when the outbreak began, 25,000 residents would leave the city. Of those that remained 17,000 would contract the disease, resulting in 5,000 deaths.

May Marshall was nearly one of them.

During a walk in Memphis on July 23, she developed a backache, chills and high fever, all symptoms of yellow fever. A doctor at the walk diagnosed her as having the disease.

She was taken to the home of a former slave woman who, violating doctor's orders, wrapped the pedestrienne in cold cloths. After weeks of suffering, Marshall slowly recovered. She stayed in St. Louis until September. "I had a hard struggle," she said later, "but I lived through it. It is an awful disease and I don't see how I am living today."

After recovering, she walked in front of 7,000 at a fair in St. Louis. She then traveled to Pennsylvania where she performed in Oil City, then Bradford, where she picked up $600, then traveled to Erie. She followed that with a trip to Philadelphia's Academy of Music, where she walked 50 miles in 10:52, eight minutes under her announced goal of 11 hours.

Her string of victories in Pennsylvania helped make up for a terrible spring and early summer failures. In spite of an up-and-down six months, her overall resume looked impressive.

By late 1878, May had completed one-hundred 50-mile walks and twenty-three 100-mile walks. She was the only walker to cover 100 miles in less than 27 hours when she recorded 26:47 in Boston. .

Her earnings from walking matches and personal appearances totaled $25,000.

But her appeal was plummeting.

As 1878 came to a close, she uncharacteristically suffered three failures inside a month. Crowds and pay dwindled. The label, "Champion Pedestrienne of the World," no longer impressed the masses. After all, where could she take the sport? Without Von Hillern's presence, or another credible rival, the typical sports argument, "Who was greatest?" didn't exist.

May Marshall and pedestrianism needed a challenger.

Some of the pedestrienne hopefuls who had spent months walking as undercards and understudies were developing their skills. The *New York Clipper*, one of the few publications that carried sports stories, reported on a vastly improved Bertie LeFranc, although she took some serious time off as she and George Avery had gotten married and were the new parents of a baby girl, Portland (ME) resident May Bell Sherman, Rochester's Bertha von Berg (aka Maggie von Gross), Carrie Ross, and Helene Freeman all gave credible performances. Even out west, where professional pedestrianism was slow to catch on, Kate Lorence recorded 100 miles in less than 28 hours.

But in Wisconsin, a young unknown was dazzling the Midwest with a series of remarkable races.

She seemed like the perfect rival. Only a few months younger than Von Hillern, she performed well, she enjoyed a positive personal image with the public and the press. She reached a high level of pedestrian accomplishment. And she had overcome numerous obstacles.

Only hers were more personal and tragic.

*   *   *

Like many of the pedestriennes, the early life of Exilda LaChapelle is not well chronicled. She was born in Marseilles, France on February 15, 1859. The young family moved to Canada where both of Exilda's parents soon died, leaving her in the charge of an itinerant uncle, who didn't appear to be much of a disciplinarian.

She began walking professionally in Canada and North Midwestern United States at around the age of 13. The pixie-like LaChapelle, with jet black hair, small nose, and dark, piercing eyes made her a target for obnoxious, inebriated men in the smoky bars where she often performed.

Likely out of desperation, she married at 15, and gave birth to a boy. For the first time in her life, she enjoyed some stability, but her happiness would not last. Within a year, her baby died.

That event devastated her and for several years at least, and in many ways, defined her life. In later interviews, she spoke of wanting to retire from walking for the simple life of mother and wife. She frequently broke down when she spoke of losing him.

In late 1877, she returned to the track.

*   *   *

By April, 1878, she was making a name for herself in Wisconsin, and even garnered some mentions in the Chicago papers and the *New York Clipper*.

Only 19, she could already perform with the best. She covered 336 miles in 100 hours in walking from Montreal to Toronto. She covered 100 miles faster than 25 hours, something no other pedestreinne had done. Like Marshall, she frequently beat men. She also discovered unwanted conflicts on the track. In December, 1878 a male competitor hit her as she tried to pass, once on the breast and once in her mouth. His backers claim she crowded him. Judges ruled in her favor, but she had already left the track so the match was declared a draw.

Overall however, the reaction to her in Wisconsin mirrored those of other successful pedestriennes, large enthusiastic crowds cheering every completed lap. And she appeared to accomplish her tasks with a minimum of visible effort or discomfort.

Throughout 1878, she walked in Racine, Oshkosh, Fond du lac, and Janesville. She received positive newspaper coverage and the admiration of patrons, but she wasn't pulling in the money of Von HIllern or Marshall.

Her victories would earn her anywhere from $25-$75, with totals leaning toward the former.

But that would no longer do. She'd proven she could go much higher in the fledgling sport.

By late 1878, she was readying herself for a bigger stage.

CHAPTER 11

Arrival in the New World

On October 22, 1878, just nine days after leaving England, Madame Anderson and her entourage landed in New York. She approached William Vanderbilt, owner of Gilmore's Garden, about hosting a long endurance walking contest at his venue.

In 1871, showman P. T. Barnum bought the lease for the New York and Harlem Railroad Passenger Depot and converted it to "The Great Roman Hippodrome," also called "Barnum's Monster Classical and Geological Hippodrome." His showcases included circuses and other performances in the roofless building. In 1876, bandleader Patrick Gilmore took over. He hosted the first Westminster Kennel Dog Show in 1877, and illegal boxing matches disguised as "exhibitions" or "illustrated lectures."

Vanderbilt became the richest man in the world when his father, transportation magnate Cornelius Vanderbilt, died in 1877, leaving his oldest son almost all of his $100 million fortune.

Lured by show business, Vanderbilt bought the building. Already it might have been the most famous entertainment venue in the world. In a few months it would earn greater fame under its new name: Madison Square Garden.

But Madame Anderson's timing couldn't have been worse. Gilmore's was in the second week of what would be an incredible six-week run of P. T. Barnum's New and Greatest Show on Earth.

Still, her new manager, Webb, tried to convince Vanderbilt to give her a shot. Vanderbilt listened patiently and then said, "The woman can never accomplish the feat, nor can any other woman; it is simply an impossibility. You may have the Garden for one week, no longer."

She couldn't get Gilmore's, but she had options, however none could match Gilmore's appeal and income potential. So, they headed across the East River to Brooklyn's Fulton Street.

In just a few years Fulton Street had developed into a thriving entertainment district. While the nightlife choices didn't rise to that of New York in either quality or variety, Brooklynites could still choose from an array of ways to spend a free evening.

Some of the more daring acts included "William Tell" shows in which the marksman stepped off at usually 30 paces then, using a gun, shot an apple off a trusting partner's head. In a somewhat less dangerous version, but still attractive to patrons who longed for an adrenaline fix, the "targeted" half of the duo would hold the apple in a hand extended overhead.

Other more traditional acts included singers, ventriloquists and "Blind Tom," the celebrated Negro boy pianist, and maybe the most popular show, Harriet Beecher Stowe's "Uncle Tom's Cabin."

Webb approached the owner of a small theatre at the corner of Smith and Fulton Street, "Captain" AR Samuells.

After some initial reluctance, Samuells agreed.

*   *   *

In many ways, Alexander R. Samuells represented the typical, mid-19th century Brooklynite.

In 1842, AR's father brought his young family, including his two-month-old son, Alexander, to Baltimore from England. The elder Samuells worked as a carpenter, and in 1850 they moved to a rapidly growing Brooklyn where they lived for several years. On August 15, 1861, the 19-year-old AR Samuells enlisted in the Civil War.

For the rest of his life, he used his "military experiences" to his advantage, and then some. He routinely referred to himself as "Captain," telling everyone he enlisted in the 14th Regiment New York State Militia.

The 14th fought in both Battles of Bull Run, Fredericksburg and Chancellorsville, a total of 17 in all. Just three weeks before mustering out they had fought at Spotsylvania and The Battle of the Wilderness, the first two confrontations between Generals U. S. Grant and Robert E. Lee. In those two battles more than 50,000 troops were killed, missing, wounded or captured.

The 14th Regiment's tenacity and distinctive crimson pants won them respect from both sides. They were the only regiment honored with three monuments at Gettysburg. Referring to their unusual red trousers, Southern General Stonewall Jackson called the regiment, "Red-legged Devils."

The won the admiration of President Lincoln, and he often requested them to protect him during battlefield visits.

But Samuells' official war record reveals a very different story.

He enlisted in the 6th Light Artillery Battery New York. Instead of being a part of, and leading men in some of the bloodiest and costliest battles in US history, in four years the 6th LABNY suffered no officer deaths either from war or disease or accident, and only 17 enlisted men died from all causes. Samuells mustered out on August 16, 1864, as a corporal.

By 1867, Samuells, now 25, returned to Brooklyn and married 17-year-old Amelia. They had their first child the following year.

The well-liked and smooth-talking Samuells dreamed big. He won big; he lost big. He frequently cycled through his own fortune and that of others.

In 1868, he purchased the City Oyster House on Fulton near Adams St. Then he signed a 10-year lease for the City Assembly Building on Washington Street near Myrtle Avenue and established the Assembly Billiards Room. The hall featured 34 Phelan and Collander's tables, one of the top billiards' hall suppliers in America.

Both enterprises proved major successes.

But not all of his ventures turned out so well. His delving into the Clarendon Hotel on Coney Island in 1872 lasted less than a year. His 1876 proprietorship with the Neptune House fared little better.

By the early 1870s Samuells, barely 30 years old, had reached many of his business goals and accumulated considerable wealth totaling $250,000.

But he fashioned himself as a bigger player.

And he saw Vanderbilt as a rival. Samuells had been successful, but his quarter million couldn't approach that of the richest man in the world.

However, despite their successes, both men sought to make it in show business. Vanderbilt used Gilmore's Garden as his theatrical outlet.

Samuells had already gotten into the game.

In 1873, he bought the nine-year-old and often troubled Park Theatre. He spent $75,000 in renovations, but the Panic of 1873 put him in bankruptcy and he lost much of his fortune, and the theatre.

However, the failure and frustration of Park Theatre did little to quell his passion to make a mark in show business.

Just two years later he found a vacant lot at the corner of Smith and Fulton Streets. It measured 50 feet x 150 feet, was landscaped with lots of trees and access to the train. The Brooklyn Bridge, when completed, would reach almost to its front door.

Samuells had found the spot for his re-entry into the entertainment world. Unlike Park Theatre it came with no excess baggage, no bad public will; no previous owners with mismanagement issues, and no unresolved conflicts with the press, public and performers.

This would be his theatre from start to finish. He would call it Mozart Garden.

*   *   *

Construction on his new venue began early in 1877, but problems started almost immediately.

He signed a 10-year lease and, in spite of securing $40,000 for its construction, a shortage of funds forced the workers to walk off the job. Samuells hocked his watch and chain to pay them. In late July two men suffered serious injuries when they fell off a ladder while raising a beam to the roof, further delaying construction and the scheduled August 1 grand opening.

Samuells saw an early August grand opening as a key to success. Most entertainment venues closed during the hot summer months. The Park Theatre shutdown until August 27. With a four-week head start, Mozart would get a huge jump on the theater season.

Samuells promised that, with the exception of Sunday night shows, admission to all programs would be free, with profits coming from alcohol sales. Bandleader Emil Seifert would headline and showcase the Garden's superior acoustics, comfort and amenities through his "Sabbath Shows," which charged twenty-five cents admission, and would prove that "legitimate theatre" would play in Brooklyn.

On the day of its August 12 grand opening, the *Brooklyn Daily Eagle* described it as a "plain capricious brick building with windows on three sides, a simple roof (made of plastic slate), which makes no pretensions to florid ornamentations."

Lukewarm media response aside, the public greeted Brooklyn's newest addition to the entertainment community with great anticipation. Hours before the doors opened, hundreds of Brooklynites lined up on both Fulton and Smith Streets, pressing around the building, everyone trying to sneak a peek through the windows and catch an early glimpse into the arena.

About an hour before the show, the doors opened and a mob rushed through both the Smith and Fulton Street doors, with police standing at both entries gently guiding people inside.

Patrons entering from the narrow Fulton Street side on the north walked into a vestibule that ran the entire 50-foot width of the building. Above them workers installed gallery seating for about 100 ladies who wanted to eat and listen to music. The vestibule featured a lager beer bar, cigar stand, and lunch counter, which would serve German style sand-wiches. Under the vestibule sat a chilled wine and beer cellar. Walking another 30 feet took them through the vestibule and into the main room.

Those who entered via the eight-foot double doors on Smith Street immediately felt the crunching of the gravel-covered floors that led into the main room. In the middle of the room sat enough tables and chairs to seat several hundred people. Along the middle of the opposing east wall, they saw the orchestra platform. An aquarium fronted the stage, which was adorned with an abundance of flowers and shrubbery, hanging baskets, vases filled with tropical plants, and a "profusion of birds in cages."

Looking up, patrons saw a ceiling supported by trusses and painted to look like the sky.

Ventilation brought in cool air from below and carried out heated air above.

While Samuells boasted that his venue would rival Gilmore's, despite him knowing that Vanderbilt's arena could hold 10,000; Mozart 2,000. Barnum wouldn't have considered putting his world-renowned show in such a small arena.

But Samuells didn't care about that. He finally had his theatre, and as usual, big plans.

CHAPTER 12
Samuells Prepares the Garden

*J*ust two weeks after opening, Samuells ran into a pay dispute with his conductor, Emil Seifert. The union musicians took Seifert's side and walked out.

Mozart closed for a week.

On September 3, he reopened the Garden under a new name, the awkward, "The Great London Music Hall Mozart Garden," although everyone still called it Mozart Garden.

Additionally, Samuells continued with a downscaled version of the Sunday night Sabbath Shows, for which he charged   fifteen cents admission.

But the Garden would grow to much more than that.

*   *   *

Even as Samuells planned upgrades for his entertainment programming, dramatic happenings were taking place that would affect him personally and professionally.

America's entertainment tastes were changing. Sports such as baseball, boxing and endurance walking were transforming the American landscape, and rapidly attracting rabid fans throughout America.

Samuells saw an opportunity.

At this point, he likely partnered with local sports promoter Mike Henry. In 1871, Samuells and Henry sat on the board of the Brooklyn Atlantics baseball team. The Atlantics exploded in popularity when on June 14, 1870, in front of 10,000 people, they defeated the Cincinnati Red Stockings in an extra-inning game, snapping their 111-game winning streak.

Like Daniel O'Leary, Henry came to America from Ireland. Similarly, he loved competition and the new concept of organized professional sports. He promoted and managed virtually every sporting event in

Brooklyn, especially baseball and boxing. Any significant athletic contest in the city had his talent, skills and personality behind it. Adding to his appeal, Henry ran one of the most popular bars in Brooklyn on Front Street, just down from Mozart Garden. Police said he ran the quietest bar in the district.

Henry stood six-foot four, with broad-shoulders easily carrying his nearly 200-pound frame. He dressed well and wore a cluster pin worth hundreds on his ascot. He adorned himself with a gold chain that he often twirled around his finger when engrossed in conversation. He earned the public's admiration in 1872, when he received a medal for saving a child's life.

On April 17, 1865, the *Brooklyn Daily Eagle* described him as "a peaceable, quiet and inoffensive man, always good-natured with nothing of the bully or of belligerency about him."

His peacemaking nearly got him killed three times.

In April, 1865, while eating in the Oyster Saloon, Henry helped dispose of a drunk. Within minutes the man returned with a knife and slashed Henry's neck, severing three arteries, and narrowly missing his jugular. Incredibly, he recovered within a week.

Henry's second stabbing occurred on May 26, 1877, when he and some inebriated friends took a carriage on a return trip from Coney Island. One requested to stop for more drinking, a suggestion Henry nixed. When the man persited, Henry stopped the buggy, pulled the man out and threatened to leave him. As Henry returned to the wagon, the man stabbed him from behind, cutting a six-inch gash in his upper left leg.

In 1881, a derelict patron would shoot Henry in his own bar after refusing to pay an $8 tab. The bullet would miss his heart by less than an inch. For days he would lay in critical condition. He remained bedridden for a month.

Besides baseball, Henry developed a love of boxing, an attractive sport for a man well over six feet tall. He refereed and managed matches and, unlike many in the business, built a reputation for putting on top flight, well promoted, honest bouts.

Maybe more than anyone else in Brooklyn, Henry saw the significance in the rise of professional sports. Samuells knew Henry held the key to promoting such contests.

But Samuells wouldn't go to a straight sports-themed program. For now, at least, he had to maintain the popular Sunday evening concerts. In spite of the many battles the once-dominant churches had lost over the appropriateness of entertainment centers in Brooklyn, the Sabbath concerts remained his most popular and profitable attraction.

So Samuells tweaked his weeknight programs. One night he offered drama, the next boxing, sometimes combined with minstrel shows or comedic talents. The new strategy worked. Wrestling, variety shows, musicals, singers, boxers, gymnasts all played to sold-out houses; patrons often stayed late into the night.

The Garden's popularity grew into the place where Brooklynites wanted to see and be seen. Temperance meetings, under the auspices of the Temperance Union of Christian Women, ran successfully there with many giving their hearts to Christ. One meeting attracted 3,000 with most ignoring the fact that Mozart Garden sold alcohol.

On February 20, 1878, a three-hour boxing match opened with Tom Nolan singing, "No Irish Need Apply." Women got "jammed in the surging mass" of more than 2,000.

Samuells benefited from any type of publicity. In late November 1877, Excise Commissioners complained about Samuells using a picture of a "half-clad" female outside Mozart Garden to entice the patronage of young men. One community leader, playing to the city's fame for large and popular worship facilities said, "Brooklyn, City of Churches and Rum Shops."

Either in spite or because of the incident, people continued flocking to Fulton Street, especially Mozart Garden.

Playing to full houses night after night, Samuells took another gamble. He would do what no other Brooklyn theatre did: He vowed to keep Mozart Garden open through the hot summer months.

Most venues closed for two reasons: inadequate ventilation attributed to heat, and performers also got some time off after a busy series of stressful performances.

Staying open all summer meant Samuells and Mozart Garden would own the entertainment district.

Night after night, throughout the summer, Mozart Garden played to packed houses. On July 26, the *Brooklyn Daily Eagle* praised Samuells and said, "Music, singing, dancing, and all the attractions of a good variety of entertainment are to be enjoyed at the Garden. . ." the *Eagle* called Samuells, "The first amusement caterer in the local field," and that Mozart Garden, "has flourished under his management." Later in August it said, "Samuells' offers is just what Brooklyn needs, from music featuring comic songs to athletic endeavors and Negro minstrels shows."

After several failures, he finally found success in the entertainment business.

But he still failed to top his perceived rival, William Vanderbilt.

That thought might have passed his mind. Publicly at least, he stopped comparing Mozart to Gilmore's.

Maybe the reality of Mozart Garden's position began to hit Samuells. He built a 2,000 seat arena that would provide a series of attractions to Brooklyn, but have little impact beyond that. By contrast, Vanderbilt's Gilmore's Garden had taken on an almost cathedral-like aura. It may have been the best-known entertainment venue in the world, playing to some of the greatest theatrical/athletic performances ever seen.

But Samuells' greatest moment lay ahead.

In late October or early November 1878, Samuells reached an agreement with Webb. He would rent Mozart Garden to Webb so his client, Madame Ada Anderson, could walk 2,700 quarter miles in 2,700 quarter hours, or one quarter mile every 15 minutes for 28 days and three hours. If she failed at any point, the contract was void, and she would receive no remuneration.

On paper, the task looked ridiculous. How could someone walk for a month and never get more than 10 minutes' sleep? How would one body respond to such stresses? Wouldn't she go crazy? Even Daniel O'Leary said publicly he wouldn't try it.

Samuells began refurbishing the Garden. Laying the track meant removing the chairs from the gravel floor, and other accommodations such as her privacy tent, which reduced seating capacity from 2,000 to 800. Patrons would be confined to limited seating around the track, some on the infield and in the balcony. He built an 18-inch-high railing on the track's perimeter. It served at least two purposes. First, it improved the aesthetics; second, it kept enthusiastic spectators from crowding the pedestrienne during the most popular hours.

Brooklyn's city surveyor measured the track for accuracy. Judges and other officials would ensure an honest race. A doctor would monitor her physical condition.

To give the event greater credibility, Samuells hired Mike Henry to promote it.

Madame Anderson could periodically alternate direction to help avoid overuse injuries. Spectators could follow her progress via a tote board on stage and a giant clock that hung from above.

To generate interest, Samuells opened the Garden two days early for inspection. Professional walking aficionados, gamblers and the curious came out to get a good look at the surroundings, to take stock of the venue's renovations, experience the atmosphere, and meet the major players. Brooklynites took advantage of the opportunity. They walked a few laps on the track. Many knelt and sifted the track's sandy mixture with their fingers. Others stood and bounced on its soft surface. A few took off their shoes and imagined the thrill of competing in front of potentially hundreds of their friends and neighbors. Excitement built as Brooklynites got a thrilling glimpse into the "real world" of pedestrianism.

Some even ventured into Anderson's privacy tent.

Anderson's temporary home hardly looked like a select place of solace. Rough, cheap wood made up two sides. The Garden's brick wall formed the third. To the entry's left sat Anderson's small, robe-covered bed, set in a pine frame. At the foot of the bed, a red curtain hung from a sagging cord, forming the fourth barrier. Furnishing the room were two tables, two chairs, a large trunk, and a chamber pot. Several bottles of wine, ale, extracts and medicines hung on the walls and lined the floor. Behind the curtain sat a makeshift kitchen consisting of a stove, table and cooking utensils. In addition to her human company, the room would be home to Madame Anderson's Maltese kitten.

For the next month, Mozart Garden, the track and this privacy tent would be Madame Anderson's world.

CHAPTER 13

Brooklyn Meets Madame Anderson

The night of December 16, 1878, with the Garden half-full more of the curious than sports followers, Madame Anderson completed her first quarter-mile in four minutes, with an easy springy gait that indicated she was in her element.

Unlike her mentor, the always businesslike William Gale, she embraced the press. A *New York Herald* reporter followed her into her tent. She sat down on her cot, covered her limbs with a rug and opened her world. After discussing her diet with him, she said, "Toward the end, I will drink champagne."

She was asked about battling fatigue.

"I never experienced very great difficulty waking up." She continued, "My problem is most often with blisters."

They were an unavoidable part of pedestrianism.

Madame Anderson preferred the more durable leather type shoe with laces on the side and harder soles.

But as her blisters worsened, she would switch to a balmoral gaiter that featured loosely-fitting laces across the foot and ankles.

Then the bell sounded and she rose to prepare for her next walk.

She covered her next three quarter miles with times of 3:20, 3:00, and 3:10, giving her an aggregate mile time of 13:30.

Only 674 miles remained.

She waited for an opportunity to showcase her entertainment prowess.

She found one early.

During her sixth quarter, the audience sat stunned as, without warning, a Hoboken man jumped onto the track, his intentions clear: He wanted to test Madame Anderson.

She immediately took comical advantage. She lengthened her stride, lowered her head, and pumped her arms at ninety degree angles.

He labored to maintain the increased pace. She slowed, let him gain some ground, then stepped in front of him and accelerated again. As the scene played out again, the crowd's snickers turned to chortles and finally to all-out laughter at the pedestrienne's game. The band added to the monkeyshines by playing an upbeat tune, inspiring Madame to push again. After just a few laps, the man dropped out, beaten in good-natured fun. The encounter resulted in the Madame recording her fastest time yet: 2:46.

While only occasionally mentioning results, the *New York Times* continued running periodic critical editorials against Madame Anderson. While commending activities such as those that required skill or featured danger, such as the trapeze artist or riding the unbroken horse, the paper wrote on December 18 that Madame Anderson's journey had none of the "skill" attributes. "...[I]t is not easy to thrill at the sight of a human creature plodding wearily around a circle of sawdust or tan-bark until nature gives way." The editorial concluded by saying the sport's pervasive gambling spirit "leads people to bet and "put up money" on any absurd performance of uncertain issue."

But few paid attention to the criticisms.

As with most top pedestriennes, frequent costume changes added to her appeal. The fashion statements attracted females, many of whom came to Mozart Garden just to see another part of her wardrobe. The outfits served another, more lascivious purpose. They often revealed aspects of the women's more desirable attributes. Not only did the form-fitting dresses highlight women's breasts, but another part of the female anatomy that rarely got a public mention: arms and legs. So controversial were these terms that even large-circulation newspapers described them via the more innocuous term: "limbs."

Early in her performance, she appeared wearing a flame-colored silk dress that reached to her knees. It had a square-cut neck decorated with a collar elaborately embroidered with a gold braid. The dress hung loose at the waist, making it fashionable and functional. The men smiled with approval; wide-eyed women looked at her, then at each other in amazement. The sight made the crowd explode with raucous cheers. Because of the lateness of the evening, only about a hundred people witnessed the scene, but its coverage in New York newspapers created increased interest in Madame Anderson.

The encounter with the Hoboken man and her style-setting costumes made Brooklynites realize that for the next month Mozart Garden would play host to an attraction never before seen in America.

Responding to Mike Henry's name, followers of baseball, boxing, O'Leary, and even Marshall and Von Hillern would soon flock to

Samuells' venue for an evening of genuine entertainment. Saying, "I saw Madame Anderson at Mozart last night," at work or the social club would generate emotions that ranged from jealousy to admiration.

No one wanted to miss the antics of Madame Anderson.

Shortly after midnight on December 18, a *Brooklyn Daily Eagle* reporter interviewed the pedestrienne about her about her sleep deprivation.

Madame brought the conversation back to her troublesome feet.

"The pain keeps me awake," she said, "and sometimes I cannot get to sleep till it is time for me to go on the track again. If my feet remain in good condition, I will sleep with ease and comfort."

She then admitted that during her inevitable "sleepy spells," she would circle the track in a somnolent condition.

The first two days, Madame Anderson had but one hour sleep. Even though she answered each bell promptly, her quarter splits slowed. And as she predicted, her feet swelled. The lift in her legs vanished; her stride shortened. Her shoulders drooped and her head slumped.

She kept most of her ailments to herself, saying, "People don't come here to see someone suffer."

The crowd witnessed another part of the Madame's theatrical skills after quarter 218, about 55 miles into her task. Eschewing a much-needed rest, she jumped on stage, sat behind the piano and, in front of an astonished crowd, began playing and singing Verdi's "Back to Our Mountains." The stunned audience listened intently to her contralto voice, as she put her musical talent on display in the tiny arena. She didn't possess the skills of a great diva; virtually all known descriptions described her voice as "passable," but no one expected the mini-concert.

When she finished, the house erupted in heartfelt appreciation for the efforts. For the next three weeks spectators would wonder what Madame Anderson would do next. Unannounced, she might sing, play the piano, make speeches, pull tricks, and constantly exhibit the skills she had developed as a performer. That "soul of an entertainer" personality had already attracted larger and enthusiastic crowds. No one could determine if people were coming more for the walk or her sideshows.

On Friday, December 19, 75-year-old former boxer Bill Tovec got caught up in the Garden's increasingly festive atmosphere and joined the pedestrienne on the track. Unlike with the Hoboken amateur, she showed the pugilist some respect. Madame pushed the pace, but only enough to allow the impressively fit Tovec to stay with her. The crowd again cheered the efforts of both athletes. The duo stayed abreast for about two more laps before he dropped out to generous applause. It marked the first time a celebrity had walked with her.

It would not be the last.

Less than one week into the walk, and the atmosphere at Mozart Garden reached unrivaled enthusiasm. Many stood during the Tovec spectacle. In what pleased Madame Anderson and Samuells immensely, women were coming in larger numbers.

But her growing and adoring public didn't see the fatigue battles inside her room. She removed her shoes and socks, plopped onto her couch, and fell fast asleep. Then time-strapped attendants struggled to prepare her after the three-minute warning bell. With Madame half asleep, they set her up on her cot. While she leaned on a helper, often Henry, they slipped socks and shoes back on her feet, lifted her, then guided her to the tent opening where she commenced with another seven-lap ordeal.

Her physical condition constantly drifted in and out of a bright and alert phase into a semi-conscious state.

She was developing a routine. Madame Anderson would stumble her way through a walk, then two hours later appear as vigorous as at the start. She emphasized that these shuffle-tramps were not to be confused with the upcoming sleepy spells. They would come later.

News of the excitement in Mozart Garden stirred the interest in another group of people, professionals whose high-profile reports would send Brooklyn's fascination with the rising star to a new level. Like many others, they would arrive as skeptics, but watching the athlete made them realize that she was a physical marvel.

Reports of Madame Anderson's quest reached the medical community.

Several doctors, including the Surgeon General to the New York Governor, were convinced no one could survive nearly for 30 days while limited to 10-minute naps four times an hour.

One physician bet $100 she wouldn't finish.

CHAPTER 14

Chaos in the Tent

At 11:30 p.m., December 20, Madame Anderson completed quarter 400. She had now logged 100 miles. In what would become a common scene, a team of 8-10 doctors surrounded her to assess her condition. Her temperature recorded ninety-nine degrees, pulse 78-80, the approximate resting rate for the average person. The physicians noted: One, her troublesome blisters inhibited her walking, and two, mental anxiety interfered with her sleep.

However, they had no explanation how Madame Anderson's body would react to the ongoing stresses she would place on it.

*   *   *

Hour after hour Madame Anderson consistently answered the bell, methodically logging quarter-mile after quarter-mile. In the early mornings the Garden resembled an echo chamber. During these times Madame Anderson chatted with the scorers and when not overcome with exhaustion, she would sit down and regale them with an English ballad at the piano.

Madame Anderson did such a good job of showcasing her skills and hiding her fatigue, the *Eagle* reported, "She shows no sign of defeat. Her achievement would embarrass O'Leary," but, the paper added, "her feet are quite lame . . . and are badly blistered and painful."

On December 21, an *Eagle* reporter entered her tent after she finished quarter 448 (mile 112).

He found Madame on the couch, blistered and swollen feet treated by two female attendants who had carefully removed her shoes and stockings. While drinking a cup of beef tea, she looked up with a bright smile and said quietly, "You see, I am taking a rest. I shall get some sleep by and by."

"What time do you sleep during the day?"

"I take most of my sleep from one o'clock in the morning to about four."

She added that she slept around one and a quarter-hour out of every 24.

"Sometimes, of course, my constitution demands a certain amount of sleep. These are what I call my 'sleeping fits or spells.'

"If I could only get a half-hour of sleep at a time once in a while, I would not mind the walking at all. The only relief I find at such times is in drinking beef tea."

Then, tipping her cup in the direction of the reporter, she added, "That revives me."

"How do you manage to endure the tremendous strain on your constitution without rest?"

"I don't know, unless I think the body sleeps while the brain remains active. In that way I account for the pain in my limbs and back, which I sometimes suffer. I cannot explain my meaning exactly, but I believe physical response is possible while the mental faculties are energetic."

Modern science backed up Madame Anderson's assertions. Even during sleep, parts of the brain remain active. With the sleep-deprived person, the parietal lobe takes over some tasks when other parts of the brain shut down.

"I have not thus far felt any particular fatigue. My back pains me at times, but I do not mind that as much as I do my feet, which are badly blistered. They trouble me a good deal now. I did not think they would give out so soon."

The warning bell sounded. Madame rose from the couch, set her cup on the table and said, "When they (the sleepy spells) are gone, I expect to make up for lost time. I am confident of success in any event."

After completing quarter 489 at 9:50 p.m. on December 21, more than five days of continuous walking, Samuells requested her to the stage.

In front of a suddenly curious and quiet crowd, he presented her with an attractive gift of cut glass, comprising of a jug, two glasses and a tray, courtesy of a new fan. Everyone stood and cheered the announcement and acceptance of the gift. Madame Anderson then raised her right arm. The crowd again quieted. She thanked her benefactor and made a short speech, saying among other things that she had sacrificed a theatrical/singing career for a more promising future as a pedestrienne. The packed house cheered.

She then stepped off the stage and began number 490.

* * *

About that time Madame Anderson's laps had worn a path around the track. While walking with her, an alert Mike Henry, whose responsibilities were growing daily, picked up some small pieces of hard foreign objects, just averting disaster as Madame Anderson missed stepping on it. A quick inspection revealed the objects were slivers of wood. Digging further, he uncovered handfuls of warm coal. The obstructions were undoubtedly subversive attempts by a gambler or gamblers who would benefit from Madame not finishing. According the *New York Herald*, they were "not the size to disturb any walker in thick boots, but quite sufficient to hurt the tender feet of the pedestrian."

Henry spent the next several minutes clearing the track while Madame Anderson carefully proceeded.

Early the next day, Madame Anderson suffered through her most severe and intense sleepy spell to date. Each time she arrived on the track only seconds before having to start. Her problems began before quarter 512, or 128 miles, when time-strapped attendants rushed to get her blistered feet into her shoes. They lifted her from the cot and Madame almost buckled from the pain. In their haste, the attendants put her shoes on the wrong feet. They offered to correct them in the tent, but the pedestrienne stopped them, saying, "I cannot afford to lose the $100 that I offered anybody finding me off the track three minutes after any quarter."

They emerged from her tent one minute and twenty seconds after the warning bell. Aides guided her to a chair where they frantically corrected their mistake.

For two fatigue-laden hours, they struggled with the weary pedestrienne. Unable to wake her, they pulled her into a seated position then, with the athlete slumping sideways on her husband, her seemingly lifeless head flopped on his shoulder, two harried assistants slipped on her stockings and shoes, careful not to irritate the blisters that now covered her feet. They lifted her by her arms, dragging the near rag-doll like body across the floor, limp feet leaving toe trails in the gravel, all the while offering words of encouragement that fell on deaf ears. They slapped her lightly. She woke enough to support herself.

Often with Mike Henry at her side, who was careful not to physically assist her and violate her agreement, she staggered around the track, eyes closed, arms limp, soles never breaking contact with the ground. Her head continually dropped to her chest. She weaved on the three-foot wide oval, increasing the distance she walked. On turns she was saved from wandering off the track only after bumping into the outside railing, revealing yet another reason why she insisted on its construction. Upon completing lap seven, she collapsed into the arms of Henry or a judge, who carried her back to the cot. But her quarters took so long to complete, she almost constantly shifted from entering the tent only to turn back around again when the horrific scene replayed itself. While few spectators witness the torturous spectacle, officials and newspaper reporters wondered if they were watching a great athlete perform, or a madwoman with a passion for self-destruction.

At least one spectator had added incentive for watching the Madame's sufferings. Convinced she couldn't continue much longer, on Friday he bet a friend $25 she would be off the track by Sunday afternoon. He watched her struggle all night then paid off the wager.

To the amazement of everyone not familiar with the woman's incredible powers of recovery, she emerged from her tent for quarter 520 rejuvenated with head up, arms pumping, walking briskly and eating a sandwich.

Excitement toward the woman's attempt at history grew daily. Almost every newspaper report told of some new reason for New Yorkers to visit Mozart Garden, even for just an hour or two.

At 7:50 p.m. on December 22, Madame Anderson completed quarter 576. The Garden could barely hold all the spectators, one-third of them women. Some took advantage of the invitation to walk a lap or two with the pedestrienne, who enjoyed the company and the goodwill it garnered.

"It's unusual for Brooklyn to be excited about pedestrianism," wrote the *New York Herald*, "but this has created a furor. She is pleasant, brimming with good nature, especially with children."

At this point Madame Anderson maintained a fairly consistent schedule, sleepwalking approximately two or three hours a night, then waking for more spirited spurts. In the early hours of December 23, her attendants again struggled to get the plucky pedestrienne off the bed and onto her feet. "It'll never do to have her lose that hundred dollars," she told one who shook her and tugged on her right ear. As Elizabeth Sparrow reached to pull her upright, the pedestrienne suddenly extended her right arm and swung it, whacking the face of her long-time friend. Sparrow yelled as everyone else gasped. The woman fell three steps backwards, barely missing the stove upon which some beef tea simmered. Mrs. Sparrow crashed against the tent wall, blood spewing from her mouth. The hand hit with such force and sound, attendants feared she had suffered a broken jaw. Paley struggled to keep his wife's balance and fought to drag the semi-comatose woman back on the track before the second bell rang. Most of the others saw to the dazed and bleeding Mrs. Sparrow, who was led to the bed that only a few seconds earlier had rested the woman who walloped her.

Medical personnel stopped the bleeding, examined her and determined that her jaw wasn't broken. Still, she had suffered a cut lip and a dislodged tooth.

Later, an astonished Mrs. Sparrow would say, "I knew Madame could walk, they told me she could sing, and now I know she can fight. I'd just as soon been kicked by a mule."

Paley led his wife to the track, where a small but stunned crowd was relieved to see her, but was also aware that something upsetting had just occurred in the tent.

Incredibly, the turmoil aroused the weary walker, and she clipped off the subsequent quarter-mile in a good time.

CHAPTER 15

General Tom Thumb

$\mathcal{A}$s Christmas approached the thousands who jammed Mozart Garden each day had even more to cheer. Madame looked strong. Her eyes, which had frequently been glazed or even shut, were now bright as at the start. Her pace quickened, and she was now the performer who loved to entertain. At times she enjoyed almost nine minutes' uninterrupted rest between quarter-miles. Women, in particular, thrilled at the life shown by the new Brooklyn hero.

But now even those who had no interest in seeing a pedestrienne walk on an undersized track had more reasons to visit Mozart Garden. While local celebrities and dignitaries had delighted crowds by walking with Madame for a few laps, what happened on quarter-mile 771 brought them to their feet.

He suddenly appeared on the track, not walking, but waddling. She slowed for him. He needed no introduction. It was not his face that made him recognizable to everyone in Mozart Garden.

It was his size. He stood barely three feet tall.

Barnum's international star midget, General Tom Thumb, in town for an appearance on Fulton St., was strolling with Madame Anderson.

Few names in show business shined brighter. In his 37-year career as a promoter, PT Barnum sold 80 million tickets, and 20 million paid to see General Tom Thumb. He once toured Europe and performed for Queen Victoria. The general played fictional and real characters, including Napoleon Bonaparte. He also did comedy shtick with a straight man, sometimes played by Barnum.

As the two paced through a few laps, smiling and waving to the patrons, the general occasionally stopped to shake hands or offer a salute to someone with whom he had made eye contact. He drew huge laughs as he "sprinted" to catch up with the star pedestrienne.

*   *   *

At 8:30 p.m. on Christmas Day, a *New York Herald* reporter was given access to the pedestrienne's tent. She looked a bit sleepy, reclining on her couch, eating from a bowl.

"How do you feel, Madame Anderson?"

"I am very well, thank you. But I could go to sleep very easily."

Her eyes were drowsy, but her face displayed a confidence of someone comfortable in her environment.

"What are you eating now?"

"This," she said between mouthfuls, "is beef and cabbage, not the good English beef, but it's as near to it as we can get here."

Additionally, she told the reporter she ate chops, beefsteaks, poultry, fish, oysters, beef tea, light puddings and cakes, and grapes. Her drinks were limited to tea, port wine and champagne. Later, she partook of cabbage, corned beef, potatoes and sponge cake.

"I think," she said, "I have done full justice to the American oysters. My appetite is always good. I can eat what I like."

"How often do you take refreshment?"

"Almost every time I leave the track, except when I go to sleep."

"Do you think your power of endurance proceeds from any special character of your diet or method of living during this trial?"

"Oh no. I get my strength where other people get theirs, and I'm grateful for it."

Then she told of her life goals, about how she dreamed of being an actress at a young age, and while she enjoyed the public's attention regarding her current undertaking, she lamented somewhat that the admiration would only last until the end of this current life.

"Why," exclaimed one lady in the tent, "you don't want them staring at you in the next world, do you? You don't want them to be pointing at you and crying out, 'There goes Madame Anderson?'"

When the Madame responded by saying that was exactly what she wanted, the lady replied, "Then while you are walking, we will be flying around looking at you, and we shan't be able to keep up with you even then."

The Madame laughed and was asked if she would accomplish her goal.

"Oh, yes," she exclaimed, spooning some cabbage crumb off her chin, "I've been working rather hard today. I am tired, but I don't ache so much as I did last night. Then I had my first aches in the body since I began."

Then the warning bell rang, and with a smile she said, "Now ain't that tiresome?"

She put down her bowl, then wiped her mouth with a napkin.

She then sprang to her feet and got back to her duty.

As the quarter miles accumulated, Anderson used her vast amount of knowledge and skills to maintain an appropriate level of intensity. She more frequently bathed, about once every three or four hours. Wearing a new outfit almost always enlivened her spirits, and those of the females who loved to see and admire her fashion sense. Doctors continued marveling at her condition. Her attendants used a combination of vinegar, water and coal tar to manage her troublesome blisters.

Many times she strolled, occasionally acknowledging the crowd with a nod of the head or a quick wave of the hand. The *New York Sun* reported on Christmas Day, "She walks erect, and her massive shoulders and limbs make her a picture of tireless strength."

She would elevate sagging interest by varying her pace. At 4:00 p.m. on Christmas Day, she dashed off a quarter-mile in three minutes, a quarter-second. When informed of the result, she said, "That's not good enough," then proceeded to clock two consecutive 2:52's. She would usually cover the last lap of these bursts in a quick spurt, disappearing into her tent as if evading a predator.

She enjoyed that environment, knowing that every new dress, each variation in her routine, any twist would impress those lucky enough to see her perform.

Brooklynites reveled in the show.

Increasingly, patrons joined her on the track. One slightly built woman wearing a brown dress and gray shawl, walked two quarter-miles with her. Another woman, supposedly from Boston and a pupil of Bertha von Hillern, accompanied her for another quarter-mile. Others paced her through laps: Mrs. AR Samuells, her daughter Minnie, and professional pedestrian Charles Harriman

They all encouraged her, and Madame Anderson responded with small talk that ranged from idle chat to insights into her personal life and that of a pedestrienne. Virtually all wanted some kind of "scoop" about her thoughts on anything. Madame Anderson proved a co-operative conversationalist, not shy about revealing herself to her fascinated followers.

As interest in the woman grew, and she continued to battle and conquer her sleepy spells, new allegations of fraud arose.

One prominent Mozart Garden visitor asked Samuells, "Where's the other woman?"

"What other woman?" asked the manager.

"The twin of this one. No one woman could keep up this walk. It is impossible."

A horseman asked for a copy of the track certification. Several "sporting men" showed up periodically to see first-hand if she was "keeping up her shake."

Still other visitors, such as US Congressman Daniel O'Reilly, called her remarkable and predicted she would finish on time.

Families packed the Garden throughout Christmas Day, as if they considered Madame Anderson part of their extended family. She received many gifts, including flowers, food, silver eating ware, and atomizers filled with perfume. Ever wary of sabotage, attendants took any potentially contaminated gift and placed it on the scorer's table. They threw away confectioner's gifts, fearing they were laced with poison.

One group of young lads presented the pedestrienne a Christmas tree and a dressed sheep. Possibly suspecting a problem, she politely declined the offer. Later, a report circulated of a missing mutton from a local restaurant.

Writing about the incident, the *NY Herald* said that the boys thought the matter was a joke on the eatery, but predicted, "The laugh will be on the other side before the matter is ended."

*   *   *

After mile 213, Madame Anderson complained for the first time publicly about the problems of the track's design.

A *New York Sun* reporter entered Madame Anderson's tent and saw an attendant wrapping her damaged feet. He asked her about her persistent problems with blisters. Her response surprised almost everyone, and intrigued readers, always thirsty for revelations into the sport and the woman.

"Blisters no," she says, "there is something worse though, something only a pedestrian could appreciate."

Before the contest Anderson believed that the track would cover the Garden floor. Without getting her input, Samuels laid boards, then covered them with the traditional track topping of sawdust and sandy loam mixture. He, like many others, mistakenly believed it was easier to walk on a spongier path.

"There is a wearing pain which is always caused by long walking over springing boards," she told the reporter. "Your whole weight comes down on your heel, the boards bend down and the forepart of your foot strikes the track. It not only has to bear your weight, but resist the upward spring of the boards, which causes an extra pressure of nearly the weight of your body. I tell you, it's awful."

But as the final bandages covered her feet, she added, "I shall go on as regularly as the sun travels around the earth until my task is accomplished."

At 10:00 p.m. on Christmas, she walked quarter 873 in 4:49.

* * *

Just after midnight on Boxing Day, a loud yell made the packed house collectively jump and Madame accelerated "as though Indians were on her trail." She turned quickly in a combination of shock and curiosity. She kept looking for the source of the disruption, then she saw a cluster of people laughing at her reaction and congratulating someone with back slaps and handshakes. She circled the track, head turning, trying to figure out the perpetrator's identity.

She, and just about everyone else in Mozart Garden, recognized him. "Texas" Jack Omohundro enjoyed the commotion he'd started with his famous "Comanche yell."

Texas Jack's legacy went beyond that of mere show business. Like his friend and colleague, Buffalo Bill Cody, his fame grew from his frontier skills as a hunter, scout, trapper, spy and Indian fighter. As a teen, he enlisted for the South during the Civil War, and infiltrated Union troops. With Cody's influence, the post-Civil War government made an exception against hiring ex-confederate soldiers and employed Texas Jack as a scout. He infiltrated a gang who had been robbing federal supply trains then turned on them and helped ensure their capture. He was rewarded with a bonus of $10,000.

His stories were retold in dime novels and in 1873 he and Cody brought their lives to the stage. The duo's performances drew raves from critics and spectators.

The audience loved Jack's outburst, for almost anything the pedestrienne did enhanced the entertainment package. Seeing Texas Jack get involved in such a humorous and creative way brought howls from the audience. For several minutes a few patrons mimicked the ear-piercing screech, each one bringing a smile and sometimes a wave from Madame Anderson.

Her impressive quarter after 948 prompted an attendee to say, "She looks as though she had just started out shopping."

After Madame completed quarter 950, a *New York Sun* representative entered her tent.

Seeing an attendant remove her shoes, he picked one up for a close inspection. Although the reporter had followed and written about the athlete for several days, he had never noticed her footwear. They were not much larger than a school girls'. The daintiness, almost toy-like characteristic of her foundation contrasted sharply against her stern athletic build and steel-like determination.

Pressing the soft leather between his thumb and forefinger, he noted their flimsiness; they resembled stockings rather than shoes. He flicked his thumbnail against the small, polished cobbler nails that secured the sole to the upper.

The shoes were thinnest at the heel and ball of the foot. While not surprising, since that mirrored the normal wear pattern of shoes, they seemed just a few laps from wearing through.

Taking the shoes from the reporter, she fondled them and said, "I have five pairs of new shoes, for I have walked nearly 7,000 miles in these." She said she wished O'Leary's shoemaker would craft a good pair for her. "After I wear my new ones a few rounds, I generally throw them across my room on returning from the track."

The warning bell rang. She sat down, slipped her flimsy shoes back on, grabbed her velvet cap and tassel, and bolted out the door for quarter 951.

The reporter, slightly taken aback by the revelation, then turned his attention to Mrs. Sparrow and asked if she thought the woman would finish.

"She is certain to do it, unless she is taken with a fatal illness."

When she returned Paley, whose presence had gone unnoticed until now, in a possible attempt to bait his wife said, "What do you think a fellow said to me over at Gilmore's Garden?"

"I am sure I don't know," she replied, startled at the sudden emotional change in the tent.

"Why, he said that after you were through here, he would walk a thousand miles in a thousand hours, and that would be a bigger feat than you are doing."

"He's an ass and never tried it," she snapped.

Officials estimated between 7,000 and 8,000 came and went during the day, and at times the Garden cheering was deafening.

But rumors of fraud continued.

CHAPTER 16

Imposter

*J*ust days before Anderson approached the halfway point, rumors resurfaced about a possible "double."

The *New York Herald* detailed a potential conspiracy.

Two women walked. One Madame Anderson performed in the day and during the packed evening rush hours; the other sped around the tan-bark track in the early morning.

The paper speculated that the duo "so resembled each other that even those familiar with both could scarce tell the difference."

A twin could quickly don her sister's dress, or an undetectable copy, while denying public access to her room. The con could be arranged late at night while many of the few remaining spectators slept. The paper offered no evidence, only her inexplicable recovery after several hours of near somnambulism.

The power of suggestion, and gamblers growing increasingly desperate, gave credence to the theory.

With the *Herald's* speculation, spectators wondered publicly about her repeated episodes of rapid restoration. They would leave for dinner seeing a woman struggling with "scarcely strength enough in her limbs to keep from falling on the track," then return a short time later to find her marching at a snappy 11-minute per mile pace.

A furious Henry said, "I've been out here since the beginning, put in 20-hours days, strained my knee, and you're asking me if this is a fraud? What kind of person would do that to himself for a fake?"

Walking judge H.B. Hazelton who, outside of Henry, walked with the pedestrienne more than anyone else, said, "Samuells wouldn't have asked me to come if he wasn't sure of my integrity. I agree, what she's doing seems impossible. I've never seen anything like it. But I've not seen evidence of any deception. I would have no motive to participate in it."

Henry and Hazelton and other officials constantly stayed on alert, monitoring the clock to note any discrepancy in the lady's mannerisms or behavior. They all looked for any tipoff to a ruse. Professional gamblers and their minions sat throughout the night. Independent amateurs stalked her tent, hoping to collect the $100 promised to anyone who actually spotted her not following the prescribed routine.

Coming to her defense, the *New York Sun* reported she had to appear at the appropriate time because, "there are at all hours persons on the watch, anxious to catch her off the track when she should be on it."

Adding to her credibility, reporters from the *Brooklyn Daily Eagle, NY Times,* and even the *Herald,* continued working in eight-hour shifts, recording each quarter split in minutes and seconds, and noting that she had started each walk at the appropriate time.

Some who believed her performance took issue with the incessant physical stresses she subjected herself to, and thought the contest should be stopped.

They wanted Henry Bergh to put a stop to the spectacle. Bergh founded the American Society of Prevention of Cruelty to Animals, and took a key role in forming the Prevention of Cruelty to Children.

But their voices fell on deaf ears. Too many people, including Samuells and the gamblers, had put too much money, time and effort into the event to allow it to stop.

Besides, the public loved it.

The walk would play out.

Talk of policing, if not outlawing women's endurance walking events, wasn't new. After the first Marshall-von Hillern match, the *Chicago Times* questioned its logic and attraction, saying, "Unfortunately, the new sport was invented, or at any rate has been chiefly developed, in the free and enlightened North."

The San Francisco *WASP* used its sardonic tone, speaking of the pedestriennes, and said, "All amusements likely to demoralize the standard of our female population must be suppressed, but this which is worse than infamy has unqualified sanction."

But Anderson continually showed a flair for either capitalizing on or quelling a nasty rumor with a dramatic response that ultimately increased her popularity. Shortly after 10:00 p.m. on December 27, she completed quarter-mile 1,065 and immediately stepped on the stage and addressed the hundreds of attendees.

"Thank you for your support and patronage," she said. "As you know, I have worked as an actress, singer and now professional pedestrian. I thank God for giving me the ability to walk; Samuells for seeing my needs are met; and especially those who were most diligent, the ones who stayed all night. For you, I will sing following my next quarter-mile."

She then addressed critics.

She vowed that she accepted her current challenge on her own terms, not at the urging of anyone else.

"I am not going to kill myself," she said. "If I find that it is likely to tell on my constitution, I promise you most faithfully that I shall stop it at once. I can always get a living, whether at walking, acting or singing, while in this world."

The *Herald* reported that she delivered the speech, "with great effectiveness, heightened as it was by her perfect poise and her hearty, vigorous physique and frank friendly bearing."

The enthusiastic throng interrupted an upbeat version of "Grandfather's Clock," with cheers. Upon its completion, Anderson added to the moment's electricity by speeding around the track so quickly that a tiring Henry had trouble maintaining the pace.

Brooklyn loved Anderson's stylish way of controlling her critics. Each rumor or personal story, every glimpse into her tent, gave the public a greater insight into the woman. And with each revelation, emotional ties between walker and city increased. When it appeared she lacked the internal strength to persevere, her growing fan base responded with enthusiasm and an encouragement that seemed to propel Madame Anderson to a goal that no longer seemed impossible.

For a moment at least, her accusers grew silent.

Qualifying their earlier assertions regarding Anderson's "double," the *Herald* said, "No one observing her freshness now and recalling the tired eyes of ten minutes before would wonder that it might have been rumored that there were two different women."

And those weren't the only stories circulating.

She responded quickly when rumors circulated that more major appearances were scheduled after her "now inevitable" Brooklyn victory.

Newspapers, most notably the *New York Herald*, reported that Boston officials had offered her a $15,000 appearance fee for a walking exhibition; she would then attempt to equal Gale's 1877 record in Australia.

Madame Anderson invited a *Herald* reporter to walk a few laps with her, granting him a semi-private interview.

Walking an ever-quickening pace, she said, "I was sorry to see that statement in your paper that I was going to walk 4,000 quarter miles in 4,000 consecutive 10 minutes. I have made no such arrangement, and I think it would be rather premature of me to talk about commencing such a feat as that before I had completed the one on which I am now engaged."

To the delight of the Garden faithful who saw the confrontation as another publicity ploy for their enjoyment, the tiring newspaperman almost immediately fell behind.

For the moment at least, the question of a double was quelled.

*   *   *

While she enjoyed increasing popularity in Brooklyn, she shared newspaper headlines in New York, where a major endurance walking contest had been going for four days at Gilmore's.

Vanderbilt, in a possible attempt to put Samuells in his place and send a message that Gilmore's would always land the superior talent and attractions, had sought the two best performers possible. He hoped for more than just good competition; he wanted a record-breaker.

The first contestant would be a rising star, a Connecticut fireman named Napoleon Campana.

In mid-November, Campana reportedly covered more than 500 miles in six days, a performance matched only by Weston and O'Leary. The feat earned him $500 and the nickname "The Bridgeport Wonder."

The record drew Vanderbilt's attention. He billed Campana as a new face in pedestrianism. Knowing Campana would never come close to filling Gilmore's, he recruited someone who would.

Daniel O'Leary. He agreed.

Campana vs. O'Leary; Vanderbilt had his dream match.

Like Campana, O'Leary's name remained fresh in peoples' minds. Just a few weeks earlier he had easily defeated John "the Lepper" Hughes in a six-day contest, 403 miles to 310. The Irishman's total fell short of his world record 520 miles set in England the previous March. He didn't consider Hughes much of an athlete.

"The less said about him the better," O'Leary said after his victory.

Few believed Campana could win, but his six-day performance in Connecticut gave him a qualified status in the sporting world.

"Weston was undefeated before O'Leary," he said of his chances.

During his Bridgeport race, the *New York Times* said, "... this one idea of completing his 'stent' seems to thoroughly possess him, almost to madness."

"I will do it or die on the track," he said.

Officials hoped Campana would add some much-needed drama in a match against the popular O'Leary. Few athletes perform at a high level when virtually everyone cheered for such a talented opponent.

O'Leary's confident manner, professional record, public persona and appeal often beat down his opponents emotionally and mentally.

About 2,000 were on hand at 12:56 a.m. on Monday December 23, 1878, when backers escorted the two men from their tents to the start line. Betting favored O'Leary 4-to1.

According to the *New York Times*, Campana "looked worried and haggard. With his thin lantern jaws, long nose and loosely-jointed frame, he presented a striking contrast to his compactly built opponent." His outfit didn't help. He wore a scarlet flannel shirt that fell to his knees, a black silk cap that partially covered a crimson handkerchief, black tights, white stockings, and black shoes. Across the front of his shirt, in black letters, his nickname appeared, "Sport," and on the back, "Old Stag," a reference to an old fire engine he once ran. He removed his outer shirt revealing the words "Old Sport" and the number 41.

O'Leary wore a white shirt, black knee-breeches, white stockings, and carried corn cobs to help absorb excess sweat. Just 12 hours into the race, O'Leary led by 10 miles.

The papers, at least, gave up on Campana early.

"If such be the fact," wrote the *Brooklyn Daily Eagle* the next day, "the end is not difficult to predict."

"[He] looks utterly fagged," reported the *Brooklyn Daily Eagle* after just three days. "His walking seems labored, and his arms, shoulders and head are brought into constant play every step he takes."

O'Leary grew so confident of winning that he let his little daughter walk with him for a few laps, a scene that delighted the crowd, already sensing another easy O'Leary win.

On December 29, O'Leary coasted to victory in front of 5,000 spectators. He needed only 400 miles to outdistance his rival, who finished drunk and due to swollen feet, without shoes. The last few laps his backers almost dragged him around the track. He recorded 357 miles after accumulating 80 the first 21 hours.

The race proved a financial success at least. Each night saw huge crowds. O'Leary collected three-fourths of the gate receipts for his efforts.

Afterward, O'Leary apologized for his poor performance: "Give me a man worthy of my steel and I will show you what I can do." Then he added, "This man, Campana, is unquestionably the pluckiest and grittiest I have met so far."

But the event fell far short of Vanderbilt's vision. He had boasted of its history-making significance and that people would talk about for years. But like so many others, Campana couldn't live up to O'Leary's dominance. Although O'Leary's post-walk comments sounded gracious, his "poor performance" reference must have made Vanderbilt wince.

The New York papers added to Vanderbilt's embarrassment and gave the Mozart Garden team an even higher profile by contrasting O'Leary's tall, deliberate walk, arms held at ninety degree angles, with that of Madame Anderson's strolling, arms at her side.

In his quest to detract attention from Samuells, Vanderbilt had sabotaged himself.

Worse for Vanderbilt, hundreds of O'Leary-Campana attendees left Gilmore's and headed to Mozart Garden to watch the woman who now might have been the top draw in America's most popular sport. After Mozart's seats filled, people stood where they could find room, in foyers and jammed the infield. The women who attended now acknowledged their hero by standing and waving handkerchiefs each time she passed.

Some of Brooklyn's finest citizens visited the Garden for the first time. Locals read about appearances by Cactus Jack, General Tom Thumb, Congressman Daniel O'Reilly and other celebrities who suddenly found it an inviting place for an evening of excitement.

Gifts to the pedestrienne continued almost unabated. One of Henry's former colleagues from the Atlantic Baseball Club and a female admirer presented her with large bouquets of flowers that were immediately placed on the stage table that now overflowed with dazzling color and aroma.

A Brooklyn physician gave her a set of cut glass and, showing that some experts now believed in her, said, "Before the unheralded English woman gets through her performance here, she will be looked upon as one of the greatest wonders of the pedestrian world."

A little girl then walked a lap with Anderson. She was followed by others who stood in line to do likewise. Mike Henry welcomed any brief rest. He had worn out two pair of shoes walking almost around the clock.

For those who couldn't get enough, the *New York Sun* gave readers some insight as to the happenings in the pedestriennes' tent. The paper reported that she slept soundly between 7:00-9:00 p. m. Her shoes were pulled the moment she hit her cot, then replaced at the three-minute warning. The paper noted, ". . . she is led a few steps in the room, and then walks out, moving slowly over the tan-bark track."

During this time she walked her last lap faster than the first six, which further excited the throng of spectators. One paper stated, "As she looms up through the tobacco smoke in the evening on some of her fast rounds, the applause grows deafening."

With his star's drawing power resulting in increased attendance of unescorted women, Samuells saw an opportunity to get good publicity and wrestle even more media attention in his direction.

He announced a seating modification. He would convert the stage to a gallery that could accommodate between 100-200 patrons. The area would be reserved for women, many of whom loved the pedestrienne, but were put off by the men's smoking, rough language and offensive come-ons.

"This will cost me $3,000," he told the *Brooklyn Daily Eagle*, "but I will be quickly repaid." The three-day project would commence on the morning of Monday, December 30.

Samuells said nothing more, but it was worth noting he had scheduled the project to commence just hours after completion of the O'Leary-Campana contest.

*   *   *

With two weeks remaining, the *New York Sun* reported that Madame Anderson was now the major topic of conversation throughout the city. The most common questions were, "Will she hold out?" And "Is it possible for a woman to accomplish the task she has laid out for herself?" And, "Are you going to Mozart Garden tonight?"

Samuells' and Anderson's camp were ever indebted to Mike Henry. He proved far more diligent than they could have imagined. He endured long nights, exhaustion, and a constant monitoring of her condition. Without him, Madame Anderson likely would have failed long ago. His dedication to integrity might have saved them all. The public's embracing of him helped keep the naysayers at bay. His word to the *Herald* in denying the existence of a "twin" convinced all but the most skeptical Brooklynite. The *New York Sun* called him, "One of the finest coaches in the country."

Henry found the obstructions on the track; his name brought out spectators before they recognized the walk's significance.

He had grown into a valuable member of her team. Like everyone else, he performed his duties with efficiency and dedication. Anything less probably meant failure.

*   *   *

Ever looking to entertain even the smallest audience, and to enliven the mundane atmosphere that smothered the arena during the lonely times, Madame Anderson pulled a prank on the good-natured Henry.

She stepped on the track, content to walk alone. Henry rested on a chair near the room.

On the second lap, she paused behind her tent. Fighting sleep, Henry lost sight of her. Fearing she had quit early, he jumped from his chair and ran toward her tent, stopping at the last minute when she emerged from her hiding place wearing a big smile. The trick worked. The handful of spectators laughed at the light-hearted fun she had with him.

But the evening's cheerful atmosphere quickly changed .

Tension mounted on the next quarter as she staggered from her room almost sleeping. Twice earlier she tried to leave the track before completing the requisite seven laps. Both times she got into shouting matches with her attendants, who finally convinced her to continue or she would fail.

Knowing she needed a boost, and playing on her sense of nationalism, during a break Samuells hung a British flag on either side of the stage. Upon seeing the homage to her country, the small crowd cheered. She smiled and increased her pace.

However, mostly she struggled through the night. Only the alert and diligent Henry kept her on schedule.

*   *   *

On Sunday afternoon, December 29, Mozart Garden filled with church goers. The enthused crowd overflowed onto the stairs and packed the balcony.

Men wore black, women were attired in Sunday best dresses of red and blue, some even replete with stylish trains. With every emergence from her tent, crowd noise rose to deafening levels. Spectators stood on chairs hoping to get a better look; those on the floor braced themselves on shoulders in front of them; they jumped when she walked by.

They screamed her name. Men removed their hats and waved them above their heads like lasso-twirling, as if the very action spurred her around the next lap.

Anderson, of course, acknowledged the legions who watched, but a business-like demeanor supplanted her usual playful expression. Instead of her usual friendly smile and wave to the crowd, she relegated her emotions to short, quick, salute-type waves of the wrist and a nod of the head, her face still bearing an almost grimace of one who would rather focus on doing her job than making friends.

And her number of friends was growing.

CHAPTER 17

Night Owls Mischief

Much of Madame Anderson's appeal stemmed from her proclivity toward pranks like hiding from Henry, who occasionally served as her target of an occasional whip-crack, which explained why he sometimes carried the accessory/weapon. Her playful attitude changed the Garden's atmosphere, even during its darkest and most disheartening desolate hours.

Reporters delighted in telling of the mischief she created.

The *New York Sun* described her first victim as a "beery old owl," whom she found slumped over the track's outer railing, asleep. After a few laps of witnessing his disinterest, she bent over and poured a handful of tan-bark on the back of his head. The few spectators found this act amusing, but he continued sleeping.

Her favorite trick involved taking a piece of burnt coal and "decorating" a sleeping spectator's face. Once, she found her piano player, exhausted from several hours of producing music, snoring at the keyboard. Sneaking up to the stage, she blackened his cheeks and nose in the shape of musical notes. He awoke a short time later and rubbing his face, realized that he'd been had. He turned to the audience, who then laughed at the sight with the same energy they used to cheer the pedestrienne. After a few moments of mirth, he spun 180 degrees on his piano stool and performed with renewed vigor.

Her antics also gave the few late-night newspaper reporters great material when their most intriguing tasks included counting laps and watching the clock.

During those times they welcomed any diversion, but they soon found that Madame Anderson had inspired some late-night pranksters.

A group calling themselves "The Night Owls" added to Anderson's spirit and carried it to levels that even she probably couldn't have imagined.

"Membership" numbers varied from night to night, but they averaged between 40 and 50. They monitored Garden activity during the wee hours, cheering the lady, but mostly they discussed and debated potential jokes to pull, including determining who would play the best foil.

During the height of the Anderson "twin" accusations, members of the Night Owls found a female dummy in a storage room. Adorning it with one of the Madame's dresses, they hung it from a high railing across from her tent and attached a sign that read, "My twin sister."

The amused pedestrienne responded to a judge, "If no one has any objections, I will take a little sleep and let my sister walk a few quarters."

But their greatest trick came at the expense of a young lad who slept in a chair just outside Madame Anderson's tent.

With the pedestrienne struggling, the Night Owls went to work. At Henry's urging, the Owls found a police mannequin prop and carefully pinned its arms so it hugged the boy's shoulders. A few seconds later, Anderson emerged from her tent and joined the pranksters in forming a semi-circle behind the victim. One member then stepped forward and held up a noisemaker so everyone could see it. Several, including Madame Anderson, smiled and smothered giggles. Everyone nodded their approval.

Making sure all were watching, he leaned over and shook the rattle, piercing the strained silence with an annoying clatter, sending both boy and mannequin crashing to the floor. Tumbling repeatedly, the boy screamed and battled his persistent rival with endless punches and kicks. For about forty-five seconds they rolled on the floor, the boy grunting and flailing to attempt to release himself from the "death grasp."

Only then did he hear the laughter.

He stopped, sweating, exhausted and panting, and looked at the audience he had attracted, then at his captor. With a smile that read more relief than humor, he slowly recovered as he lay supine, adjacent to the track. He then glanced at his lifeless protagonist, still pinned to him, almost mocking him, unwilling to let the joke die.

A rejuvenated Anderson returned to the track with new life. When the jocularity faded, some of the spectators returned to a state of slumber. But the pedestrienne again took advantage of the situation. Armed with burnt cork, she marked their faces.

*   *   *

After thin late-night crowds, women returned in larger numbers around 9:00 a.m., most staying for two or three hours. During this time Anderson clocked quarters of around five minutes.

In the afternoon of Monday, December 30, she exited her tent wearing a purple velvet dress trimmed with white fur reaching to her knees. Her outfit included a black velvet cap and white trunks that displayed the well-developed muscles of her lower limbs. Unable to find suitable walking shoes, she still wore her old 7,000 mile pair. She said she was tired, but thought she might improve after completing the halfway point that evening.

She then said to a *New York Sun* reporter, "I shall sing a song when I have finished the last quarter of my first half of the journey."

A few minutes later, a man walked with her, at times almost sprinting to keep up. After completing his mini-tramp, he wiped the sweat off his forehead and said, "Very few men can keep up with her." He then asked Paley if she could actually complete her task.

"You can judge for yourself," said Paley, "[In England] she set out to walk 2,660 quarter miles in as many quarter hours, which she did on time. She then rested two days. After this short rest she announced that she would walk a quarter of a mile every five minutes twelve hours a day for a week, and she did it."

At 8:00 p.m., just a bit more than an hour before Madame Anderson would reach her highly anticipated halfway mark, near tragedy struck.

While cooking, an attendant started a fire in Madame's room. Smoke quickly filled the small arena. Spectators choked and wiped their burning eyes, and waved away the pollution. Men covered their mouths with handkerchiefs. With each passing second, the atmosphere grew more dangerous.

Madame Anderson kept walking.

Within 10 minutes, Mozart was enveloped in a blanket of a combination of smoke from the fire, the ever-present haze from tobacco, and residue from the gas lamps.

Patrons would have had justification to panic. Lax building codes, numerous open flames and frequent overcrowding all contributed to potentially deadly conditions. And Brooklynites had experienced it first-hand. Just over two years earlier, on December 5, 1876 a massive fire destroyed the Brooklyn Theatre, killing 278.

Madame Anderson's journey, so secure just minutes earlier, now seemed in jeopardy.

Leaving the track for any reason meant defeat. Keeping her wits and her focus, she fought the pollution and heat. Sweating profusely, she coughed and squinted her way through the next quarter.

Officials contained the fire, then opened all the vents, skylights and windows. The cool air gave the spectators an initial shock, but the refreshing blast calmed them and the atmosphere as the clean crisp air replaced the smothering, choking cloud.

Had the fire continued for a few minutes longer, Madame Anderson's walk would have ended in tragedy, and dozens, maybe hundreds, would have died.

As conditions in the Garden improved, Samuells gave her a gray ulster to protect her from the cold but refreshing air. Within minutes, everyone settled back into their places.

The near-disaster brought to the forefront the pollution battles she had been fighting almost since the beginning. On December 31, the *New York Sun* reported, "The atmosphere in which Madame Anderson has walked has been abominable and measures should be taken immediately to put a stop to the burning of poor tobacco and smoky fuel."

An hour later, with the air inside Mozart Garden cleaner than maybe it had been in more than a week, Madame Anderson completed quarter 1,349 in 3:51.

At 9:15 p.m. the pedestrienne emerged from her tent dressed in a purple velvet tunic and her hair hung in a braid. Walking with Mike Henry, who this time served more as an *avant-courier* to keep the track clear of enthusiastic spectators' feet, hands and heads, she marched to the inspiring music of "Whoa Emma." In an increasingly common scene at Mozart Garden, hundreds pressed against the rail, cheering and reaching for the pedestrienne. The applause drowned out the songs, but the musicians, who were also not immune to the excitement, continued playing with vigor.

Walking confidently, Madame Anderson completed the quarter mile in 3:13 to what the *New York Herald* called, "a perfect storm of applause."

It marked number 1,350. She had reached the halfway point.

Upon completing the milestone, Samuells seated Anderson on stage and took a few moments to settle the crowd. He smiled.

Making no mention of the near disaster, he said, "The quarter just ended completes half of Mrs. Anderson's promised walking performance, which is to walk 2,700 quarter miles in the same number of quarter-hours, beginning at each quarter hour. She is now enjoying good health, and is determined to complete her task."

Again to thunderous applause, Madame Anderson rose and said,

Ladies and gentlemen, I had on two or three occasions before thanked you for your personal cheerful encouragement. I could not go on without your assistance. You have done your part, and I thank God I have been able to do mine. In every 24 hours I have fits of sleepiness, which are very severe.

While I sleep I suffer. Sometimes I wish that I could never sleep; it is so painful to wake up. I used to think that in old England the people are very cheery, but here it is more so, for the inhabitants are more numerous on account of the great extent of the country when I first began my walk I asked the ladies for their presence. I think from the number of ladies who came that they are satisfied. It is the goal for women to see how much a woman can endure. When I first came to this country I heard that American ladies would sometimes walk two blocks. I did not know how much two blocks meant, but supposed that it must be two miles. Now I don't think it good for a lady to ride two blocks when she can walk. As a lady experienced in walking, let me say it is beneficial to walk. I do not want all the ladies to walk as much as I do (laughter), but a reasonable amount. Now I find that like some women, I have done too much talking. At the end of this quarter mile I promised to sing a song, but as there is no one to accompany me on the piano, I have made a little speech instead. Mr. O'Leary promised to come over here tonight. I know you will all be glad to see him, for I think he is a very good man.

The warning bell then rang. Madame took multiple bows. The cheering continued through the next quarter mile.

Someone found a piano player.

After number 1,354, she stepped on stage and sang "Nil Desperandum," following it with a 4:03 quarter.

May Marshall in photo dated 1882. Note medal on dress.
Courtesy of Gerry and Charlotte Curtis

Poster announcing Mary (actually May) Marshall's April 27, 1877 walk of 50 miles inside of 12 hours at Mechanics' Hall, Worcester, MA. Adult patrons could watch for fifty cents, children twenty-five cents. Courtesy of the Antiquarian Society

Miss Bertha Von Hillern
CITY HALL.

G R E A T

R   **R**

CLOSING EXEMPLIFICATION OF

Physical Culture.

88 MILES

IN *26* CONSECUTIVE HOURS,

WITHOUT SLEEP !

E   **I**

Begin 8 P. M. Friday, Aug. 10,
Finish 10 "   Satur'y, "   11.

A *Main Hall,* (Reserved),   -   *50 cts.* **A**
Gallery,   -   -   -   -   *25 cts.*

Tickets now on sale at Stockbridge's Music Store; Sturgis, Druggist; Schumacher's Picture Store, and at H. C. Bagley's, 482 Congress Street.

T R I A L

HALL OPEN
DURING ENTIRE WALK.

Announcement of Bertha von Hillern walk in Portland, ME August 10-11, 1877.
Courtesy of Maine Historical Society

MADAME ANDERSON IN HER WALKING COSTUME.

Madame Ada Anderson Courtesy of Frank Leslie's Illustrated Newspaper
February 1, 1879

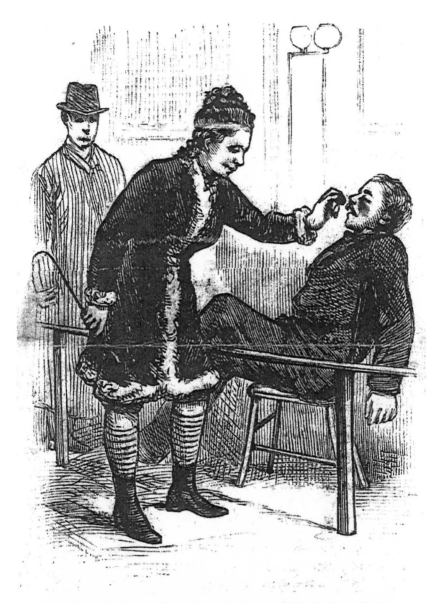

Engaging in her favorite prank, Madame Anderson chalks the face of a sleeping patron during her month-long walk at Mozart Garden in January 1879. Courtesy of Frank Leslie's Illustrated Newspaper February 1, 1879

After completing quarter-mile 2,698 of 2,700, Madame Anderson made her way through the throngs, stepped on the Mozart Garden stage and sang "Nil Desperandum," or "Never Despair." Courtesy of Frank Leslie's Illustrated Newspaper February 1, 1879

After spending several days hospitalized for exhaustion, Madame Anderson's
diligent coach, Mike Henry recovered enough to lead the pedestrienne around
her last quarter mile at Mozart Garden. Courtesy of Frank Leslie's Illustrated Newspaper
February 1, 1879

Police kept fans at bay as a triumphant but spent Madame Anderson is carried from
Mozart Garden after completing 2,700 quarter miles in 2,700 quarter hours. The
accomplishment earned her more than $8,000. Courtesy of Frank Leslie's Illustrated
Newspaper February 1, 1879

Fannie Edwards' sex scandal with Frank Leonardson often overshadowed her impressive endurance walking achievements, and contributed to the pedestriennes' downfall in New York. Courtesy of the Bancroft Library Univ. of CA Berkeley

PROGRAMME

OF THE

INTERNATIONAL PEDESTRIAN TOURNAMENT,

TO BE HELD AT THE BROOKLYN RINK,

DURING MARCH AND APRIL.

A. P. BLIVEN, Manager.
W. A. WAKEFIELD, Ass't Manager.

Programme.

FOR THE WEEK ENDING MARCH 8, 1879.

PEDESTRIANS.

Track No. 4.
Miss MAY MARSHALL and MADAME WALDRON,
in their great and unprecedented walk of
4000 quarter miles, in 4000 consecutive quarter hours.

Track No. 5.—Mr. AUGUSTUS H. SMITH,
in his great undertaking of walking
3000 half miles, in 3000 consecutive quarter hours.

Track No. 3.—Mr. EDMUND CARMER and
Mr. JAMES A. COBB,
in the Amateur Six Day Walk.

Track No. 2.—Miss ETTA ADAMS,
in the great Six Day Walk.

Track No. 1.—Miss NELLIE EDWARDS and
Madame ANNIE LAMB SPORT,
in the Two Hour Walk. (Monday night only.)

Track No. 6.—Masters ARCHER AINSLIE and
JOHN F. WALDRON,
in their One Hour Walk. (Monday night only.)

Track No. 7.—The petite MISSES HIGBEE,
AGED 5 AND 8 YEARS,
in their One Hour Walk. (Monday night only.)

Other Competitors will be announced by bulletin.

BILLIARDS.

YANK. ADAMS,

The greatest Living Expert of Finger Billiards, will give exhibitions every afternoon and evening, in conjunction with

Mr. JOHN BISSENGER,
AND HIS SISTER,

Miss LENA BISSENGER,
THE QUEEN OF THE CUE.

MUSICAL PROGRAMME.

MONDAY AND TUESDAY, MARCH 3d and 4th.

PART I.

1 Grand March, "Rebeka,".......................Barnby.
2 Overture, "La Patronne,"....................Suppe.
WERNER'S 23D REGIMENT BAND.
3 Non e ver,...................................Mattei.
Mr. CH. FRITSCH.
Cavatina, from Lucia,.........................Donizetti.
Miss JENNIE BACH.
5 Grand Air from The Poacher,.................Lortzing.
Cornet Obligato by Mr. J. SALCEDO.

PART II.

d Selection from The Chimes of Normandy...Planquette.
telice, from Ernani,.........................Verdi.
Mr. A. SOBST.

For balance Musical Programme, see Third Page.

Completing this 4,000 quarter miles in as many quarter hours walk took nearly six weeks and earned May Marshall $5,000. Courtesy of Gerry and Charlotte Curtis

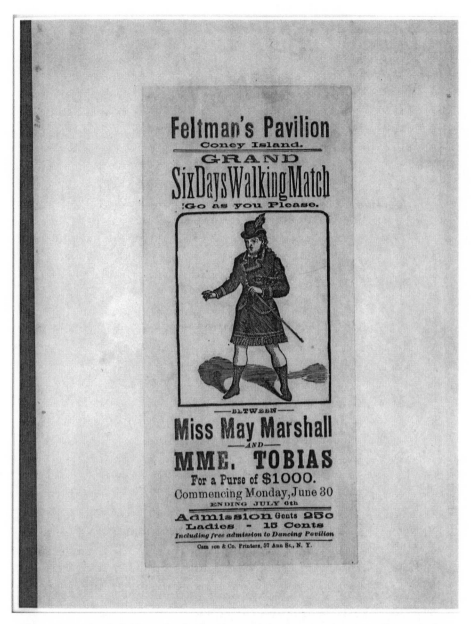

In June 1879 Sarah Tobias, who finished last at the International Six-Day Championship just three months earlier, topped May Marshall, 312-302 miles. Courtesy of Gerry and Charlotte Curtis

Mme. EXILDA LACHAPELLE,
PEDESTRIENNE.

Houseworth. Photographer.   12 Montgomery St., S. F.

Exilda LaChapelle's dominating performances in San Francisco made her the darling of the west coast and drew the ire of her rivals. Courtesy of the Bancroft Library Univ. of CA Berkeley

New York's Amy Howard moved west and temporarily elevated the sport and propelled other pedestriennes to superior performances. Here she poses with the Rose Belt, one of many such trophies presented to champion walkers. Courtesy of National Police Gazette Enterprises, LLC

Madison Square Garden hosted many pedestrian competitions, including this men's contest circa 1879. Note the walker's elaborate privacy rooms on the infield. Courtesy of Ed Sears

THE NATIONAL POLICE GAZETTE. 9

On December 16, 1879, an inebriated John Dermody attempted to crash the International Women's Six-Day Walking Match at Madison Square Garden. Police arrested him before he completed one lap. Dermody's garb included a dress, mismatched shoes, and a veil. Courtesy of National Police Gazette Enterprises, LLC

MISS BERTHA VON HILLERN.

Bertha Von Hillern, the first Pedestrienne.

One-time actress Amy Howard, the greatest pedestrienne, was still a teen when she left the profession in 1881. She returned to the stage, but tragically died during childbirth in 1885. She was 23. Courtesy of Heather Whiteside Ward

CHAPTER 18

Welcome 1879

"*I* did not think it was possible for her to do what has already been done," said one woman. Later in the day another said, "I came with my husband this morning, but grew so interested that I had to return."

Doubts of Madame Anderson's performance still lingered under the surface, but representatives from at least two newspapers had been present throughout every hour since the start. Her effort gained more credibility when a "long" bath put her 13 seconds late to the start. An alerted patron ran to the entourage.

"You said you'd give one hundred dollars if she wasn't in her proper place when the start bell sounded," he told Paley.

They paid the man. While Madame Anderson lost a c-note, the story legitimized her effort and made the audience more attentive.

Just after midnight on Monday, December 30, 1878, Madame Anderson broke into one of her mini-routines; she walked steadily, not recording spectacular times, but avoiding public signs of sleepy spells. Clocking most of her quarters in the 5:00-5:30 range, she exhibited the strength and consistency that elevated her to America's newest athletic star.

The following afternoon one of Daniel O'Leary's cousins visited Madame Anderson in her tent to offer some encouragement and showed her O'Leary's Astley belt.

"Daniel would have come himself," he said, holding the prize toward her, "but his feet are swollen from his victory at Gilmore's."

Madame stood motionless, hesitating to take it. He stepped toward her.

Madame Anderson slowly raised her hands and took it from him. Her arms fell a few inches from its weight (it reportedly weighed four pounds).

She admired the intricacies of its workmanship; she caressed it as she would a valuable gem or priceless artifact.

She ran her fingers along its silver plates, taking special notice of its raised impressions of runners and walkers. Her eyes locked on the solid gold buckle that every professional walker dreamed of: "Long-Distance Champion of the World."

Maybe more than anything else, the Astley Belt took pedestrianism to the level of popularity it now enjoyed.

Sir John Dugdale Astley, a member of the British Parliament, became so enthralled with endurance walking that he had a belt commissioned and named, then made it part of a prize package awarded to the winner of any of the five six-day races he backed in 1878-1879.

Each victor would take home a minimum of $4,000 and a percentage of gate receipts, enough money to attract the world's top walkers. The winner would also have to defend his belt against anyone of any nationality, "civilized or barbarian."

Any competitor who won three consecutive races kept the belt permanently.

Madame Anderson put the Astley Belt around her waist and admired it. She took it off.

"Thank you for the meeting," she said, returning it. "And tell your cousin I hope he gets better soon." She then smiled and said, "I know how troublesome feet can be."

The warning bell brought her back to reality. Within seconds she returned to the track.

*   *   *

As 1879 approached, everyone in Brooklyn wondered how Madame Anderson would ring in the New Year.

Fans packed the Garden on December 31. Men stood on wooden chairs. They stretched their necks, some nearly toppling as they contorted their bodies in an attempt to catch a glimpse of the pedestrienne each time she passed.

Notably missing from the excitement was the omnipresent Mike Henry. Twice the pedestrienne passed her tent beyond the requisite seven laps, but now her motive was enthusiasm, not weariness. If not for Henry's diligence, she would have covered an extra lap or more.

Just before midnight on December 31, the usually boisterous crowd turned silent as Samuells stepped on stage and poured Madame Anderson a glass of champagne. She turned to the audience and offered a simple toast.

She wished everyone in her adopted hometown of Brooklyn a happy 1879. With that, she drank to her old and new friends, and then sang, "Two O'clock in the Morning."

Then the warning bell rang.

According to the *New York Sun*, "She began walking in the New Year with the cheers of her admirers in her ears."

Usually around 1:00 a.m., Mozart Garden thinned. The band retired, leaving just a few hard-core followers, judges, gamblers, and those who used the venue for a cheap hotel.

But tonight would be different.

Attending included those who couldn't get enough of Anderson, the Garden or the evening. Some of the stylish New Year's Eve balls that often continued celebrating, some until almost dawn, broke up early. Many of the revelers left to make a late-night, or early morning visit, to the Garden.

For two hours well-to-do-couples made grand entrances wearing the finest New Year's Eve formal attire. Women's stylish outfits featured tight waists, long trains, bustles and square necklines. Floor-length dresses mostly hid shoes. Shoulder-length hair was pulled back, making a decorative-looking bun; some wore straw bonnets featuring ribbons, bows and lace. Accordion-style hand fans completed the ensemble.

While some men wore military-type garb, most donned black suits, white shirts, with canes that served more of a fashion statement than practical function. Their personal grandeur was accentuated with a top hat, a step up from the bowler, the headgear of the common outing. Mustaches added to the air of distinction.

For the first time the festive atmosphere in the Garden filled the early morning hours. The most influential of both Brooklyn and New York stayed and talked, bragged, "showed up" the commoners, and made several laps through the Garden, ensuring they were at least seen, if not their presence recorded in some appropriate periodical, all done for posterity of course.

For the moment Madame Anderson became little more than a sideshow. Although responsible for the spontaneous early-morning soiree, few paid her any attention.

These "proper genteel bluebloods" couldn't let on that they had any interest a woman's walking match. In their high society, none would have given a thought to Ada Anderson; but they could justify giving Madame Anderson a few minutes.

In the early hours of 1879, even New York's upper crust couldn't risk not being seen at Mozart Garden.

Their status demanded it.

*　　*　　*

Just hours later the pedestrienne's demeanor dramatically changed.

By 10:00 p m. on New Years' night, the *New York Sun* described her as ". . . a very tired woman," and that she was "creeping over seven laps." Then according to the *Sun*, ". . .she glided like a heavy ghost over the next quarter in 6:04. Even the applause on her last lap failed to quicken her almost benumbed limbs."

As usual, Mike Henry gave an optimistic, and pretty much accurate assessment, "She's sleeping now; in two hours she'll come out with the spring of a gazelle."

*　　*　　*

As she continued in the second half of her journey, spectators began focusing on two large flags that adorned the stage; to the patrons' left, the Stars and Stripes; to the right, the Flag of England, which hung almost directly over her privacy room.

Madame's tent drew stares and caused whispers as it became the topic of curious conversation.

They wondered what went on behind the door. How did she hold up outside the public eye? What did she eat? Did she sleep? How did she spend time during her brief respites? the *New York Sun* said, ". . .men and women endeavor to penetrate the hidden mysteries of her retreat."

A long look might have shocked them.

During the late afternoon hours of January 1, she slept on her right side, arm extended beyond the bed's edge. She almost looked relaxed, except that the light from the Garden window highlighted her pallid face, clenched hand and twitching eyelids.

Hearing the warning bell, her skilled attendants slid their hands under her shoulders, lifted her torso upright, then guided her feet to the floor. With each one taking a side, they helped her stand. Only then did her eyes exhibit life, as she wearily reached for the door. Mike Henry, who seemed to communicate with her telepathically, then assisted her through the opening.

It added to the increasing surreal moments. The exhausted athlete, fighting fatigue, left the solace of her room to enthusiastic masses cheering her to continue. She seemed oblivious to the upbeat band playing to lift her spirits, and a throng of followers cheering her every move, celebrating the moment, enjoying the attention and prestige she was bringing to Brooklyn.

New York papers began chronicling her missteps. Several times in the previous 48 hours she had run into the railings and or the wall. The casual observers might have thought they were witnessing the woman's demise. But her experienced support team expected them.

"It's only due to her overexcitement during New Years," said Miss Sparrow with a smile. "Soon she will be stronger than ever."

Somehow, she managed to show some life to those who supported and cheered for her the previous fortnight. Unlike earlier attendees, the majority of the Garden's new visitors weren't pedestrian aficionados.

The Garden filled more with curiosity seekers and those who sought to experience the new Brooklyn pride that now enveloped the city. The pedestrienne and Samuells didn't even worry about attracting female spectators anymore. They had outgrown that goal.

But Madame Anderson would soon face a challenge that went far beyond fatigue.

And it threatened a victory.

CHAPTER 19

Henry's Troubles

S amuells selected New Year's Day to make a major announcement.
He had signed on as Madame Anderson's manager.

This arrangement would potentially send the sport of endurance walking to another higher level, and maybe even exceed the glory days of the Von Hillern-Marshall rivalry. Madame Anderson, the woman whose athletic achievements humbled even the great O'Leary, would go on a national tour. The spectacle would draw even more attention to Brooklyn.

Samuells would become the key member of her entourage. He would organize, plan and schedule her appearances. It seemed destined for success. At some point she might even outdraw Barnum.

Following her current performance, she would enjoy a two-week recovery in Brooklyn. Her tour would likely commence in Boston, the city that had embraced Bertha von Hillern in 1877-1878. Samuells had already made arrangements in Pittsburgh and Buffalo. She would then visit the Pacific slope.

"In the spring she will return from San Francisco," Samuells announced. He then paused, smiling widely and said in a booming voice, "...and walk at Gilmore's Garden."

The masses cheered the news. They raised it a notch when, as if on cue, the pedestrienne emerged from her tent.

*   *   *

Activity in the Garden was now never-ending.

On January 2, the *Brooklyn Daily Eagle* reported, "It is fair to assume that Madame Anderson yesterday had more New Year's callers than any lady in the land..." The line outside her tent numbered in the dozens throughout the day, forcing Samuells to limit access.

The paper continued, noting the endless gifts of flowers presented to Madame Anderson. Hundreds of people stayed all night forming pedestrienne watching parties, and ". . .enlivening their vigils with sundry decoctions of gin and sugar, which appeared to keep up their spirits wonderfully well."

Hundreds remained through the night. Impromptu musical sessions became commonplace. A man playing a mouth organ joined a piano player. A quartet sang at three in the morning, and Madame jumped on stage and formed a duet. Later, they all sang, "I Dreamt My Boy Was Dead."

However, when the band started playing, "See the Conquering Hero Comes," she immediately demanded they stop, saying, "Be kind enough, gentlemen, to reserve that until I have completed my task and done something to deserve it."

She rarely walked alone. Female representatives of CB Hazelton's recently organized Ladies Walking Club accompanied her. They took turns walking laps or even a quarter mile with the pedestrienne as they encouraged women to engage in regular exercise. An ex-district attorney joined her for quarter number 1,640. Although he struggled, the immense crowd appreciated his effort. Shortly afterward the Chairman of the Board of Supervisors gave the "walker" a bottle of wine and quipped, "I didn't think he'd go that far." Later, the appearance of Commodore Nutt, Barnum's "other" midget attraction, thrilled the crowd as he went a few laps with her.

News of the pedestrienne spread across the country. Newspapers from New York, Chicago, San Francisco and smaller towns such as Cedar Rapids, Canton and Salt Lake City all ran reports of her progress.

But as the accolades went national, Madame Anderson faced a new problem.

Mike Henry, her near constant companion, coach and morale booster since early on, was suffering.

In a few days Henry's body had transformed from a large, boisterous, friendly figure into a weak and frail shell. He shuffled with pain. His strained physical state found him fighting for sleep and loss of appetite. He stopped fraternizing with Garden patrons. Each day he sat in a chair outside Madame Anderson's tent, face growing more ashen, skin drying, moving more slowly and losing concentration. His lack of color accentuated the lines in his face. .

He might have been worse than Madame Anderson at any point in the last two weeks. However, most felt confident she would recover; he might not.

Doctors noted Henry's distress.

Long walking days ranging from 12-21 hours took its toll on the untrained Irishman. His boots had destroyed his feet. Large strips of skin had ripped away from his heels and forefoot, exposing oozing, tender flesh, making them prone to infection. Huge blood blisters surrounded his toenails, which pulled the nail from its bed necessitating removal. His knees had swollen. Ankles stiffened. Muscles ached. He suffered from the same maladies that had doomed many endurance walkers: dehydration, exhaustion, dizziness, and headaches.

Mostly, he just didn't have the athletic background for such an arduous task.

Doctors ordered Henry home.

Madame's team immediately needed a substitute; one capable of long-distance walking with little sleep, and still possessing the personal skills to offer much-needed encouragement and specific direction for Anderson during her "sleepy spells."

Fortunately, Samuells had a competent replacement in the Garden.

Race judge Charles "CB" Hazelton had an endurance walking background, and occassionally joined Madame Anderson for a few laps.

Hazelton accepted the challenge. For the extent of Henry's recuperation, and no one even knew if he would return, Hazelton would "coach" Madame Anderson.

* * *

"There seems to be literally no end to the endurance of that woman," said one at Mozart Garden on the evening of January 4.

"I can well believe," said another, "that she could keep up that gait until 1880 just as readily as she has walked for the past three weeks."

A doctor who had been constantly evaluating her condition said, "There's no telling how long she can keep this up."

After days of struggling through sleepy spells and slowing quarter times, Madame Anderson finally enjoyed a good streak. For more than a week, even her good quarters were rarely dipped under 4:00. Now, she covered a dozen in just over three minutes. For the first time in days, she walked quicker and looked better than since she started.

Hazelton continued organizing legions of women who continually lined up to go a few laps with her. Most struggled to keep up for even a short time.

Their encouragement inspired Madame to make more stage appearances. The Mozart Garden faithful wanted to hear her sing. It renewed their confidence in her.

* * *

Some papers questioned how Madame Anderson could walk so much and not lose weight.

According to the *Herald*, she ate or drank something virtually every break for 24 hours beginning 8:00 pm on January 3. Most of her calories came from port wine, oysters/lobsters, tea and beef tea.

Her advice came from Gale, and they had some science behind them, or at least trial and error, and under the circumstances, might have been her best nutritional choices.

Port wine is a dessert wine, more sweet than alcoholic. Reportedly provided by a physician, it provided her with critical carbohydrates, the type of fuel needed most in endurance training. It was basically a 19th century Gatorade without the glucose polymers.

With Madame Anderson burning approximately 3,800 calories per day, and about 2,500 of those expended through walking, she would have needed increased fat and protein intake that the shellfish provided. The beef tea, a combination of round steak, water and salt, would have given her electrolyte replacement lost in sweat. The rest of her diet: pineapple, candied fruit, peanuts, bread, potatoes, and onions was apparently eaten in small portions but added some nutritional value.

Since the *Herald* didn't publish the portions, one can't give actual caloric consumption. But even modest intake, the numbers show that on this day (when she apparently suffered few ill-effects from sleepy spells), she consumed a surplus of around 1,500 calories. While this 24 hour period was probably not a typical eating day, it does illustrate her ravenous appetite, fueled not just by her tremendous physical activity, but by her malfunctioning hormones, which were telling her to eat even though her stomach was full.

Even small amounts of sleep deprivation decreases the body's manufacturing of leptin, the hormone that works with the brain to regulate appetite, and increases the production of ghrelin, a hormone that boosts hunger. In other words, Madame Anderson might have been overeating, even though she was walking 24 miles a day.

Long-time Brooklyn gynecologist Dr. Alexander JC Skene, one of the many physicians who examined her, said he had never seen such a fine specimen, and except for her droopy eyelids, claimed she was "in perfect condition." He said he considered her a physical study and was confident she would finish.

*   *   *

At 1:49 p.m. on January 4, she completed quarter mile 1,800, bounded into her tent and shouted, "Only 900 more quarter-miles and my task will be finished."

Soon after an ambitious amateur woman, inspired by the moment and not of any carefully thought out preparation, impetuously jumped out of her chair and forced her way to Hazelton, demanding the right to walk, not just with Madame Anderson for a lap or two, but against her in a quarter-mile.

The novice told the women in line that Madame Anderson appeared not to exert herself while walking, with the ladies saying, "She should do so on this occasion, as she would have an opportunity of showing her best speed."

The confident Anderson emerged from her tent, suppressing a chuckle.

Word of the challenge passed quickly through the crowd and they hushed as the two approached the quarter-mile mark in front of the judges' stand.

They lined up and Madame Anderson looked down, smiled, turned to her opponent and stage whispered, "Good luck."

The bell sounded and the duo took off at a solid clip.

Anderson's "rival" found out almost immediately that yes, Madame Anderson hadn't been pushed by any other woman. And she wouldn't be pushed this time, either. The challenger struggled to maintain the pace set by the pedestrienne. Arms flailing and gasping, she trailed by 20 feet after just one circuit.

The crowd continued cheering as Madame pulled away, building her lead to almost a half-lap. At that point, the challenger broke into a run and slowed only when she caught the pedestrienne.

Madame Anderson responded by accelerating again to a one-half lap lead, the crowd alternately laughing and cheering. Now gasping for air, the dispirited woman stopped in front of the judges' stand, sweating profusely, bent over, hands on knees, her quest finished. She failed to complete even one quarter-mile. The crowd delighted at the scene, then cheered even more when the grinning pedestrienne lapped her rival, giving her a pat on the back.

The cheering and laughter rose to the rafters.

"If I had gotten this much support in England," she said referencing her failure in the Plymouth circus tent, "I might have finished."

She walked well in front of a packed house the rest of Saturday. Usually a member of Hazelton's walking club accompanied her, but many struggled.

Through it all the enormous crowds cheered her every move. According the *New York Sun*, "The excitement eclipses everything since her New Year's toast and songs," and, ". . .she walked like the 7th Regiment on dress parade."

As further evidence of her improved condition, and growing confidence she would complete her task, bets on her finishing were now even.

As she neared quarter 1,900, the press began speculating about her inevitable victory. The *Brooklyn Daily Eagle* said, "During the past three weeks she has faithfully fulfilled her agreement of walking a quarter-mile in every consecutive hour, and the public has yet to find her off the track beyond the time specified for her appearance."

". . . her triumph over physical exhaustion will be as great as her admirers could desire. Enthusiasm of the fair sex grows every day . . ."

But a few noticed a change in her appearance, holding out predictions of a victory.

The *Sun* stated that her one-time rosy cheeks were replaced by a dark, almost menacing appearance, causing some to remark, "She looks as though she has some Indian blood in her," and, "she has the look of a Malay," referencing a group of dark-skinned people who lived primarily in the Malay Peninsula of SE Asia.

The paper also commented that she wore no cosmetics, and her foot pain subsided, thanks to her getting a new pair of shoes. She gave her first public comment on her condition since Henry's departure, pronouncing herself, "very well."

Wanting to maintain enthusiasm, Samuells increased the drama. The bell at the judges' stand would now not only ring at the three minute warning and at the start of each quarter, but would now sound after she completed six laps. Later that tradition would be called the "bell lap," a ritual at any track meet. While Samuells would never admit it, this adjustment might have been a response to her increasingly miscounting laps.

Those struggles seemed far away now, and everyone focused on the energy in the venue.

In early 1879, everyone wanted to visit and be seen at Mozart Garden.

*　　*　　*

During a walk in Cincinnati, a male pedestrian was discovered using a ringer to get through a race. That event, coupled with a local performance of Shakespeare's "Two Dromios," a musical comedy that involves a pair of mischievous twins, refueled rumors of Madame Anderson having a double. In answering the accusations, she offered to pay the expenses of anyone to stay all night and to visit her room anytime they desired.

For the masses, Madame Anderson had now achieved what would later be called superstar status. Brooklyn pastors increased their criticism of the walk, since parishioners were leaving church early to visit the Garden.

Due to a midweek rain, the crowds were smaller on Wednesday January 8, and Samuells cut admission back to fifty cents. But two unexpected events highlighted the evening. The crowd cheered when Mike Henry, after a three-day respite, returned and walked one quarter with her. Unfortunately, his return was temporary. He struggled to maintain her pace. Afterward, her pulse was 72, his 120.

Doctors sent him back home.

She would miss him.

During quarter 2,143, the crowd gasped. Her stunned walking partner turned and realized she had left the track after completing only three laps. Rushing into the tent, attendants found Madame passed out on the couch. Her crew begged her to return. She insisted on being left alone. Sparrow sat next to her friend, took her cheekbones in her palms and almost nose to nose, and convinced Madame to immediately return to the track.

Sparrow, the ever-present assistant, demanded that her employer follow her command or she would lose with less than a week remaining. Outside the tent anxious spectators sat and said little. Women twisted handkerchiefs. Men gripped their umbrellas. Sleeping fans were awakened. They nervously looked at the clock on the wall. Everyone knew time was running out. Her quarter times had slowed for days. Reports of her deteriorating physical condition had dominated conversation throughout Brooklyn. Those most familiar with Madame's periodic bouts with exhaustion had seen this scene play out before. They had also come to expect a recovery, sometimes within minutes.

But now, with precious time ticking away, this delay could end the walk only five days from victory.

If she didn't come out soon she would have spent more than three weeks and recorded 535 miles, and leave with nothing.

The crowd relaxed a bit when Sparrow led Madame Anderson out of the tent. The droopy-headed pedestrienne shuffled across the track. Sparrow held up her head and pointed to the giant tally board that proved that the pedestrienne still had four laps remaining. Madame Anderson opened her eyes, rubbed them, squinted, then rubbed them again. She turned to her assistant and nodded. Somehow, the weary pedestrienne processed the message and continued. Scattered cheers rose throughout the Garden. But Madame had lost a precious three minutes. The pedestrienne took a big breath, gathered herself and refocused, with the crowd suddenly inspired and cheering madly as she fought through the final four laps. She then stumbled into her tent and plopped on the couch.

The quarter was her slowest yet: nine and a half minutes.

Two and a half minutes later, the warning bell rang. She had three minutes before she must start 2,144.

From the beginning, Madame Anderson talked in surprisingly candid terms about the devastating effects of her sleepy spells. While she had wandered into walls and at times seemed to be sleepwalking, she had now miscounted laps several times. Two days earlier she had walked an extra lap while in a stupor. Even rabid followers of the sport had never seen this level of exhaustion. Many who watched couldn't believe that, after more than three weeks, this would happen.

However, her entourage knew what to expect. And thanks to the experienced Elizabeth Sparrow, who had seen Madame Anderson through so many contests in England, she survived. The struggle would continue for five more days, but conquering number 2,143 might have proven the major turning point.

Some in the Garden were horrified; others amazed. All were impressed.

*   *   *

"I'm overwhelmed," said Madame Anderson after entering her tent on the afternoon of January 9.

The raising of admission prices to a dollar during prime time hours encouraged the attendance of a higher-income crowd, and they, like virtually all who preceded them, cheered the woman and her pluck.

But now the atmosphere offered an added touch. These people, unlike most of the earlier attendees, had disposable income, and they took turns lavishing gifts on the woman.

While Madame Anderson had received many presents, mostly bouquets of flowers, the latest gifts wowed her entourage.

Almost every hour she received something in the order of a bonbonniere or a straw basket. She was presented a handsome Russian leather box filled with cut flowers, books, pencil cases, card cases and vases, and a gold mounted riding whip. Someone gave both she and Henry a gold-headed cane.

She walked and handed some of her floral gifts to cheering ladies. The *Brooklyn Daily Eagle* noted all the "jeweled fingers" that reached over the railing hoping to get a prize. At 11:30 p.m., she sang, "Alice, Where Art Thou?" Then she walked a lap backwards. Women arrived for a short visit of "just one more quarter," but stayed for hours.

Later, in true Night Owl fashion, she blew a horn in the ear of a sleeping man who drew laughs from the hundreds of witnesses when he ran screaming out of Mozart Garden. He returned later and said, "I thought it was Gabriel himself, and this was Judgment Day."

He might have had some insight. The man was an undertaker.

And the small crowds that had visited the day before, undoubtedly depressed due to a storm, were now replaced by hundreds. On the evening of January 9, just four days from victory, 2,000 came and went during the evening.

The new enthusiasm again encouraged the pedestrienne. She received an ovation every time she emerged from her tent.

Her feet improved and she returned to the familiar 7,000-mile pair; she planned to stay with them until the finish.

The hundreds who stayed just beyond midnight witnessed an unexpected treat. About 1:00 a.m., a large contingent entered Mozart Garden, capturing everyone's attention. In marched Colonel Sinn's Company from New Park Theatre. With the spectators rising in sections, the group looped around the track and upon the stage. A week earlier the names might have been unrecognizable to the lower-class patrons, but new fans of Madame Anderson were well-versed in local theater, and they pointed and whispered their names almost immediately.

While all drew their share of attention, patrons reserved their greatest applause for Kate Claxton, one of the era's most well-known and respected actresses.

Claxton led a group of about a dozen show business people to the stage.

The company marched in single file, and each one sat in a chair.

Madame Anderson finished her quarter mile and joined the group. For the next few minutes the performers allowed the audience to hear them talk about differences in the acting profession between America and Great Britain. Anderson told them about Gale encouraging her to come to America, the risks and expenses she took to get there, and some of the hardships involved with such an ordeal, but the goal made the effort worthwhile.

"I love to entertain," said Madame, smiling to the crowd.

"You could entertain in England," said Claxton.

"I love money, too,"

As if on cue the bell rang and Madame rose, laughter filling the arena.

But this time she couldn't conceal her afflictions.

She gingerly descended the stairs, each step bringing a controlled grimace and clenched teeth, but amid the Garden's festive atmosphere, few noticed.

A look of relief enveloped her face when she reached the floor, and she returned to her task.

At 8:45 p.m. on January 10, she completed quarter mile 2,500. Only 200 remained.

CHAPTER 20

Madame Anderson Victory

*O*n January 12, the last full day of Madame Anderson's epic walk, the *Brooklyn Daily Eagle* slammed an editorial in another paper, which still questioned Madame Anderson's now inevitable record: "There seems to us not the least reason to doubt that she has done all she has promised to do."

But even with only hours remaining, some doubters persisted.

After watching Madame Anderson struggle through a quarter mile and totter into her room, one woman said, "She'll never come out again."

A dozen women or so echoed the comment.

"They say I won't come out again," Madame said to Miss Sparrow as she curled up on her couch.

"And indeed you will then," came her friend's reply.

She completed the next one in just over three minutes and returned to her tent, applause still ringing in her ears.

"I think they might be better occupied on Sunday than in kicking up a jolly row."

She followed that comment with,

I shouldn't be surprised if I came in next time with the head of an old woman in my mouth."

"Why?" asked Paley.

"Well, there's an inquisitive creature, about 70 years old, sitting close to the rail at the upper end of the track. She is dressed in black and her face is framed with one, long, corkscrew curl on each side. Her nose is sharp and her eyes are piercing. Every time I pass her she shoves out her head and peers into my face as much to say, 'I'm bound to find out if you are the same woman every time.' I'm afraid I shall snap her head off if she keeps it up."

She continued playing pranks, and during the wee hours she still delighted in charcoaling the faces of sleeping spectators.

Over the last few days, Mozart Garden had looked more like a variety show than an athletic contest. The votaries of Terpsichore showed up for a "flying" visit, a pianist played, "Don't Get Weary," a woman who claimed she "could keep up with Madame Anderson if she just had a walking outfit," was given one. She lasted six laps and was laughed off the track. A Barnum performer sang about 50 verses of a song he'd written for the pedestrienne, then walked a quarter with her.

An estimated 4,000 paid one dollar each to visit the Garden on Monday, January 13, 1879.

Before work, after work, skipping work, leaving church early, nothing had kept Brooklynites and now New Yorkers from Samuells' venue. Women stayed all day; men left work early and remained through the night.

But not all the devotion was positive. A woman left her 18-month-old baby in the company of a young man while she and a friend went to Mozart Garden. Time got away from them, and when they returned they found the sitter drunk on the floor, unaware of what had taken place. A fire had broken out and the baby would die from severe burns.

* * *

With only a few hours remaining, people stood on the chairs, tables or the stairway. Men climbed on each other's shoulders, any place they could to catch a glimpse of the celebrity. Women clapped, waved their handkerchiefs, and gathered outside her room. The gift table on the stage overflowed with flowers and other gifts of admiration.

Madame clocked a 9:30 on quarter 2,624 when she stopped and listened to a four-year-old girl sing. Shortly after noon she sang "Tis But a Little Faded Flower," then followed that with, "Thy Voice is Ever Near," a tribute to her husband. From 6:00 to 7:00 p.m., the crowd dwindled to about 200. Newcomers sat stunned as they had watched a semi-comatose woman as they left for dinner, but a bright-eyed, fast-paced pedestrienne when they returned.

A reporter from the *NY Herald* described his view from the stage:

> One can only see a sea of heads and a narrow lane on the left in which the woman in the purple velvet walking suit is making quick time. With the completion of each quarter mile, spectators go from standing at attention to at ease. Some women rest on rails. When she comes out of her tent, they rise in segments again. Some men try to find a spot on stage."

For quarter 2,691, victory now a forgone conclusion, an adrenalin-charged Madame Anderson exploded from her room dressed as the

Goddess of Liberty, wrapped in a blanket design of stars and stripes, and carrying an American flag in her right hand. More than 2,000 screaming fans drowned out the band. Men doffed their hats and swept them from side to side.

Meanwhile, chaos ruled outside Mozart Garden. Hundreds clogged the intersection of Fulton and Smith, getting as close as possible to the history-making moment taking place inside. Police arrived and blocked the doors, denying further entry into the overflowing Garden. Inside, officers fought through the jammed house to keep the track clear from the madness that threatened to smother Madame Anderson and keep her from finishing. Every mini-break meant a lull in the enthusiasm, but it always came back stronger when the warning bell sounded, and then rose to the rafters when she appeared. The *Brooklyn Daily Eagle* wrote that the hall was so packed that, "people couldn't raise their arms above their heads."

She finished 2,698, stepped off the track and pushed her way through the frenzied throng, all of whom reached for a quick touch or at least to catch a glimpse of her. She climbed on the stage and raised her hands, signaling for silence. Two minutes passed before the crowd settled down. The she said,

> I want to sing you a song. They tell me that the betting against my accomplishing this feat has been very great, but I should be ashamed to mistrust the people of Brooklyn, who have stood by me through my weary task. I should be ashamed to think that an unkind thought to me would be harbored for one moment by any man not withstanding any amount of money he might have bet against me. I am now going to sing, 'Nil Desperandum.

She then pointed to the pianist, raised her eyebrows and briefly hummed. He struck a note and she said, "Half a note higher." Then she smiled and said, "There is a good deal in knowing how to do things."

All eyes were focused on her. She briefly scanned the packed house, soaking in the moment. This had been her goal for 20 years. For the last four weeks, she had dazzled Brooklyn with a remarkable ability to entertain, and this, supposedly her favorite song, would be her finale. They applauded after every verse. When she finished she left the stage for the track, the crowd reluctantly giving way. With the noise shaking the rafters the entire quarter-mile, she completed 2,699 in 3:12 and dashed into her tent.

A few seconds later, a Mr. HH Wheeler stood and waved the crowd silent, and said, "I am requested by the management and judges to

128

announce that on the completing of the next quarter-mile by Madame Ada Anderson, she will have completed the task of walking 2,700 quarter miles in 2,700 quarter hours."

He then listed her fastest and slowest times:

Fastest quarter: Number 6. Time: 2:46 at 9:15 a.m. on December 16.

Slowest quarter: Number 1,282. Time: 10:00 at 4:15 a.m. on December 30.

Fastest mile: Number 17. Time: 17:10 at 12:47 p.m. on December 17.

Slowest mile: Number 656. Time: 32:06 at 3:55 a.m. on January 13.

With silence nearly overwhelming Mozart, the final warning bell rang. Within three minutes Madame Anderson would for the last time emerge from her room, her solace and home for the previous 28 days.

The crowd barely moved. Incredibly, for the next few seconds the Mozart Garden was engulfed in an eerie quiet. Mike Henry, who had given of himself more than almost anyone, the man who had spent days at home recovering from his crushing coaching duties, and who had only made sporadic appearances since, stepped onto the track. He would lead her to victory. It was a fitting tribute to the man who brought Madame to this moment. She emerged from her tent for one last trip, one last quarter mile that would conclude what had been a performance never before seen in America, not by May Marshall or Bertha Von Hillern, or even the top men walkers, Daniel O'Leary and Edward Payson Weston.

As the final seconds ticked before the start, the Garden stayed quiet. All eyes were on her and Henry as they stood at the start line. Samuells looked at his pocket watch, counting the seconds. He reached for the bell. His hand hesitated for just a moment. When he pulled the cord, the thousands erupted in a deafening roar. In an instant Mozart Garden broke into pandemonium, a crescendo that waved from inside to the hundreds outside, the ones who couldn't get in, but had to be at the Garden, if not in the Garden. Madame Anderson took off like she hadn't in any of her previous 2,699 quarter miles. With Henry fighting to stay ahead, he barely kept the inside lane clear of errant feet and hands, clearing the path for Madame. She ran the first lap, legs more shuffling than sprinting, keeping a short distance from Henry. She covered her first lap in 16 seconds, the second and third laps in 17. Fatigue bettered her on number four and she clocked a 20. She hit the line and dropped the shuffle in place of a brisk walk pace, but the cheering continued unabated. With the deafening celebration easily drowning out the band, the throngs outside could hear the cheers and knew the triumph was only seconds away. She clocked both laps five and six in 28 seconds.

Then she started her final lap, number 18,900 out of 18,900. Although no one could hear it, Samuells repeatedly sounded the bell signifying the occasion. With ear-piercing cheers throughout the Garden, the near mob-like atmosphere crested when she crossed the line one last time.

She clocked 2:37, the fastest of 2,700.

Mozart Garden shook as thousands inside and outside celebrated the accomplishment. Inside, handkerchiefs waved, hundreds of hats were thrown into the air, and people shouted themselves hoarse.

The timers couldn't make an official announcement for nearly a minute after she finished.

With the crowd still cheering, she again made her way through the throng, climbed on the stage, and sat in a chair facing the 2,000 enthusiasts. When all was quiet, only then did people notice the ringing in their ears.

Too hoarse to speak, Samuells gave the floor to Corporal James Tanner, the Brooklyn tax collector and Civil War veteran who lost both legs in the Battle of Manassas in 1862. He gained his greatest fame as the stenographer who chronicled President Lincoln's last moments. Cpl. Tanner read a humorous letter from Corporation Counsel Clinton DeWitt. Tanner then made a speech in which he commended Madame Anderson for showing Brooklyn women what they were capable of doing. According to the January 14, 1879 issue of the *New York Herald*, he said, "I am happy to say that the Brooklyn people by their patronage enabled Mme. Anderson to bank $8,000 last Friday, and in this case I, the laborer, is worthy of the hire."

He concluded with, "Madame Anderson's visit may have been more than passing benefit to the ladies of Brooklyn and teach them to make more use of their limbs and take daily perambulations that may benefit their health."

Then it was Madame's turn.

She commented about the superior strength of men over women, but also believed women possessed an advantage in endurance. She then gave a brief summation of her professional frustrations, saying,

> As a girl of 18 or 20, I had a really beautiful contralto voice, but that did not make me a name. I then tried the stage, and although I held an honorable and responsible position, I was not chronicled on the banner of fame. My next effort as a clown in a circus was also a success in its way, but still the long, looked for reputation was not reached. I then became a manageress, and got some reputation for losing money, and finally on September 12, 1877, I commenced my present business. I took the advice of Gale, the

famous long-distance pedestrian, and when he told me, 'Go abroad and they will give you a name.' I came here and now I will go back with the name for which I have struggled since my girlhood. I sincerely trust that He who has given me the strength to make it will give me strength to keep it. The lesson I give to the women of Brooklyn is that they must learn to do their part in life. Do the best you can; that will mean a great deal.

She then turned her attention to those who had criticized her for walking on Sunday.

I have done the work contracted to do, the same as the servants that cook their dinners on Sunday and the car drivers that drive them to church. I thank you all for your kind patronage, and I hope that in a year's time I will be able to retire and lead a quiet life.

Amid the cheers that had been a part of the walk for several days, she took Samuells hand and he helped her off the stage. Officials carried her out of Mozart Garden, police continued pushing back against zealous fans.

Attendants lifted her into a waiting carriage.

Hundreds followed it down the street.

She was taken to a Turkish bath house, given a warm bath and some beef jelly and port wine before going to bed.

While that took place, the official scorers and surveyors certified and swore to the accomplishment.

*   *   *

Madame Anderson spent the next few days recovering in a local hotel where doctors okayed her health, but also recommended she not try such a stunt again. Meanwhile, Samuells remodeled Mozart Garden, in preparation for a benefit to honor Brooklyn's newest hero.

On January 17, 1879, hundreds followed her carriage back to the Garden. Tables and chairs now covered the track and infield area. Colorful bunting hung from the rafters, and British and American flags decorated the railing.

About 200 paid $5 each to attend the reception. Gifts to the pedestrienne included cut glass, silver service sets, food and more flowers. Maybe the most valuable gift was a six-piece silver service set, inscribed with the following:

Presented to Madame Anderson by the citizens of Brooklyn, Long Island, as a token of their admiration of her physical endurance, under the Direction of AR Samuells and JH Webb.

New York dignitaries made speeches, expressing their admiration for the achievement. Madame Anderson rose and gave thanks to God and the people of Brooklyn. She drew great applause when she said, "I always thought the time would come when I would meet with success, and it has come."

They gave her the $8,000. The average annual household income was $500.

In just one month, Madame Anderson had 'made a name,' helped Samuells better Vanderbilt, and elevate the status of Brooklyn and Mozart Garden.

On a larger scale, she had infused life into a sport that desperately needed a boost.

Over the next few weeks, the sport would experience a renaissance with more pedestrienne hopefuls, new stars and skyrocketing popularity.

Unfortunately, its critics would grow in numbers and intensity, requiring the pedestriennes to find a new home.

Then they would face a new set of problems.

CHAPTER 21

Proxy Rivalry

*L*ike most people in late 1878, May Marshall probably didn't take Madame Anderson's announcement of a month-long walk seriously.

In early January 1879, she traveled to Washington, DC for a 27 hour, 100-mile walk against hometown pedestrian William Crawford in Ford's Opera House. The sawdust track measured 10 laps to the quarter mile, and in an unusual set up, half the track sat on stage, the other half, supported by beams, extended into the audience.

But Marshall couldn't ignore Madame Anderson's daily accomplishments, especially since the *Washington Post* and other papers carried daily updates.

Marshall vs. Crawford commenced at 8:00 p. m. on January 8, and crowds were kept small at least in part to inclement weather. However, expected enthusiasm never materialized, and the event flopped. Gate receipts totaled only $175, with the venue lessee taking $100 and Miss Marshall's manager receiving the balance. Invoices from the band and newspaper ads went unpaid. Crawford badly beat Marshall, completing the 100 miles with 48 minutes to spare. The pedestrienne logged only 94 miles before dropping out. As with many of her recent performances, a swollen leg crippled her. She hobbled more than walked her last few laps.

While experiencing another stinging loss, the press' growing interest in Madame Anderson might have humiliated her more. On the same day the *Washington Post* announced Marshall's defeat, it mentioned that Madame Anderson had completed 2,272 quarter miles. The paper also reported the large crowds at Mozart Garden, sharply contrasting against the echo chamber where Marshall performed.

In spite of her game leg and emotional letdown, Marshall and her agent quickly put together a plan to equal Anderson's new mark, but they figured her doing 2,796 quarter miles in 2,796 quarter hours, or 24 hours more than Anderson's total. She would do it in the E Street Gymnasium. She enlisted the help of several doctors. Surveyors certified the track at 24 laps to the mile, six per quarter mile, including the distance from the track to her privacy tent, set up on the building's SE corner. The configuration required her to walk three stops up or down on each lap. Six judges and scorers were sworn in to keep an accurate count of the number and time of quarters walked. Two officials would be on hand at all times, working three, eight-hour shifts. She also hired "two colored women" to assist her, each working 12-hour blocs.

On the evening of January 20, May Marshall made a short address, stating that she wanted to beat Anderson's record. She told the crowd that she had more than 125 professional walks behind her with more than 9,000 miles logged. She also said that 22 times she had defeated a male opponent. She said mentioning her achievements were more to re-establish her credibility with the American public and make them forget about Anderson.

She toed the line. At 8:30 p.m., the starter shouted, "Go!" and the crowd cheered her entire first quarter, which she completed in 2:25.

Two days later she revealed her pride and confidence to a *Washington Post* reporter who visited her between quarters.

"So you think you will go through with your task, do you?" asked the reporter.

"Oh, I know I will. I am a woman of iron heart and can do anything I undertake. I am the best human walker in the country, and can do anything that an Englishwoman can do."

"Iron heart is well enough, but it takes iron limbs and an iron constitution. Unless you have these it is iron check to make the effort," said the reporter.

"Well, I have never failed yet, and I know I won't now. My business depends on it, for unless I do it I can't get another engagement."

"And this is your only reason for thinking you will do it?"

"Well, if I can walk six days, or twelve days, or 100 miles, why can't I do this? I have the best physicians I can get."

But the physicians don't walk for you. Have you had much training?"

"No, I only walk around and see the sights while I am in cities."

"And made dietary preparations?"

"Oh no! I eat what I want, but I don't want much. Tea and toast will be on my diet on this walk."

"Pardon me for asking you if you have contemplated the chastening corn."

"Never grew a corn in my life. I've a small foot, but wear a big shoe."

"And won't your limbs swell?"

"No, they are hard as iron."

"What about the importance of sleep?"

"The doctors will have to attend to that. After the first four or five days the trouble will commence. I think Madame Anderson was often brought on the track asleep, but she walked just as well."

"Then you think you can walk sleeping as well as awake?"

"The Englishwoman did, and so can I. When Von Hillern, the German, came over, I beat her and I'll beat this one. Why, I'll bet this room full of money that I can beat Von Hillern any walk she names, and if I succeed in this, I'll bet two rooms full that I can beat the female world."

She vowed to complete the feat or be carried off the track dead. Early crowds were small, but were larger than early attendance for Anderson's walk.

*   *   *

Four days after Marshall began her quest in Washington, Exilda LaChapelle, the one-time small-town walker from Wisconsin, sought the same goal at less than prestigious Folly's Theater in Chicago. The track measured 28 laps to the mile, the same as Mozart Garden. Similar to Mozart, a railing circled the track on the infield side.

On the evening of January 25, and in front of a small crowd, she recorded her first of a proposed 2,700 announced quarter miles in 2:25.

For the next three and a half weeks, May Marshall and Exilda LaChapelle competed through newspaper reports, vying not just to better Anderson's record, but against each other.

After a week Marshall began attracting attention. Dr. Mary Walker, one of America's first female physicians, was a constant visitor to the track, and even attempted to walk a quarter with the pedestrienne. Marshall struggled at times, and needed physical guidance to maneuver the distance from the track and into her tent. An unknown admirer gave her a basket of flowers, the first of many.

At 9:00 p.m. on January 27, Miss Marshall clocked her 675th quarter mile in 3:09, completing ¼ one-fourth of her task. Actors, politicians and national celebrities were routinely on hand to watch and participate.

Like Anderson, she experienced sleepy spells, the worst occurring around 2:00 a.m. when a young man volunteered to help steady her when necessary.

In Chicago, the first few days went well for Mme. LaChapelle. For both women, crowds and enthusiasm grew through the first week. On January 30, Chicago Mayor Monroe Heath came to watch the pedestrienne. To the delight of some, and the chagrin of others, she performed without tights. In spite of this exhibitionism, or because of it, throngs of ladies continued filling Folly Theater. At 11:00 p.m., she completed quarter mile number 491 in 2:01.

Word spread throughout the gymnasium that Miss Marshall had planned something special for quarter number 1,350, her announced halfway point. As the flap from her 12 x 20 tent opened, the eight-piece brass band played "The Wearing of the Green," and she appeared wearing a garnet dress reaching below her knees. Her striped stockings accentuated the great muscular development of her lower extremities. As she accelerated throughout the walk, necks craned and chairs emptied as everyone strained to catch even a glimpse of "that funny woman who never sleeps." Women waved their handkerchiefs, men stomped their feet and tapped canes on the floor louder and faster with each completed lap. She finished, turned and bowed to the appreciative audience, and disappeared into her room.

A writer for the *Washington Post* entered her tent, and found her eating some oatmeal.

"How do you feel Miss Marshall?"

"As bright and sound as a $100 gold piece," she replied with a smile.

"Aren't you fatigued?"

"Not a bit."

"What do you subsist upon, generally?"

"I don't have any regular diet. Beefsteak, eggs, oatmeal, or most anything I like. I take tea, but no coffee."

"Do you sleep much?"

"Sometimes not for two days. When I do, I take ten-minute naps for about two hours."

"Do you not feel ill-effects from so much loss of rest?"

"Sometimes I am drowsy, and then I feel very mean, but I manage to walk it off."

"How are your feet?"

"Why, they are all right now. I haven't had a single blister on them. The doctors say they are as smooth as a person's hand."

"How is your record so far, Miss Marshall?"

"Way ahead of Madame Anderson's."

"Is there anything special you wish to say to the people through the Post in the morning?"

"Only that I am a real live American woman, and I don't want other live American men and women to forget it, either."

The bell then sounded for Miss Marshall to commence with quarter number 1,352.

In Chicago, Mme. LaChapelle struggled. Big crowds had yet to materialize. Unlike Marshall, she was an unknown. She had to earn respect and develop a following.

On February 4, LaChapelle completed 1/3 toward Anderson's total. Every evening the Folly audience grew in number and enthusiasm. But the stressful days and nights were having a cumulative effect. She looked haggard, and appeared groggy. During a sleepy spell, she ran into a support beam, injuring her shoulder. The theater manager responded by positioning guards at the pillars. During the last few days she had received numerous gifts, including a colorful array of flowers, a whip, and a pair of walking leggings. By midnight, Madame LaChapelle completed quarter 976.

The following day Miss Marshall began showing major signs of fatigue. She fell into a shuffle and her times slowed.

Like Madame Anderson, Miss Marshall loved putting on a show. In some regards, the audience's angst and "wanting to see a train wreck" propelled her athleticism to another level. She responded to the challenge of reaching a difficult goal. She also embraced the pressure of carrying the pedestrienne flag for America against a German, a Brit, and now a Frenchwoman.

She believed that by outdoing Anderson, she could claim a proxy victory against all three.

But she might find that claim difficult to attain.

At 5:00 a.m. on February 5, LaChapelle recorded quarter 1,000. At 3:00 a.m. the next day, Marshall completed number 1,467.

Three days later a crowd of more than 500 watched Mme. LaChapelle, cheering her almost every move. She complained of pollution burning her eyes, so the gaslights were turned as low as possible, but men pretty much ignored frequent requests to stop smoking. At 10:00 p.m., Mme. LaChapelle totaled 1,256 quarter miles; Marshall, 1,739.

The next day, in a curious, if not disturbing development occurred at Folly. From midnight to 8:00 a. m., a mysterious team of "watchers" showed up and kept tabs on LaChapelle. They talked to no one, but were diligent with their task, taking notes with each completed quarter mile.

On Monday evening, February 10, a good crowd saw May Marshall complete quarter number 2,000. She took the opportunity to officially announce her intention of completing 96 more quarter miles in 24 hours to beat Anderson's record. To generate interest, management introduced a Saturday matinee special. From noon to 6:00 p.m., admission prices were reduced from twenty-five to fifteen cents. The move proved so successful that they offered it again for Tuesday. The lower rate encouraged families to attend the gym. Marshall invited children to walk with her, but it was also a painful reminder that her son was in Chicago, under her mother's care.

Newspapers, which Miss Marshall read each day, reported on LaChapelle's struggles. Getting updates on the Frenchwoman's nightly sleepy spells, the headaches, and haggard looks all contributed to Marshall's belief that she alone could beat Anderson's record. She probably figured that since LaChapelle had been so focused on equaling Anderson, she wouldn't have the stamina to continue if she even if she did make 2700. Marshall's extra 96 would make the public forget Anderson, put LaChapelle in the background, and elevate May Marshall as undisputed Queen of the Tan Bark.

At 11:00 a.m., February 10, LaChapelle, still complaining of a headache and running a slight fever, passed 1,500. At 3:00 a.m. on February 11, Marshall totaled 2,042.

As with Madame Anderson, both pedestriennes experienced their most difficult times in the late evening. But whereas Anderson generated some interest and had a nocturnal following such as the "Night Owls," Marshall and LaChapelle hopefuls were left with mostly the sound of their dragging feet and a few encouraging words that often sounded more like hopeless haranguing than enthusiasm. While both struggled, LaChapelle suffered more, which seemed her lot in life. Unlike Marshall, who loved competition, and Anderson, who loved performing, LaChapelle walked to avoid the personal tragedies that had followed her since a child. Not walking left her living with of the loss of everything she had known, from her parents to her baby. Those proved a much greater pain than any endurance contest could inflict on her.

She also knew that after a few hours of "sleepwalking," the adoring crowds would lift her spirits.

The two "watchers" continued their ritual. Every night the sequestered duo counted laps, and seemed to record the pedestrienne's every move.

Even though her sleeping spells increased in both frequency and intensity, May Marshall remained confident of victory. Less than a week from finishing, she fared better than LaChapelle, whose evening stretches had turned into a series of comatose stumbles. On many occasions she would have collapsed had a nearby volunteer not grabbed her. Her quarter times slowed, virtually eliminating her brief respites.

LaChapelle received reports, too. The *Chicago Tribune* periodically updated Marshall's progress. While not descriptive, their brief recounts made it clear that Marshall would complete not just her task, but even go another 96 quarter miles. The Frenchwoman responded with mixed emotions. With days remaining, even 2,700 seemed impossible, but Marshall had given her a deadline. She now had a new focus, if not life.

Marshall's plan might backfire. The message of an extra 24 hours didn't discourage her antagonist, it had inspired her, and everyone in her tent, everyone in Folly Theater, maybe everyone in Chicago.

LaChapelle's mood improved and she had more fun. In the early hours of February 12, she roused a dozing attendee, "Weak up, sir," she said in her French accent, "you are here to watch me, not sleep."

However, she still faced several battles. Of the three walkers who had attempted such a multi-week feat, she was the youngest, least trained and least experienced. Three weeks into the event, she showed signs of breaking down. On February 13, with still 10 days remaining to reaching her announced goal, she suffered from uncontrollable arm twitches. Her legs swelled. She eschewed breakfast, and constantly suffered from fatigue. She only survived through Dr. Dunne's continuous treatment of her blisters and the administering of stimulants.

The next night, Folly Theatre received some special guests. Sitting in a reserved area were AR Samuells, William Paley, and fresh from her two-week walk in Pittsburgh, where she successfully completed 1,350 quarter miles in 1,350 quarter hours, Madame Ada Anderson. In a few days she was in town for an upcoming walk of 2,064 quarter miles in consecutive, 10-minute segments. The Anderson team had made no secret of their desire to trump LaChapelle, saying, they wanted to "take the shine off anything she accomplishes."

And in what might be a coincidence, after the Anderson team's visit, the papers never mentioned the watchers again.

On February 15, the crowd lifted LaChapelle's spirits as they acknowledged the pedestrienne's 20th birthday. She received other gifts, the most notable a diamond ring.

At 11:30 p.m. on February 17, May Marshall finished her originally announced task, completing the historic 2,700th quarter mile in 3:20. Her longest and most severe sleeping spell had occurred the day before around 10:00 a.m. With only 24 hours remaining, everyone felt confident of victory. The gymnasium was packed to suffocation, and the press couldn't wait to announce the achievement. A group of locals, somewhat embarrassed at the lack of patronage during the event, rented a band to parade through the city during the day and play at the hall during the evening. Auditors counted the take, paid expenses, and put the remainder in a bank account for Marshall. It was hoped that the impressive attendance from the last day would equal an appropriate remuneration for her month-long effort.

The *Washington Post* reported, "Though this walk will not make her much richer, the reputation of it opens a wide field for her, and her splendid physique will take care of the rest."

They wrote that even as she continued her quest for 24 more hours. At 3:00 a.m., she completed quarter number 2,710.

More than 1,500 crammed into the gymnasium for May Marshall's anticipated grand finish. After 2,760, she quickened the pace, and made each of her last 15 quarters faster than four minutes. She was cheered at every turn of the six-lap quarter, and her blushed face and bright eyes indicated that she was overwhelmed by the adoration. As she completed quarter 2,796, the building shook with applause.

She was presented with a gold medal on behalf of the Gymnasium Association. Her presenter said that Miss Marshall was a triumph of physical culture and showing how the body and mind can work together.

Taking the stage, she bowed to the audience, but was either too excited or fatigued to reply. She disappeared into her tent, her new award dangling from her neck.

Afterwards, officials collected a purse for the pedestrienne so she would be appropriately compensated. The event had been well attended, even during periodic stretches of inclement weather, but the matinee fees had hurt Marshall's take. To make up for it, four men passed hats through the crowd.

Her quarter mile times sent shock waves throughout the endurance walking community. She appeared to have finished in much better condition than Anderson. She clocked 2:14 for number 1,350; her slowest, 6:40 on 2,138. For the 29 days, she had averaged four minutes, twenty seconds per quarter, meaning she had walked a total of seven days and six hours.

All of her cumulative times bettered Anderson. And she walked an extra 24 hours.

Feeling thrilled and exhausted at the same time, Miss Marshall was wrapped in a blanket, carried out a side door, put in a carriage, and taken to a friend's home. There she immediately received a Turkish bath and a rub down, and another one before heading to bed. When wakened after 30 minutes' sleep, friends restrained her from getting on her feet. They required her to read a paragraph from a newspaper to test her mental state. They repeated the test 30 minutes later.

Several spectators, officials and officers testified that she had indeed completed her task, so no one could legitimately accuse her of fraud. In addition to the medal, she reportedly received a paltry sum of $600.

As she slept, May Marshall took comfort in regaining the title: Queen of the Tan Bark. She had defeated the German, Von Hillern, and had now eclipsed Anderson's record.

Adding to the excitement, papers reported that Marshall accepted an invitation to walk 2,800 quarter miles in 2,800 quarter hours in New York beginning March 5. If successful, she would receive a guaranteed $2,000.

That offer might have encouraged her to quit at 2,796. When Marshall stopped, she knew LaChapelle continued, but even if the Frenchwoman tied the new record, Marshall needed only four more quarters to beat it. Besides, if Marshall set a new record at 2,800 or even better in DC, that would reduce the attraction and probably the money, and maybe even kill the whole New York offer.

But in spite of her increasing troubles, Exilda LaChapelle had not left the track.

*   *   *

Although LaChapelle now controlled the proxy rivalry, she still struggled. She ate little, her diet now consisting of sherry and eggs every two hours. She complained of headaches, pains in her shoulders, and tender feet. Her resolve seemed greater than any walker. Her times between quarters 1,700 and 1,900, more than two days of walking, were almost all between four and a little over five minutes.

On Thursday, February 20th, a reporter asked about her tribulations. "I will win," she said, "but I was frightened this afternoon. I was taken so sick, I felt for sure I should have to leave the track."

"You are certainly looking well."

"No one knows what I have suffered, but then I have the will not to say anything about it. I have the endurance to get through this."

At that point the warning bell rang and as she left her tent, Madame LaChapelle said, "I'll be back in a minute."

The crowds grew to near capacity every night, with more and more ladies present to see, marvel, cheer and sympathize with the little French girl. Many would join her for a few laps. Some wanted to keep her company; others to experience the thrill of witnessing history.

Since the beginning, undercard walks for amateurs and professionals had taken place in conjunction with Mme. LaChapelle's performance. That particular evening, five women completed a one-mile competition. Officials scheduled a 'fat man's race,' limited to those weighing more than 200 pounds. Coinciding with LaChapelle's finish, a short walk for school girls was set.

But LaChapelle now suffered from a noticeable limp, and she often tramped with a drooping head.

As with Marshall and Anderson, LaChapelle went through her most trying times in the evening, when few, if any, were on hand to offer encouragement, and the hall sounded hollow as her shuffling moccasins echoed throughout the empty cavern. Numerous attempts were made to arouse her to rise for each quarter. Her joints and muscles, always strained, ached even more without the crowd and music to encourage her.

After she completed her seventh lap, she collapsed into her cot for a short rest before the uncomfortable scenario replayed itself. During those times an attendant constantly accompanied her to make sure the strained athlete didn't fall against the rail, a likely possibility had she been on her own. At 4:00 p.m. on February 20, she completed quarter 2,509.

As the night turned into day for the last time, she perked up and brought a cat onto the track, which followed her for several laps. Madame LaChapelle had now passed the last of these tough spots, and at 11:00 p.m. that evening she would have accomplished her announced task.

The next night, Exilda LaChapelle had covered 2,602 quarters. Most expected her to finish; she was preparing to make pedestrienne history.

The large enthusiastic crowd, and the uplifting tunes from the band all boosted her spirits. The exhaustion and her painful and swelling headaches had dissipated, but tired legs continued to take a beating.

Most businesses closed due to George Washington's birthday, so many people sought entertainment. At noon the crowd filled Folly Theater and cheered as the plucky pedestrienne covered quarter number 2,656. By 8:00 p.m., with every seat taken, LaChapelle finished 2,689.

From that point on, every emergence from her tent brought deafening cheers from the crowd. Wearing her favorite red suit, she accelerated. A local professional pedestrian and her manager were now constant companions. At 10:00 p.m., after walking 2,696, she smiled as fans presented her with a floral tribute in the shape of a ship. Her manager carried the flowers, and beamed at the interest taken in his protégé. Two fast-paced women joined her for 2,697, and she recorded 2:36. The male pedestrian joined her for 2,698. With everyone screaming, she clicked off a 2:59.

After the next quarter, Dr. Dunne climbed onto the stage and hushed the crowd. With a dramatic pause he announced that the Madame would not only equal Anderson's record, but beat it by completing another 300 quarter miles in the next 50 hours - one quarter every 10 minutes in just over two days. As if on cue, Mme. LaChapelle appeared for number 2,700, the crowd cheering louder than ever.

She had just accomplished what few thought possible. But now, in a perfect example of one-upmanship, in two more days of walking she would beat Anderson's record with her in the city, break Marshall's four-day-old record, and even top her proposed 2,800 quarter-mile contest in New York.

With the crowd screaming, she and her male companion sprinted the seven laps, where she recorded a remarkable 2:04.

When the excitement died out a bit, she stepped on stage where her Manager gave her several gifts, courtesy of her admirers. Presents included a pedometer, an elegant gold watch, and a gold medal from local actors.

Most notably, she received another larger gold medal with a figure of a pedestrienne on one side and an inscription on the other:

Presented
To
MME. EXILDA LA CHAPELLE
Champion Pedestrienne of the World, by Her Chicago Friends
February 22, 1879 at Folly Theater, on the Completion of her walk of 2,700 quarter-miles in 2,700 quarter hours, under the Management of the Davies Bros.

Mme. LaChapelle bowed, and 10 minutes after finishing 2,700, began the first of 300 more, recording 4:21.

The shortened breaks meant that for the next two days she would get virtually no sleep. She finished the next day in front of a packed house at 1:00 a.m., about half of whom were women who waved handkerchiefs and cheered her every move during the final two hours.

In just a couple of months, Madame Anderson, Exilda LaChapelle and May Marshall had redefined pedestrianism. Just weeks earlier, Marshall had struggled to keep the sport and her career alive. After three never-before-seen performances, women's pedestrianism enjoyed more popularity than ever.

All over the East, immigrant women heard about the pedestriennes and saw the sport as a way out of poverty.

Von Hillern, LaChapelle and Anderson fought and succeeded, and they faced the same struggles as any of the millions of immigrants who lived in a nightmarish existence. Additionally, Marshall overcame widowhood and single motherhood.

In 1870s America, anything could be accomplished. And many of them believed they could do it. They saw it. The women walked; they took breaks. What could be simpler?

In early 1879, everyone believed it, and they all wanted a part of the pedestrienne madness and prosperity.

But while following and participating in the sport reached unprecedented popularity, the pedestrienne hopefuls weren't prepared for grueling days and the long ordeal. They weren't trained and they lacked the professional help that made the established athletes so successful.

Most would face huge disappointments through high profile failures. And the criticism, once limited to an occasional editorial questioning the wisdom and usefulness of such spectacles, would soon question the sport's legality.

CHAPTER 22

Pedestrienne Madness

"*B*artell's off! A 10-mile race upstairs!" shouted the ticket seller at New York's Brewster Building on the afternoon of February 2, 1879.

Annie Bartell, nicknamed, "The Westchester Milkmaid" after her hometown and that she carried a milk pail with her, started in the Brewster Building a walk of 3,000 quarter miles in 3,000 quarter hours. During her performance, she received 473 bouquets of flowers, three dogs, and two riding crops.

In spite of big public support and innumerable gifts, the task overwhelmed her.

After less than a week, with a mere 566 quarters completed, she quit, suffering from blistered feet, and twitching, swollen legs and hips. Her last few hours, according to the *NY Herald*, had been a "funeral march." She staggered off the track and collapsed. There she slept for two hours, unaware that two more pedestrienne hopefuls had supplanted her.

On February 3, The *NY Herald* reported,

She could not see the track and had to be guided more carefully than a blind beggar on the king's road. Moreover, she had to be held up or she would have fallen fast asleep on the sawdust. At last all consciousness, save that of suffering, seemed to pass away, and when she left the track the last time she was as completely unaware of it as if death instead of mere exhaustion had stricken her down.

Madame Anderson's accomplishment in January 1879 had an immediate and profound impact on women in New York. Not only did she affect the professional walkers, but for the next several weeks, any empty building, any space large enough for a track in New York City would play host to a woman's walking event.

And the public couldn't get enough.

One magazine publisher said, "If I should publish in my next Sunday paper a new essay by Emerson, I should sell an extra 500 copies. A full report of the walking match will sell 25,000."

Not many were interested in the professional formalities of hiring doctors or judges; any relative, neighbor or fan would suffice. The process consisted of three steps. Find a track, draw a line, walk.

The empty three-story Brewster Building became the most famous host. The retired Bartell was quickly replaced by Millie Reynolds and Mrs. M. A. Scott. A walker named Abbott replaced Reynolds after just three days. A second track was laid in the Brewster Building, for more walkers, including Lulu Loomer. Then On February 13, just 11 days after her embarrassing failure, Annie Bartell gave it another try, this time on track two. On Monday, February 17, the same day May Marshall finished her task in Washington, a third track on the top floor was built for another hopeful. They were all shooting for Exilda LaChapelle's record.

Throughout February, all over New York and even beyond, women with little or no experience suddenly appeared with hopes of duplicating or even beating one of the champions' records. Most failed miserably and were never heard from again.

On Valentine's Day, the *New York Times* ran the headline, "Pedestrianism Gone Mad." Two days later, "Walking in Six Cities, Sawdust Rings Encircling the Earth; Pedestrian Fever in New York, Brooklyn, Jersey City, Hoboken, and Williamsburg—The Latest Returns."

In Williamsburg's Adelphi Theatre, a pedestrienne called Madame Franklin was more than one-third through a 2,800 quarter miles in 2,800 quarter hours. Jersey City teen Macie Burns hoped to complete a 24-hour walk.

Two women dressed in sealskin sacques and diamonds showed up at a walk wanting to see how many quarter miles in a similar number of quarter hours they could finish. The crowd loved the spectacle; not so the manager, who insisted they leave. When they refused, he ordered them arrested. Officers escorted them to the local police station, the manager in tow. Only then did they realize their predicament, and pleaded for release to their husbands.

They spent the night in jail.

When Bartell dropped out at Brewster the second time, officials needed a new main attraction. Madame Franklin agreed to move her

2,800/2,800 attempt at Adelphi Theatre to the Brewster Building, and extend a new record of 3,500/3,500.

However, maintaining the walk's integrity necessitated the closing of several streets between the two venues.

A surveyor rode in front of her entourage, which included police and a brass band. Madame Franklin finished her quarter mile at the Adelphi at approximately 1:05 on March 1. She got in a carriage and rode until a timer instructed her to resume. She exited the carriage and walked the just-measured quarter mile. She repeated this process until she reached Brewster.

A few new pedestriennes got good reviews, such as Fannie Edwards, May Bell Sherman, and 17-year-old Lillie Hoffman, who completed 500 quarter miles in 500 quarter hours in Providence.

But the successes were few. Most failed in spectacular fashion.

On March 11, five women started a six-day walk in Harlem's Sulzer's Park. After 21 hours, the leader had but 53 miles.

But the most shocking and highly publicized collapse was Jennie Sinclair at Mozart Garden.

At 8:00 p.m. on February 24, she neared the two-week mark of her attempt to break Madame LaChapelle's record. She completed number 1,340. But instead of heading to her tent, her coach CB Hazelton, who assisted Madame Anderson so capably, led her to the middle of the quarter stretch and sat her at a waiting table. Hazelton presented her with a watch and chain. Afterward, she thanked the citizens of Brooklyn for their support. She closed by saying, "...I hope to show the people of Brooklyn that what an Englishwoman could do a Yankee girl is sure to do."

She then returned to her tent. She answered the bell for the next two hours, clocking a slow 7:29 for number 1,359.

But she failed to answer the 11:45 signal for number 1,360. The crowd had dwindled to 300, and all eyes were transfixed on the woman's tent. Five minutes passed. Spectators stomped their feet; 10 minutes later she appeared at her door with "a face as haggard as death." She took one step, then fainted. Hazelton caught her and carried her into her room, laying her on her bed. With the crowd standing silent, Hazelton emerged and announced that Jennie Sinclair would make no more appearances that night. The disappointed crowd walked out in shock.

Her manager and a half-dozen other men were dispatched for a physician. A brief examination revealed she had suffered a cataleptic fit.

She lay unconscious on her couch for an hour. She came to but resisted medical help. She awoke about 10 the next morning and was taken home.

Less than a week later, the *Brooklyn Daily Eagle* ran the following announcement: "Pauline Von Clusberg and Katie Morris began yesterday a competition walk in Mozart Garden. It will continue until March 9, unless one or both of the contestants fail before that time."

For most however, the successes of Anderson, Marshall and LaChapelle remained fresh in everyone's mind, and the walking madness continued unabated.

But the criticisms increased. The Women's Christian Temperance Union, always opposed to the spectacles, officially protested the sport. Newspapers published more frequent and scathing editorials. On March 17, the *New York Herald* and the *Eagle* printed a sermon by the Rev. W. G. Steele of Third St. Methodist Church titled, "The Evils of Pedestrianism." In it he denounced walking matches for, among other reasons, holding contests on Sunday. He said, "It's barbarous and never ought to have a place among civilized amusements."

The same issue ran an excerpt of a sermon titled, "Lessons of the Great Walk," by the Rev. N. B. Thompson of the Second Baptist Church. "As was to be expected," he said, "this popular subject drew together an unusually large congregation." In addition to breaking the Sabbath, he denounced the gambling and drinking, all done while "applauding the walkers."

Later that week Brooklyn city officials met regarding the lawfulness of allowing professional walks on Sunday.

Citizens complained of Sunday walks and the disruptions from loud, vulgar patrons. Brooklyn Mayor James Howell said he believed that Sunday should be reserved for church, charity, medicine or farm work. While the mayor had approved a resolution for professional walking in Brooklyn, he claimed he never intended it to stretch into Sunday.

Some precincts allowed Sunday walking, but forbade the venues from charging admittance fees. On March 24, in an article titled, "Stopping Sunday Walks," the *New York Times* reported that at the Brewster Building pedestriennes Florence Levanion and Fannie Edwards were trying to equal LaChapelle's record. However, since officials denied public admittance on Sunday, no laws were broken.

*　　*　　*

As the pedestrienne novelty wore off, failures and controversies escalated.

Even the popular Madame Anderson wasn't immune from the growing criticism.

In Allegheny, Pennsylvania, her first walk after Brooklyn, Madame Anderson ran into trouble for Sunday walking during her two-week trek. While many protested, the mayor said he had no authority to close the walk, only to fine those in charge. Madame was fined, but allowed to continue. Paley and Samuells were both arrested for violating the "Sunday Law of 1794." The fines totaled $85.30.

Madame Anderson finished in front of a thrilled crowd of 2,000 and delivered harsh words for those who admonished her, saying, "I am doing nothing more than using the gifts that God gave me." Then she thanked the mayor for allowing her to finish.

Her next exhibition, in Chicago's Exposition Center, was worse.

Scheduled to walk 2,064 quarter miles in 10 minute segments meant she would get virtually no sleep for the entire two weeks. On March 4th, just one day into the walk, she showed some weariness, but denied being tired or sore. A week later she was dragging her feet constantly, drawing sympathy from the ever-growing crowd.

With just five days remaining, she fell into a deep sleep on her couch. She was awakened with great difficulty, and complained to Paley about her painful feet and "things in general."

Paley said if he had his way, his wife would leave the profession. Samuells fired back that they should all live up to their contracts, including the one they had with him. The two men almost came to blows when Madame told Samuells she'd quit if he hit her husband. Samuells backed down.

But the next day city officials tried to stop the match. For the first time, spectators in significant numbers had turned on her, shouting "barbarous" and "inhumanity" to her on the track. The perturbed pedestrienne sometimes argued with them.

But everyone noticed her slowing pace, stumbling and sleepwalking. Criticism had reached such a level that city officials had to act.

A detective arrived at the Exposition Building and took Paley, Samuells and two assistants to the chief of police to query them about the walk and suffering they were inflicting on Madame Anderson.

The law in question stated it illegal to endanger the health of any "child, apprentice or other person under his legal control, and shall be fined not exceeding $500 or imprisoned in the penitentiary not exceeding five years."

However, a doctor examined Madame and found her in 'perfect health.'

As the Madame prepared for quarter 1,462, she turned to him and said, "Doctor, I want you to walk with me."

"But my dear Madame, I really can't. I'm lame and really…"

149

"Oh, but I want to talk to you, and haven't sufficient time off the track."

The doctor agreed and the duo's appearance drew huge cheers.

The Chicago-Daily Inter Ocean suggested that the doctor might not have talked much. She led him around in 3:05.

The doctor's report said that Madame Anderson walked "voluntarily for money and fame, and so, far from being compelled to do it, walks against her husband's wishes."

The matter ended when the doctor couldn't find any reason to remove her from the track.

Then Webb dropped a bombshell.

He said that during the LaChapelle walk, he saw her fall on the track numerous times, and that scorers swore that later she slept four or five hours a night, facts that the press ignored.

He said officials responded by asking him to leave Folly Theatre, and he did so.

Webb's accusations seem unlikely. If she had failed with so many watching and reporting, someone would have said something, or at least backed up Webb's claim. Besides, professional gamblers, with so much riding on her failing, would reveal the truth immediately. And none of the papers reported any hint of cheating.

It marked the first time Webb made a public statement accusing the LaChapelle walk of being dishonest.

*　　*　　*

With three days remaining, 24,000 tickets had been sold, a decent result, but below expectations.

The next day Madame Anderson took a 40-minute break. She justified it by saying that the track was two feet too long and she'd get credited for 21 extra quarters.

On March 17, she finished in front of 2,000 fans, but overall the walk produced only lackluster enthusiasm. Afterward, she blamed the mediocre response and performance to inclement weather, her age, a cold that kept her from singing, and the controversy surrounding LaChapelle's dishonest record. (Anderson still claimed she could prove the French-woman cheated).

She walked another mile and a half, then took a carriage to her hotel.

The next afternoon 1,500, including many professional gamblers and prostitutes, watched several men participate in a 25-mile walk, then as a local flower girl won a 10-miler.

But while Madame Anderson and her entourage claimed victory, the *Inter-Ocean* disagreed. "She twisted the rules for her situation," it reported.

She then cut off relations with Samuells, and announced that when his contract expired she would also terminate her relationship with Mr. Webb.

Madame Anderson was projected to enter and be the heavy favorite in the inaugural International Six-Day Walking Championship scheduled for Gilmore's Garden beginning on March 26. For whatever reason, fatigue, injury, Paley's insistence his wife not walk, or trauma from the firings, she didn't enter.

Maybe she knew something. That race would sink the pedestriennes in New York.

CHAPTER 23

LaChapelle Unhinged

Not all the pedestriennes saw tough times in March 1879. May Marshall, fresh off her remarkable 2,796 performance in Washington accepted an invitation to the International Pedestrian Tournament at the Brooklyn Rink. The total purse was $50,000 with $5,000 available for the featured women, the biggest payday in pedestriennes' history.

According to the official program, the facility consisted of seven tracks and entertainment options that included billiards and an extensive music schedule. May Marshall and a Madame Waldron would circle track number four from March 3-April 14, covering 4,000 quarter miles in 4,000 quarter hours.

The other tracks were reserved for undercard events of either six days or 100 miles. One night on track seven, fans could see the "Petite Misses Higbee, ages five and eight, to engage in a one hour walk."

And while the top three pedestriennes inspired other competitive walkers to join the professional ranks, their achievements were overshadowed by the dozens of poorly-trained and talentless women who lined up at Brewster and other abandoned buildings hoping to achieve pedestrienne greatness.

With civic organizations, politicians, press, and now the public turning against the women walkers, the sport needed a high profile race to prove the country still supported the pedestriennes.

The onslaught of amateurs took stage at The International Six-Day Walking Championship scheduled for March 26 thru April 2 at Gilmore's Garden.

Officials charged fifty cents admission. The race would feature 18 participants representing nine countries. The top three would take home, $1,000, $500, and $250, all of which had been deposited in a bank. Additionally, the winner would receive the Tiffany's designed Walton Championship Belt. It was named after meet director F. T. Walton and valued at about $1,000. The *NY Times* described it: "Maroon velvet, backed with red kid and bears four square plates of silver, one at the front another at the back and one on either side."

The contestants who lined up looked like anything but world-class athletes. They were of varying ages, heights, weight and idiosyncrasies. The unimpressed *New York Herald* compared the field to recent lineups at the Brewster Building, with the emphasis on quantity, not quality. The unusual Wednesday start meant that the walkers would quit at 11:00 p.m. on Saturday night and take Sunday off, then start again just past midnight on Monday.

Knowledgeable patrons could separate the top walkers from the amateurs just by looking. The more experienced women employed handlers/assistants, planned thought out nutritional and sleep schedules, and better supplied their tents with all their needs. They went through warm-up routines, and some talked easily among themselves. The novice entrants seemed oblivious to their surroundings. They meandered, nervously pacing as if waiting for their husbands to return home from an evening of carousing.

The pedestriennes wore an array of colors, with seamstress Bertha Von Berg, Exilda LaChapelle, Sarah Tobias, and 16-year-old Bella Kilbury standing out in their silk dresses, which marked a stylish contrast to the peasant-style attire of their inexperienced counterparts, who resembled servants more than athletes.

With Marshall walking at the Rink, and Madame Anderson taking time off after the Chicago debacle, that made LaChapelle, just four weeks removed from her record-setting performance in Chicago, the heavy pre-race favorite. Only three or four had any chance of defeating her.

At precisely 11:00 p.m. the inaugural women's International Six-Day Championship commenced in front of 1,500 mostly male spectators.

Trouble began within an hour.

Just before midnight Marion Cameron's husband complained that judges were cheating his wife out of laps, and that they had denied her request for a privacy tent.

She told a *NY Herald* reporter,

> My only reason for withdrawing from the contest at Gilmore's Garden was on account of unfair scoring and ill treatment. I was promised the same treatment as extended to the professionals from Brewster Hall. They were given a tent by themselves while I was put into one with another person whom I had never seen before, and compelled to disrobe in the presence of strangers, two

of whom were gentlemen. When I complained I was told by Mr. Walton, in a rough manner that, 'if I did not like things I could clear out.'

Mr. Walton waived Mrs. Cameron's $200 entry fee due to her dire financial situation, telling the couple she could pay it back if she won enough to cover the debt. He said that private tents were drawn for, and he didn't know if she had been a lucky one.

"We only had 14 tents and 18 contestants," he said.

Mr. Walton also said that regardless of Mrs. Cameron's complaints and withdrawal, he objected to her husband's verbal abuse.

"For that," says Walton, "he was removed from the building and his wife, without support, followed almost immediately."

On the track, LaChapelle took the early lead, recording five miles and three laps the first hour.

As LaChapelle increased her advantage, three more marginal walkers dropped out before dawn. Attendance was solid, although not great, as about 500 were in-house for next day, and 2,000 in the evening. LaChapelle completed her 50th mile just before 9:30 a.m. Wallace, Von Berg, Kilbury, and Tobias all walked strong.

Before the next 48 hours passed, four other contestants retired. A swollen right leg was already slowing Cora Cushing, one of the few who could challenge the leaders.

The crowds were still delighted with LaChapelle and her record. She spent much of her time smiling and acknowledging patrons, and delighting them with occasional, effective bursts of speed that other walkers couldn't duplicate.

After two days, she led Von Berg by seven miles. Some thought the Frenchwoman was merely playing to the crowd, planning on big spurts and an ever-increasing pace for the race's second half. She was clearly in control. Secretly, she planned on logging 190 miles the first half, and 200 after the Sunday break. Just as she did in Chicago, when she waited until nearly the end to announce her intentions of breaking May Marshall's record, she would create drama by announcing her intentions late in the event.

As the third day progressed, the crowd grew larger and more excited. Then LaChapelle inexplicably left the track for several hours, just before their off day. At 11:00 p.m. on Saturday night, an official fired a pistol, the walkers stopped, and their positions were marked. At 12:05 Monday morning they would return to their respective spots.

LaChapelle's unexplained three-hour absence had cost her. Von Berg led with 199 miles, Wallace moved into second with 186. LaChapelle fell to third with 184.

The pedestriennes' conflict with Blue Laws proved one of the sport's most controversial characteristics. Someone suggested beating it by requiring them to wear a US Post Office logo on their dresses. That would symbolically make them federal employees, meeting exemption requirements.

The track remained mostly empty on Sunday, with the exception of Williams, Farrand, Rich, and Von Klammasch, none of whom could afford better accommodations.

The only track action Sunday was an exhibition by three men who attempted to walk 120 miles in 24 hours. They started immediately after the women left the track Saturday night. However, after covering only 17, 19 and 48 miles respectively, all three determined their time would be better spent in pursuing other endeavors.

At 12:05 Monday, 10 walkers returned, far better than the *Herald's* prediction of four or five.

But as they began the second half, attention focused not on the race, but to a mild disturbance in the crowd. An inebriated man stumbled through the stands, trying to pick up women. Once rejected, he simply moved on to another one that tickled his fancy. Insulted husbands simply brushed off the drunken offender and he moved on to his next target.

But then the finger-pointing shifted from the man in the stands to one of the pedestriennes, and the full weight of a humiliating situation. With hands covering mouths, spectators whispered, "That's her husband!" "It can't be!" "How embarrassing!" "What? He's actually married to one of the walkers?"

He made these moves in full view of his wife, who continued plodding.

The inebriated man was William DeRose, husband of Exilda LaChapelle.

At first she tried to ignore his indiscretions, hoping it would end soon. At points on the tiny track she could almost hear his come-ons. During those moments she could feel the unwanted attention.

Finally, she sucked in a stream of air and approached the judges' stand. A teary-eyed LaChapelle told officials she was withdrawing.

"This has nothing to do with any omission or commission on part of the management," she said, "it is purely personal."

For several minutes they reasoned with her, encouraging her to stay. Still crying, she stood her ground.

"I wouldn't take $1,000 if I only needed one lap to finish," she said.

Then she turned and saw her husband, still on the make. The other pedestriennes stopped as she marched across the tan-bark track and into the stands. Some stared, others looked down, a few fought back tears.

Unaware of the unfolding drama, DeRose continued chatting with a young female patron, speaking softly into her ear as she tried to look away. When he reached to turn her chin toward him, he suddenly yelled as his wife grabbed his arm, pulled him backwards, his head snapping against his back.

With a filled arena watching in silence, the beloved Exilda LaChapelle, the pre-race favorite, and best hope for a successful race, stormed out of Gilmore's Garden, her hands squeezing her husband's right arm.

Few realized that Exilda LaChapelle viewed her husband's behavior as a violent personal attack.

He hadn't just disrupted her job or invaded her space, he had violated her solace.

Unlike May Marshall and Madame Anderson, Exilda LaChapelle didn't enjoy performing. She made it clear to the public that her life's goal was raising a family. Walking offered her a way to make a good living. More than that, it provided her an escape. Pedestrianism took her mind off overwhelming personal problems that haunted her, the early death of her parents and baby, and a philandering husband. When walking she could shut off all that misery.

But now even that small sliver of her life, the one that offered her maybe the only isolation from her life's pain, had been ravaged.

*   *   *

For the seven remaining pedestriennes (two others dropped out on day four), the bizarre scene changed the whole dynamic of the International Championship. No one knew when, or if, LaChapelle would return, but for now the walkers took advantage of this time to put distance between themselves and the Frenchwoman.

They walked with one eye on the Gilmore's entrance.

For the next few hours, no one knew what had happened in Exilda LaChapelle's shattered world. She might have waited for DeRose to get sober. She might have left him and sought some solitude elsewhere. She undoubtedly cried.

Eventually she regrouped. She was a professional, and professionals don't quit. She'd let people down. Worse, she had allowed a personal issue to interfere with her profession. The very activity she chose to escape her otherwise cruel life had been stolen from her. That thought pierced her soul. She had to rectify it.

She needed to get back in the race. She gathered herself and made a long and painful return to Gilmore's.

She arrived and pleaded with the referee and other officials. With a combination of determination and desperation, she asked for re-entry into the race, credited with the 206 miles she'd already walked. Her 14-hour disappearance cost her any hope for a victory. Returning would at least restore her pride. Finishing would give her a semblance of peace. No title and no amount of money meant more than that.

Officials preferred the race's top draw to walk, even if she wouldn't win. But the other pedestriennes had the final say. Letting her return would not serve their purposes. During her absence, Von Berg increased her lead over LaChapelle from 14 miles to more than 30. Wallace and Kilbury had her by approximately 30 and 20, respectively. With only two days remaining, even taking third would have been almost impossible. Maybe the remaining pedestriennes felt her early "playing to the crowd" showed them up. Perhaps they believed her presence would garner more sympathy from a public that already adored her. Or possibly they thought her persona would detract from someone else's winning effort. It could have been any or all of those reasons, or even a host of others, such as jealously, fear or spite. Whatever the rationale, they collectively said no.

*   *   *

Of the second half returnees, Cushing seemed the most likely to withdraw, as she suffered with a limp before the break. During day four, the intriguing story of Rosa Von Klamasch began circulating. According to her, her father fought in the Austrian army. She married a Virginian and five of the couples' six children died. The husband squandered what money they had, then died, leaving her penniless in a strange country. Seeking a better life in a bigger city, she moved to New York and found employment as a seamstress. At the height of pedestrian fever, her landlady suggested she "take to the track."

Promised $100 for competing in a multi-day exhibition in Norwalk, she received only $5. She had eaten but one meal a day for the two weeks leading up to the World Championship. Like many of the inexperienced walkers, she did not have the resources to get her through the ordeal. However, her upbeat attitude had won her many friends who provided for her.

By Monday evening, 2,000 people filled the arena. The scores at 11:00 p m., March 31, after four days of walking: Von Berg led Wallace by 19, and Kilbury by 25. The others just couldn't keep up. Farrand and Rich both withdrew during the day. Farrand, a former ballet dancer and at 54 the oldest walker in the field, left with fever and chills. Her high-profile struggles created distress among the attendees. She was taken to a hospital.

Fannie Rich also told a compelling story.

The *NY Herald* reported that she'd hoped to make a name for herself in the International Championship Walk. She claimed walking experience, "…but I had no authenticated record of my account." She only had four dollars, but Mr. Walton offered to pay the $200 entry fee and she would only have to repay if she covered it with first or second place winnings. She made similar arrangements to secure walking shoes and an outfit.

Rich and tent-mate Eva St. Claire were left with a "useless" female trainer. Their quarters lacked privacy and with regards to St. Claire's condition, became "a most disagreeable refuge for a tired and suffering woman. Men came and went at their own discretion, and soiled the floor with tobacco juice. The vessels were not removed and cleaned for several hours at a time, and the atmosphere was rendered almost suffocating with the smoke from the oil stove and lamp, which were not properly dressed and cleaned."

She left complaining that referee Plummer continually ran in and out of her tent demanding either money or her outfit.

"He forced me to shake my whip at him," she said, "then he pulled out a revolver and said, 'If you dare touch me with that whip, I'll fire at you.'"

Plummer's version varied only in that he denied ever drawing a pistol.

She also told of another pedestrienne who walked 25 miles without eating. "It was only after a time that her condition became apparent and help was given to her."

Then she said that Eva St. Clair went through the most agony.

Although suffering through intense pain, backers forced her out onto the track.

"I spoke to her on the track after she had moved to another tent and asked her about her condition," said Rich.

"'Oh, Miss Rich,' she said, 'I am dying, I think.'"

A carriage came to pick up Mrs. St. Clair from the Garden. Her backers had put $50 on her and wouldn't let her leave sooner. Someone found her on the fifth floor of a house, wondering when or even if she could walk again.

The pedestriennes' negative press extended beyond the track.

On March 31, the *NY Herald* printed the story of the Fannie Edwards, Frank and Delia Leonardson love triangle.

Frank Leonardson and pedestrienne Fannie Edwards had been seen in public together frequently since January. During Edwards' successful 3,000 quarter-mile walk at the Brewster Building, Frank had served as her trainer and taken her last name. Delia Leonardson, Frank's wife of seven years, said she understood Frank had made $800, but that she and their two children had gotten no support from him since he took up company with Fannie.

Delia filed for abandonment.

The case came to trial on March 30, when Frank claimed he'd only made $21 for all his work at Brewster's, and that he and Fannie only made $13 a week training Bessie Krohn, currently walking at Gilmore's.

Fannie sat quietly in the courtroom and "looked anything but an angel when she rested her eyes upon Delia, the complaining wife."

The judge agreed to Delia's abandonment charge, and placed Frank under $200 bond and alimony of $3 a week for a year.

Upon hearing the ruling, Fannie Edwards opened her purse, pulled out the entire amount from a wad of bills and said, "That's cheap enough. I'd pay a thousand dollars to be rid of her."

The couple then walked out of the courtroom leaving Delia alone, "...crying as if her heart would break."

*　　*　　*

Surprisingly, the crowd size seemed unaffected by the loss of the French girl, or the bad press regarding Edwards and Leonardson, and the painful tales of the other pedestriennes. The numbers dwindled late in the evening, but the stands stayed comfortably filled during the day.

Cora Cushing, who had struggled even before the Sunday break, left the track for good Monday night, having recorded a mere 198 miles and seven laps. Sick and exhausted, and suffering from swollen legs, she was taken to the Putnam House and remained in bed for several hours. Her retirement left only Von Berg, Wallace, Kilbury, Von Klamasch, Tobias, and a walker known only as Williams. In the morning Williams retired for a five-hour rest, then returned, limped through one lap, then retreated to her tent. That afternoon she announced she was abandoning the race, having covered 191 miles and three laps. A doctor visited her tent and found her right leg inflamed from her ankle to the knee. She'd lost two toenails, and large blisters covered both feet. Later in the day she would get chilled and feverish. Hours passed before she showed signs of improvement. In some ways she and St. Clair became the symbols of the pedestriennes' problems.

On the track, barring a late breakdown, Von Berg would claim the title: Champion Pedestrienne of the World. With first locked up, attention turned to the suddenly interesting battle for second between Wallace and Kilbury.

Almost from the start Wallace had stayed in the top three, with the 16-year-old Kilbury never trailing by more than a few miles. Late in the race, however, Wallace shadowed her even though she led the teen by several miles. In an attempt to dissuade her pesky rival, Kilbury would occasionally make a U-turn, or throw in a short sprint, but Wallace covered every move.

The crowd turned against Wallace, hissing her at every opportunity. About 11:00 p.m., Wallace's trainer jumped on the track. In front of the scorers, he shouted at the spectators and officials, complaining of their treatment of his charge.

"Go into your tent," someone shouted. "You're a chronic squealer."

About 4:00 a.m. the next day, Kilbury's six days' shadowing of Wallace finally paid off, as she passed her limping rival. Wallace claimed that someone stepped on her foot, but no one saw it happen or owned up to it. Although Kilbury now enjoyed a slight edge, Wallace refused to go quietly. Wallace targeted Kilbury, subjecting her to verbal tirades and even threatened her life. For an hour a judge was obliged to walk with her. Kilbury's pluck won over the crowd; she received the loudest cheers and was swamped with numerous baskets of flowers. The peoples' response lifted her spirits, and she alternately walked and ran several laps. She beat a drum on mile 325, using the audience's cheers as accompaniment.

With only 15 minutes remaining, and the spots set, four of the five remaining walkers, Von Berg, Kilbury, Tobias and Wallace walked abreast around the track arm in arm. Von Klamasch, trailing by a half-lap, broke into a trot and joined them. Von Berg and Kilbury each took an arm as she ran up panting. All five walked that way for several minutes. The crowd cheered this rare display of togetherness. The band played Yankee Doodle and applause crescendoed through the building. Tobias, Von Berg, Kilbury and Wallace finished together at 11 o'clock. Von Klamasch, wanting to total 300 miles, walked 20 minutes longer.

More than 3,000 spectators watched as Colonel Frank Whittaker presented Von Berg the Championship Belt and the $1,000 cash prize. Mr. William B. Curtis of *Spirit of the Times* also paid Bella Kilbury, who had her $200 entry fee deducted from her prize of $500. Of the 18 starters, she alone paid the fee. Mrs. Wallace received $250.

Backers promised Von Klamasch $50 if she stayed until the finish, then they gave her $60. A rumor circulated that a gentleman who admired her courage presented her with another $200. One of O'Leary's backers made a $3,000 bet that Kilbury would walk 349 miles, then reportedly gave her the winnings. Madame Tobias strolled through the last few miles, knowing she had no chance of winning anything.

Final mileage totals: Von Berg (Maggie Von Gross) 372 miles, 1 lap; Bella Kilbury, 351/5; Mrs. Ada Wallace, 336/6; Mrs. Rosa Von Klamasch, 300 miles; Mrs. Sarah Tobias, 292/6.

Controversy continued after the race. Walton claimed he and Von Berg had a verbal contract that $200 of her winnings should go to him, since he sponsored her entry. She denied making such an agreement.

For an increasing number of people however, the walk's long-lasting images would be the tragic figures who didn't finish. Eva St. Claire's "I think I am dying," quote; Cora Cushing sitting in a chair not far from the winners, looking pale and sick; and an ambulance moving the infirmed 54-year-old Mrs. Farrand to Bellevue Hospital.

And the personal tragedies created headlines and headaches for Walton: Fannie Edwards and Frank leaving Delia crying alone in a courtroom; and a tearful Exilda LaChapelle, the heavy favorite, abandoning the race because of her husband's public indiscretions

More than ever newspaper editorials questioned the purpose of long-distance walking, citing the sport's brutality, and the false hope it gave poor immigrants who saw it as an escape from poverty, and it was all contributing to its demise.

The energy and euphoria Madame Anderson brought to New York just 11 weeks earlier had vanished. The pedestriennes again needed new life, a new strategy.

They were no longer welcomed in the East.

CHAPTER 24

Pedestriennes Move West

"If a prisoner were treated in this fashion, the community would demand the warden's removal. And yet, these creatures are actually dragged around in their sleep," Dr. Benjamin Lee to Philadelphia Mayor Strumberg Stokely, May 1879.

*   *   *

In March, the Philadelphia Medical Society passed a series of resolutions condemning women's endurance walking for forced lack of sleep, risking a woman's sanity, and the barbarities now being inflicted on the women under the false-assumed name of 'exemplification of physical culture and pedestrianism.'

Newspapers, while never in unanimity in their opinion of women's endurance walking, took a dramatic turn against them. Referencing the recently completed International Championships the *New York Times* ran the headline, "The Cruel Tramp Ended," and a month later printed an editorial called, "The Walking Torture."

As more unqualified women attempted longer and more stressful walks, their physical collapses were reported in more detail. Just weeks earlier people bought papers to read about pedestriennes' successes, but now they reported more on their horrific failures.

Even the off-track scandals wouldn't stop. In early April, Exilda LaChapelle filed for divorce from William DeRose. The next month Madame Anderson's new managers brought a $3,000 suit against her.

The *New York Times* said the sport had no place to go, "...the 4,000 quarter miles must be increased by successive thousands...quarters must become halves. Let there be a match to hop furthest or stand longest on one leg."

On March 30, the *NY Herald* ran an editorial titled, "Athleticism and Cruelty." The medical community, once so curious and impressed with the accomplishments of Bertha von Hillern and Madame Anderson, checked their vitals constantly and walked away in wonder before finally admitting they were in "perfect health." The doctors couldn't explain how they were doing it, and had no reason to demand they stop.

But they needed no examinations to inspect the legions of hopefuls that now stepped on a makeshift track laid on any concert hall or theatre. They could see the deterioration and collapse in so-called "athletes" who just didn't have the background, support, determination or genetics to perform such an arduous task.

On March 29, during the International Match at Gilmore's, the *New York Sportsman* ran a poem titled: The Walking Mania. It mentioned how the craze had no end, that followers couldn't get enough, and that they wanted to see them perform until they collapse. The last stanza summed up the writer's wish:

> *And so it goes! Perhaps the world will one day find relief,*
> *When pedalmaniacs, fully gorged, shall some at last to grief*
> *For whatsoe'er the signs portend—Whatever folks may say—*
> *The trouble soon must have an end; May Heaven haste the day.*

In what might be called "unintended consequences," the sport expanded again, and this time not for the better. Public sentiment opposing pedestrianism grew as preteen children were highlighted for taking long walks. One man allowed his 10-year-old son to walk 24 miles in just under five hours. Many social reformists, most significantly Henry Bergh, intervened. He once stopped a nine-year-old girl from walking 25 miles.

In May, the *New York Times* suggested that a bill introduced the previous spring "prohibiting certain gymnastic feats, knife-throwing, and the shooting of apples from a living person's head, be brought up again, and it might be well to devote a section to brutalities in walking matches."

The sport had suffered due to rapid expansion. In some ways, it had become a victim of its own success. The top pedestriennes had inspired the untrained and only moderately talented to hit the tan bark.

With the possible exception of Exilda LaChapelle, the top walkers, the pioneers, benefited from the talent and experience of outstanding coaches and mentors. Anderson had William Gale, Marshall and Von Hillern, Daniel O'Leary.

Those experts cut the learning curve; physically and mentally preparing the walkers for the grind was a part of being a professional athlete.

Without that guidance and an experienced and knowledgeable support team, the walker faced long odds for success.

The sport died in the East because too many unprepared hopefuls entered the profession with little understanding of their tasks. The big eastern cities were home to too many unscrupulous venue managers who saw the women as a way to make significant dollars in a short time. Had someone controlled the competitions and monitored entrants, it might have survived; instead, it became unmanageable.

As 1878 ended, the women walkers floundered with no major draws outside of May Marshall. By late January, Madame Anderson brought it to new heights. Now, less than three months after her Mozart Garden triumph, the sport found itself in trouble again. Only this time, instead of lethargy, they were battling an increasingly critical and hostile public. The tide had turned against the athletes, and they knew it. This time a new personality couldn't pull them out of it. They needed an organizer, one to manage the walks, control the venues, and determine the viability of contestants. Such control was almost impossible in the big eastern cities.

By April, even the successes of Mme. Andrews 3,000 quarter miles in Boston, Marie Rockwell's 4,047 quarter miles at Mozart Garden, and May Marshall's new record of 4,125, earning her $5,000, were hardly noticed.

For it to continue, the professionals would have to radically change their strategy. Start by moving. They needed a smaller home with limited facilities so a small group of professionals could maintain some semblance of control over the events. Limit their numbers and monitor the venues, and the spectacular failures that created so many negative headlines in Philadelphia, New York, Chicago and other big cities would give the sport a more professional environment in which to work.

If the small group of pedestriennes wanted to continue walking, they needed more control over the sport.

And they would need a manager to keep the competitions lined up properly and make sure the women didn't compete for the same followers.

But who could they get? And where could they move?

*　*　*

Almost nothing was known about Edward G. Cotton. The 31-year-old was married and worked as a theatrical manager in New York.

For unknown reason or reasons, he agreed to manage the pedestriennes. Maybe he had tired of show business or, like Mike Henry, he saw sports as the next wave of entertainment in America.

He apparently had a business relationship with fellow theatrical manager, C. E. Locke. Locke lived in San Francisco, and the two worked out an agreement.

Cotton would move the pedestrienne hub to San Francisco.

Thanks to the gold rush, San Francisco's population grew from 1,000 in 1848 to 25,000 in 1849. Companies such as Levi Strauss and Co. and Wells Fargo and Co. opened in the early 1850s. The railroad's arrival in 1869 helped propel San Francisco to become the 10th largest city in the United States. And while the city enjoyed a thriving arts community, it offered little in the way of organized sports. They held some endurance walking matches, but they didn't attract big crowds or have the star power of the top East Coast Pedestriennes.

Out west the pedestrienne mystique lived, and San Francisco residents wanted the pedestriennes to compete in their city.

The prime choices to move west had the greatest accomplishments and largest followings: Madame Anderson, May Marshall and Exilda LaChapelle, and thanks to her recent victory at Gilmore's Garden, Bertha von Berg.

Others were likely considered: Lulu Loomer, Cora Cushing, Marie Rockwell, and Fannie Edwards. All had completed at least 3,000 quarter miles in 3,000 quarter hours, the standard of excellence in the pedestrienne world, although Edwards, after breaking up Frank and Delia Leonardson's marriage, carried personal baggage that detracted from her appeal. However, she would probably bring Frank, who had proven himself a top performer.

Madame Anderson might have deserved the most consideration. On top of great athletic performances, she could entertain. But she carried lots of downsides; she had already filled her spring walking schedule and she'd had several run-ins with managers. And at 36, her age presented a problem for Cotton, who wanted a long-range commitment.

May Marshall, the most prolific walker, had earned $30,000 from pedestrianism, and was fresh off her remarkable walk of 4,125 quarters in the same number of quarter hours. But in addition to a young son, she had two years on Anderson.

The appealing and youthful LaChapelle had already earned national headlines with her Chicago victory.

Not all would make the trip.

When the steamer left New York for San Francisco in the spring of 1879, the passenger list included: Mr. and Mrs. Edward G. Cotton, Bertha von Berg, her husband Joe Russ, Fannie and Frank Edwards, and Exilda LaChapelle, who also brought her husband, William DeRose.

DeRose might have used Cotton's West Coast offer to convince his wife for a reconciliation. No one in San Francisco knew of their marital problems. They could move west and renew their commitment to each other.

Whatever his strategy, she bought it.

Frank and Fannie Edwards would also start over. Out west, they would bill themselves as a great brother-sister walking team. Not only could they dominate the newspaper headlines and potentially earn a substantial income, they could conduct clinics and endurance walking training sessions. By training the athletes for competition, Cotton's group could avoid, or at least limit, the spectacular failures that doomed them in the East.

San Francisco only had two or three arenas capable of holding major walking events. Thanks to Locke, Cotton already had an "in" with management. As long as the managers/owners stuck with him and his troupe, the pedestriennes would fill their houses. After all, who didn't want to come see three of the most famous and accomplished endurance walkers?

On paper, it looked like a strong plan.

CHAPTER 25

Destructive Coalitions

S hortly after their steamer arrived in California, a perturbed EG Cotton told the *San Francisco Chronicle*, "I've had to contemporaneously manage star actresses and rival premier danseuses, but from opposition female pedestriennes, preserve me."

*   *   *

Cotton had secured Platt's Hall for three months.

The first contest would commence on May 25.

Days before the first event, hundreds of visitors filled the venue and watched as workers constructed a track, elevated approximately six inches above the floor and measuring 20 laps to the mile. The women's privacy tents stood on either side of the main entrance. A piano and band instruments sat on stage, along with the judges' tally board.

People watched the hammering and sawing, marveled, ask questions, and filled Platt's with excitement. On the streets, in the papers, it seemed all of San Francisco couldn't wait to see the star pedestriennes.

Cotton should have been thrilled. He wasn't.

Before their ship docked, the women were already fueding. Fannie Edwards and Bertha von Berg did not like Exilda LaChapelle, and she returned the sentiments.

Cotton's biggest challenge might be keeping the athletes' inner conflicts out of the public eye.

It would prove too much for one manager.

The first race featured Edwards vs. LaChapelle in a walk of 1,000 quarter miles in 1,000 quarter hours. But the advertisement didn't tell the whole story. In reality, he had scheduled a test of survival with no official finish time or distance. It was a pedestrienne version of a boxing match in which the winner stood and the loser collapsed. And since both had covered 3,000 quarter miles in 3,000 quarter hours, the event could last for weeks.

Patrons who entered Platt's on opening night came not just for the walk, but to see a new invention, a light bulb that illuminated "with the power of 6,000 candles." Visitors paid twenty-five cents for children, fifty cents for adults, and a $5 "commutation ticket," good for 25 admissions that included under card performer and local pedestrian John Armstrong, who would walk a half-mile every quarter hour for 20 hours a day. If successful, he would earn $250.

For their part, the women were walking for $2,000 plus a percentage of the gate money.

On the evening of May 25, EG Cotton, in front of a packed house, marched across the Platt's Hall stage. He waited a few moments, and looked at his pocket watch. At 7:57, he rang a bell. As the piano player pounded out an upbeat tune, applause slowly built as Fannie Edwards emerged from her tent. She wore a dark colored, form fitting basque, and a short skirt trimmed in blue. Flowers adorned her long black hair, which she covered with a jaunty black cap. She also carried a riding crop. With an easy and natural gait, she finished her first quarter-mile in three minutes, fifteen seconds.

Edwards returned to her room.

A few moments later, Exilda LaChapelle emerged. Her appearance drew thunderous applause. She wore a scarlet dress with white lace with her dark hair cut short. She completed her first quarter in 2:30, then returned to her tent.

The first quarters set the tone. For the race's duration, the athletes' goal was to avoid seeing each other. Additionally, they would often walk in opposite directions.

Just hours into the race, LaChapelle and Armstrong passed Edwards' tent when the curtains parted revealing the face of Bertha von Berg, who said to the Frenchwoman, "You are putting on lots of style, aren't you?"

Then she disappeared behind the tent flaps.

LaChapelle stopped for about 10 seconds with rigid body and clenched jaw. She finished her quarter and entered her tent. Seconds later she dashed out with fire in her eyes, a riding whip "twirling in her hand."

She sprinted into her rival's tent, but before she could complete her task, Edwards' attendants grabbed and held her. She fought their grasp for a few seconds before she collected her wits and relaxed. They "escorted" the subdued pedestrienne back to the track, putting an end to the scene. The audience sat in stunned silence. It happened so fast, few realized what they had seen. Shortly thereafter, a distressed-looking Cotton again rang the bell, and Edwards began her quarter-mile as if nothing had happened.

The episode set the tone for the walk, and the *Chronicle* quickly picked up on it, saying the two, "love each other with the passionate love of two rival prima donnas."

The competition had already turned personal. Patrons wagered on any element of the walk. Predicting a quarter-mile time, who would walk faster? Even the color of the next outfit.

In spite of Edwards' attempts to win people over, LaChapelle, with her dark complexion and her pixie-like features that included size 2 shoes, and her faster walking made her the crowd favorite. Her demeanor contrasted sharply to Edwards. She often did a little clog dance as she entered her tent, where she lay down, her feet elevated on a stack of towels, and chatted and joked in both English and French.

Edwards' projected a more sedate and business-like demeanor. She suffered from blisters. Her "brother" Frank often joined her. Just days into the race, Edwards struggled during the late-night treks. At times her assistants almost carried her around the track. Cotton warned of a possible disqualification, but that was unlikely so early in the race in front of potential days, or even weeks, of an ever-growing, enthusiastic, paying crowd.

As they neared 1,000 quarter miles, both walkers looked strong and were presented with innumerable numbers of vases of flowers, and other substantial gifts. LaChapelle received an engraved, gold-mounted cane. Later, an admirer gave Edwards an engraved, ivory riding crop and a diamond ring, and 100 shares in the Etna Mining Company.

As in other cities, local celebrities often joined the walkers, giving the audience additional reason to cheer. As a demonstration and promotion Von Berg walked for several hours a day, attracting even more attention, and likely LaChapelle's ire, especially when she wore her championship belt.

But the controversies and conflicts kept the writers busy and the stands filled.

A janitor found some chipped glass on the track. Edwards told the *Chronicle* someone planted the obstruction to cripple her since she wore such thin-soled shoes. Then she added, "But I am not saying LaChapelle did it."

For her part, LaChapelle said she felt sorry for Edwards, since she didn't really walk 3,000 quarter miles in the Brewster Building, claiming her friends carried her for many laps. She said Edwards' accusation that people taunted her and threw broken glass and nails on the track was nonsense.

Calling her rival 'poor thing' on several occasions, she claimed no personal animosity toward Edwards, but added, "Her legs are awfully swelled and she is paralyzed on one side, and it's very cruel to make a woman try and do something she can't do."

LaChapelle then slammed Edwards, claiming she had no record at all, and that well-meaning friends had fabricated her 3,000 quarter mile record at the Brewster Building. She concluded her comments with, "Now I have a printed record."

The reporter then changed topics and said, "Miss Von Berg is a powerful walker."

To which LaChapelle replied, "Yes, she is very big and fat."

After nearly three weeks, the women had extended their battle zones to include PR supremacy. Each one had received a generous number of flowers. Fannie Edwards' table had 107 bouquets, all in Fredericksburg beer glasses; and LaChapelle, 106 in solid, cut-glass Budweiser schooners. The score stayed that way for about 15 minutes when one of the Frenchwoman's florist friends brought to her a dollar's worth of posies split into two vases.

As she finished 1,999, Edwards, tiring of a male spectator who frequently hurled insults at her, stopped in front of him, waved her whip above her head and "poured forth a volley of vituperation that proved she was remarkably swift of speech, and a facile command of a variety of unwritten brief and angular Saxon thought to be usually confined to the sterner sex..." It would not be her only confrontation with a fan. She was also battling a publicity nightmare when the media reported of her true relationship and identity of "her brother," Frank.

They reached 2,000 with neither athlete giving in. Each walker looked strong, but LaChapelle was by far more dazzling and faster. All that and her attractiveness made her the crowd favorite. She said a foot shampoo left her feeling "Exilda-rated." Edwards' persona had taken a hit. Although she was less elegant and lost popularity, she continued, and that alone had won her admiration of some fans.

However, as June drew to an end, race officials grew nervous. A men's six-day race was scheduled to begin July 10, another women's race for July 17, with all three East Coast pedestriennes entered. If the women were still walking for another 1,000 quarters, they would call the race a draw. For the first time, the women had a deadline. The announcement virtually guarantees the outcome.

As the days wound down, all three the walkers showed signs of wear. Armstrong had lost 17 pounds and his leggings now hung loose. Delirious, he knocked over an equally exhausted LaChapelle, spraining her ankle. She finished her quarter mile. Attendants treated her and recommend that she quit. The *Chronicle* speculated she might retire by days' end. The next day she ran a quarter mile in under two minutes and said, "Maybe I should sprain both ankles and run it in one minute."

Four weeks into the event, and Platt's was almost always filled. Local dignitaries frequently visited. Armstrong enjoyed a short private meeting with Imperial Majesty Emperor Norton. Armstrong walked away smiling and shaking his head, making a *San Francisco Examiner* writer speculate that maybe the Emperor had offered the pedestrian part of his "empire."

Joshua Abraham Norton arrived in San Francisco from South Africa in 1849 and in 10 years, made and lost a fortune when he failed to corner the rice market. In 1859, he declared himself "Emperor of these United States and protector of Mexico." His decrees included abolishing both republican and democrat parties, and charging a high misdemeanor for uttering, "the abominable word, 'Frisco.'" He even printed his own money, which many local merchants honored. He died on January 8, 1880. His funeral procession stretched for two miles.

Women now made up more than half of the attendees, and they cheered when a pedestrienne walked with a patron, child or even when one emerged from her tent.

The relentless schedule had also taken a toll on the entertainment. One piano player who had been working fifteen to sixteen hours a day almost since the beginning had his fingers lanced of corns. He still played, but he left the keys dotted with blood. Doctors had forbidden him to play upbeat tunes such as "Father Jack Walsh," and "The Wind that Shakes the Barley O." He sometimes kept his legs propped on the keyboard to keep his feet from swelling.

Even the pianos suffered from the exhaustive schedule of the women's long journey.

The *Chronicle* said, "Six pianos have already been carried away, utter wrecks."

According to the paper, the song "Mockingbird" had played so often that the "hammers had hammered their way through the wires and through the bottom of the piano, leaving an accurately perforated copy of the rests and breves and quarters and flats and sharps of that sweet Southern aria."

As the walkers passed four weeks and 3,000 quarters, excitement built as the forced end finally neared. The hall stayed packed at all hours and the floral gifts, just days before a point of consternation over who had more, now overflowed Platt's. The *Chronicle* described the scene as, "the perfume of a thousand times 10,000 different kinds of flowers the three females now meander all day like the Sultan of old through a garden of spice."

Even toward the end, Exilda LaChapelle claimed she would have already won if Edwards' friends hadn't been assisting her. Then she challenged Edwards to continue without help. She also said Edwards and Von Berg were trying to keep her out of the upcoming six-day contest. Unlike similar accusations she'd made in regarding previous walks, these had some merit. Von Berg, who had been walking about two hours most days, said LaChapelle would have nothing left (for the upcoming six day race) "once Edwards was finished with her."

An estimated 3,500 people packed Platt's for the 24 hours leading up to the expected completion of both races.

As 1:45 a.m. on June 25, in front of a standing room house, the meet referee announced the final two quarter miles would complete the more than month-long contest. At 1:48, Edwards and Mr. Leslie Blackburn, a Von Berg cohort, emerged from her tent for quarter 3,000. Platt's Hall shook with applause as she walked her last quarter mile wearing red, white and blue, and carrying an American flag. She finished in 3:08, and with the noise almost deafening, she was presented with a gold medal. Within seconds, Platt's went silent, all eyes shifting their focus and waiting for Exilda LaChapelle.

Outside her tent stood Armstrong's trainer holding a handkerchief in a hand extended above his head. He looked at the timer on stage. With a "whoosh," he swiped his arm toward the ground. With that, LaChapelle sprang from her tent wearing a pink and white suit and medals on her breast. She sprinted around the track, the crowd never letting up. With each completed lap, the cheering intensified. She dashed across the line for the last time, prompting Armstrong's trainer to again signal the timer, this time to stop. With LaChapelle bent over gasping for air, medals dangling, beads of sweat falling onto the tan bark track, the timer and other officials studied the watch in disbelief. After a few moments more, the pedestrienne stood upright and paced in front of the stage still breathing heavily. The official time read one minute, fifty-four seconds, the fastest time of any of the 6,000 completed in Platt's, the fastest ever by a pedestrienne, even faster than any professional pedestrian had ever done.

Both walkers returned to their tents, apparently resigned to accept the uncomfortable situation that a winner could not be declared after more than 30 days of walking.

But while both pedestriennes agreed verbally to tie, neither one moved toward concession. Representatives from both sides tried to work out an agreement, but neither budged.

Minutes later, Fannie Edwards began number 3,001.

Frustrated and exhausted officials, friends of the pedestriennes and spectators watched in amazement.

172

How long would this continue?

At 7:00 p.m. the next night, Armstrong completed the last of 1,200 half-miles, following LaChapelle most of the way. Women waved handkerchiefs, men clapped their hands, stomped their feet and whirled their hats. During the entire last half-mile, the cheers drowned out the band. So many floral offerings showered on him, he finished with, "his path strewn with flowers."

Stopping short of his room, his friends carried him for two victory laps.

Meanwhile, the pedestriennes continued.

For two days officials and friends tried to convince the walkers that everyone had had enough. They would have to stop. Just before midnight on June 26, Edwards entered LaChapelle's tent and the two shook hands in front of a handful of friends. They walked another four hours to bring the total to 3,199. In an unprecedented display of unity, they locked arms and carried American flags as they completed number 3,200. For five laps the crowd, although a bit smaller than in previous days, cheered and showered flowers on the pedestriennes.

Publicly, the athletes blamed their differences on "meddlesome friends."

The pedestriennes approached the stage. LaChapelle was presented with an elegant gold ring mounted with diamonds and amethysts. Edwards received a gold medal.

In spite of lacking a definitive winner, the women won over San Francisco. All the local papers exalted the accomplishment and said that both deserved the title, "Champion Pedestrienne of the World."

So after the first women's walk in San Francisco, pedestrienne superiority remained in question. Exilda LaChapelle obviously walked faster and became the crowd favorite. But Edwards hung in even though she likely received some physical assistance and probably chemical help as well, something LaChapelle denied ever doing.

In some ways, the outcome couldn't have worked out better. The West Coast saw some impressive walking. LaChapelle and Edwards exceeded expectations. The people of San Francisco embraced the pedestriennes. Cotton had to be pleased. The women's performances had, for the most part, overshadowed personal attacks. Edwards had overcome her temper and scandal revelation regarding Frank. In the end, both received high marks from the press and achieved public adoration.

Contradicting Cotton's statement regarding pay, the NY Clipper later reported that the women did not receive $2,000, but a weekly salary that increased the longer they walked.

Platt's would be busy in the next few weeks. The women's six-day race would start July 17. But before that the men, including Frank Edwards, would compete in a six-day walk. Before that a contest would start in Platt's on June 28, just one day after completion of the LaChapelle-Edwards marathon match.

The next women's six-day match would be a championship for $1,000 and the Diamond Belt, valued at $1,500. Cotton expected a small but strong field that would include all three of his East Coast stars. Such an event would attract huge numbers of spectators, especially now that the first event had provided San Francisco with such excitement.

The pedestriennes were revitalized. So far the gamble to move west looked like a good one. Cotton saw the first race as a warm-up to a series of walks that would prove, if managed correctly, the pedestriennes could become a productive and vital part of America's burgeoning sports world.

At least that's what he had planned.

CHAPTER 26

Von Berg Extortion

F rank Edwards won the men's six-day race. He took home $1,000 and the diamond belt. His friends also gave him a hunting case, a barrel of whiskey, and a gold watch.

Cotton designed an impressive belt. It contained 12 ounces of gold and 24 ounces of silver. The belt was composed of four large bands of solid silver about three inches in width, and connected by large gold rings, adjustable to fit the walker. Two bands were blank for name inscription. On the belt's front was an 18-carat gold medallion with a shield in the center, surrounded by a semi-circle of diamonds. The shield contained a laurel wreath of tinted gold with laurel berries. In the shield's center was an image of a man walker and above it an engraving, "Palmam qui meruit ferat" (Let him who has won bear the pain). A gold eagle with extended wings supported the shield and beneath the medallion was inscribed, "California Belt, donated by EG Cotton." The women's belt was similar except for a slight difference in the Latin phrase, and it had a female figure.

It was valued at $1,500.

Cotton scheduled the next women's six-day race for July 17-22. In addition to the three East Coast pedestriennes, three locals would fill out the field: actress Carrie Maynard (aka Carrie Woods), 16-year-old Sadie Donley, who'd recently completed 700 quarter miles at Platt's, and May Belle Walton. Several other entries were denied due to weak walking histories.

Heavy bets were placed on both Edwards and LaChapelle, one man wagering $1,000 against another's $500 that the latter would outdo Frank's winning total from the men's race that had just ended a few hours before.

But only five lined up as the race start neared at 1:00 a.m. on July 17. Bertha von Berg was absent.

Von Berg refused to walk over a money dispute.

She, LaChapelle and Edwards signed a contract for $500 appearance fees. They also agreed to receive a weekly salary of $150 for eight weeks of walking. Von Berg claimed to have, but never produced, a contract stating that she got paid whether she walked or not.

While the other two met their contractual obligations Von Berg fell in with some blackmailers who insisted, as International Champion, she deserved a $2,000 appearance fee. Von Berg demanded more money..

For days an increasingly frustrated Cotton sent liaisons to her managers, who included Leslie Blackburn, Edwards' trainer, during her match against LaChapelle. Neither side moved.

As the field lined up, the crowd chanted, "Von Berg, Von Berg, Von Berg."

The starter raised his hand for silence, and asked for quiet several times, but the mantra continued. Finally, he announced the international champion would not compete, and an atmosphere of disappointment filled Platt's.

At 1:00 a.m. on July 17, the starter shouted, "Go!" and the five women took off.

Edwards strode to the early lead. Few noticed she was dressed in a short, black and white checkered dress, silk brown hat, white and brown stockings, and low shoes. The attention-getter was wrapped around her waist. She was wearing Frank's Championship Diamond Belt. But LaChapelle would have none of it. After 22 hours Edwards, who claimed to have a cold or bronchitis, trailed LaChapelle by 11 miles. The on-site doctor said the affliction shouldn't affect her walking.

But another scandal would soon rock the pedestriennes.

*　　*　　*

The Von Berg story wouldn't go away.

On July 17, just hours after the race started, blackmailer Leslie Blackburn approached one of the race managers and demanded money. His request was denied. Blackburn left and said, "I will go for you every chance I get. I will make it cost you more than the amount I ask you for."

It was later revealed that part of Blackburn's motivation to destroy Cotton stemmed from him not getting a contract to serve liquor at the women's race after he did so for the men's six-day walk.

Two days later a letter from Cotton's business partner, Charles Locke, appeared in the *Chronicle*, proclaiming that their races were honest. Locke admonished the paper for giving credence to their accusers, who claimed Locke and Cotton had shorted Frank Edwards' pay and were lying about the existence of a women's diamond belt. Locke closed the letter by advising, "Let me express a hope that when you desire information regarding my business that you will get it from myself or reliable outside parties, and not from men recognized as blackmailers or as being from disreputable antecedents."

But between Locke writing the letter and its publication, a more dramatic event occurred, one that would damage the sport and drive a bigger wedge between the pedestriennes.

According to a *SF Examiner* reporter, four men entered the office of Locke and Cotton about 11:00 p. m. on July 18. Inside were Cotton, two other men and Mrs. Cotton.

A few moments later the reporter heard a crash, turned and saw Cotton, supine on the floor, and a man named Con Mooney on top of him clutching his throat. The reporter jumped in to help, but another man pointed a gun at him and ordered him not to move. At that moment an alarm sounded and a special officer arrived. The officer blew his whistle for help, but none came for more than a minute. The pavilion track watchman entered the room and tried to pull Blackburn out, but other gang members overpowered him and hurled him over Cotton's body. Mrs. Cotton also tried to intervene, but someone threw her to the floor.

A handful more men entered, surrounded the two men and some began kicking Cotton. Included were Mooney's brother-in-law James Nolan, and Leslie Blackburn, the latter presumably the man who pulled the pistol on the reporter.

They finally stopped when a doctor came and evaluated the bleeding Cotton. He said he found no potentially fatal wounds, but discovered his head and face were "shockingly bruised." A carriage took Cotton and the doctor to the Palace Hotel.

About 10 minutes after the assault, a police captain arrived and immediately ordered the assailants arrested. Blackburn and Nolan were arrested on the charge of assault with a deadly weapon. Warrants were also issued on Con Mooney and others.

Papers slammed the police inaction, calling it "cowardly" and "irresponsible." Later, one policeman on the scene claimed he couldn't do anything without a warrant. Those reports horrified the public.

At the Palace Hotel two hours later, Cotton lay in a semi-conscious state, face almost unrecognizable, and eyes bruised and swollen shut. He also suffered from a damaged back. The medical team feared he faced permanent paralysis.

Later, Cotton said Mooney entered his office and queried him about allegations Cotton had made about Mooney being involved in a blackmailing scheme. Cotton answered, "Yes," and he would "publish their names throughout the state." At that point Mooney grabbed his throat

177

and pushed him against some glass globes, breaking them. Someone slammed him to the floor and Mooney jumped him. He could recall nothing else. He wouldn't recover for weeks, and his wife would take over many of his tasks.

Rumors circulated that the police did nothing because Cotton had lodged a complaint against one of them for an unknown offense. Police had already fallen under scrutiny when an officer, while attempting to remove a drunk from the men's race, randomly shouted, "Look out, he's drawing a pistol," putting the large crowd in a panic.

* * *

Throughout the ordeal, the women continued walking.

Edwards and LaChapelle engaged in what the *Chronicle* called "A wordless war." At one point Edwards, walking slightly ahead of her rival, stopped. LaChapelle ran into her and fell.

It was another public cheap shot by Edwards. With LaChapelle again trouncing the field, most turned their attention to the battle for second between Edwards and Donley.

Edwards still complained of a cold, and admitted she had been crying on the track. The tears might have resulted from Cotton's beating and Blackburn's role in it. She might have feared her own implication, since she had publicly aligned herself with both Blackburn and Von Berg.

Edwards took some stimulants. She picked up the pace, and made up some ground.

The Frenchwoman remained unconcerned.

She took a break.

Her tent stood out from the others. A gift from an admirer, it was striped and decorated with carpeting and a California light wood bedroom suite. She also enjoyed the assistance of a French maid and her husband. Like virtually all pedestrienne tents, the scents of liniments and ointments permeated its interior.

With another victory seemingly within easy reach, LaChapelle changed her tone with the press.

While interviewing in her tent, DeRose popped his head in and said, "She [Edwards] is flying around the track because she knows you are off. She thinks she'll make two or three miles on you now."

"Let her," said LaChapelle smiling and eating some beefsteak. "I will take my time eating and resting, and make myself comfortable and then, just as she is tired out, I will start out and make up that time, e-a-s-y."

She took issue with a mention that she drank sherry to help her get through the night.

"I never take stimulants," she said.

"Do you expect to walk against Von Berg here?"

"When this match is over the management intend backing me for $2,000 to walk against Von Berg. I shall not challenge, you understand, but they challenge."

"Will she accept?"

With a shrug she said, "Oh, no! I don't think so. She doesn't want to walk against me. She is afraid to."

LaChapelle again revealed her desire to leave the walking profession, that she did it just for the money. She said her true aspiration was to save her money, retire at age 24 or 25, and live her days out as a mother.

Two nights later, with 3,000 jammed into Platt's, LaChapelle again sprinted to victory with 307 miles, easily defeating Edwards' 262. Donley's sprained ankle limited her to 248 miles. Maynard finished with 228. Walton, who early on blamed a stomach disorder on eating some bad plums, recorded only 134.

LaChapelle took home $1,000 and the California Championship Belt (the one the blackmailers denied existed). Edwards won $750, Donley $500, and Maynard $250. In addition the walkers made peace with the scorers, who some accused of cheating them out of laps. They apologized and gave them pictures of themselves. The five finishers took a victory lap together, LaChapelle holding the belt high for everyone to see.

Donley returned home, but battled delirium and a lack of sleep. She made numerous efforts to continue walking. Miss Walton said she had lost money, including $200 on costumes, and vowed to never do another six-day walk. Harry Maynard claimed Donley deliberately kicked dust in his wife's shoes, and that he spent hours cleaning them.

Edwards suffered a bitter loss. Likely out of frustration, she challenged LaChapelle to a quarter-mile series walk. LaChapelle couldn't help but take a shot at Von Berg. "If she had been in the race, I would have gone 400 miles," she said. "Edwards could beat Von Berg. I don't think she could have even taken second or third place."

About a week after that LaChapelle victory, Blackburn and Von Berg traveled to Virginia City, Nevada for a six-day walk. There Von Berg defeated Madame Tourtilotte 308-276. The victors were quick to point out that Von Berg had beaten LaChapelle's total by one mile, and Tourtelotte also beat Edwards' runner-up total.

Legitimate questions arose about the track's accuracy, since Von Berg's husband managed the event and she reportedly covered 16 miles in one hour. Regardless, the contest enjoyed a good turnout and Von Berg returned with a silver brick and $1,000.

While Von Berg had, for the most part, avoided implication in Cotton's beating, she still employed Blackburn, one of the instigators in the vicious crime. Von Berg's reputation already took a hit at Gilmore's when she failed to follow through on a promise (which she denied had been made) to pay her $200 entry fee for the International Championship.

While Fannie's affair with Frank created a scandal, and sullied the pedestriennes' reputation, she tried to keep her professional and personal lives separate. Her friends even suggested Von Berg's likely involvement in Cotton's beating now not only caused her great personal embarrassment and pain, but drove a wedge between herself and her former friend.

The three pedestriannes owed their livelihoods to Cotton's vision, daring and belief in them. He gave them all a second, and probably last chance at careers as professional athletes.

But now, thanks to some conspirators who tried to extort money from the man who had given them so much, they faced an even more uncertain future.

In September, with little fanfare, Fannie and Frank Edwards left California and returned to New York. Fannie Edwards wouldn't walk in San Francisco again.

That left LaChapelle and Von Berg, who despised each other, and a badly beaten Cotton, who had to question his plan and his faith in the pedestriennes.

LaChapelle had made many unfounded accusations against her remaining rival, but soon none of that would matter. Von Berg couldn't keep dodging her. LaChapelle knew, if not for her husband's overt flirting, she would likely own the International Championship Belt, and Von Berg would be back in Rochester, not as Bertha von Berg, but seamstress Maggie von Gross.

LaChapelle would get another shot, and she would repay Von Berg for what happened on the track in New York and off the track in San Francisco. Winning wasn't enough; she wanted to humiliate her.

Beginning September 11, Exilda LaChapelle would get revenge on her rival.

CHAPTER 27

Cotton Ousted

A *Chronicle* interview revealed the depths of contempt between Exilda LaChapelle and Bertha von Berg. The Frenchwoman again admonished Von Berg's record for taking seven days for a six-day walking total of 372 miles. She stuck to her unfounded claim that officials gave her laps.

When told that Von Berg sprained her ankle when getting out of a carriage just before their upcoming match, LaChapelle replied, "Anything for an excuse, you know."

The paper speculated that the two hadn't competed yet because each looked to conquer other worlds. After the International Championship, Von Berg waited six months before defeating Tourtilotte in Nevada. LaChapelle had beaten all other challengers on the West Coast, including Edwards.

That left only each other.

In a pre-race interview, LaChapelle said she felt better than when she'd started at the pavilion.

"What do you think of Von Berg's chances?"

With eyes 'flashing lightning,' she said, "Well, I don't know, of course, how it will come out. Von Berg says she'll walk the shoes off me, but I— I say if she walks the shoes off from me, I'll walk the blood out of her."

She added that she could do as much on the track as anyone in the world.

Von Berg sounded equally confident, pointing to her undefeated record in 26 races and that her upcoming opponent lacked toughness in New York, saying, "She gave up because I was beating her. I am 35 miles more on my (six-day) record than she is."

However, she stopped short of predicting a victory.

"It is never possible to tell sometimes. They may chloroform me. They put chloroform on bouquets; but I always hold them off, and still the chloroform may

181

make me sleepy. Sometimes they lean over the rail and drop poison on the track. Oh, I tell you, it is worse than horse races."

The atmosphere inside LaChapelle's tent was more business-like than in her previous race. Her support team quietly made last-minute preparations, ensuring her numerous outfits lined up, and that she had all the liniments, wrappings and medical supplies on hand and in place. But the Frenchwoman never missed an opportunity to run down her competition. LaChapelle planned a quick pace knowing Von Berg couldn't match it.

"She's too big to run," she said.

That would neutralize Von Berg's strategy of dogging her opponent, which worked for her at Gilmore's. "I ran her off the track there," said Von Berg.

Rumors swirled that if Von Berg tried it this time, LaChapelle would slap her.

A nearly full house greeted the two as they lined up just before 1:00 a.m. on Thursday morning, September 11. Von Berg appeared first, then LaChapelle emerged from her tent wearing a headdress. As men lay wagers on the race, the starter explained the rules to the competitors. In the silence, the two barely acknowledged each other, although LaChapelle glanced at her opponent and noticed drops of sweat forming on her bare forehead.

The rules were finished, and the starter stepped off the track and shouted, "Go!"

They took off. The crowd cheered, the band played a lively march. Both kept to their plans. LaChapelle, who lined up on the inside, allowed Von Berg to lead, but she accelerated and overtook her. Running much of the way, LaChapelle covered the first 24 laps in eight minutes, but led by only a step. While the Frenchwoman strode the first mile, Von Berg strained, eyes focused on the back of LaChapelle's bobbing headdress, sweat already pouring off her face.

After one day LaChapelle had built a 69-55 mile lead. Von Berg's handlers claimed she had a "secret weapon." She never blistered and she would make up the difference in the second half. The two hadn't spoken and didn't intend to. Professional and amateur gamblers laid bets as to how long they would maintain their silence.

By day two LaChapelle lapped her plodding rival again and again. Perhaps already sensing her strength and Von Berg's weakness, she periodically slowed and dogged her, thus employing Von Berg's announced strategy.

The heavier Von Berg struggled in the warm air, and LaChapelle, already showing confidence of winning, ran much of a 7:52 mile, giving her a lead of 150-118 miles after three days.

In spite of the near certain outcome in the featured contest, people still came, in part to see the shorter race featuring Steve Brodie, "The New York Newsboy," who walked 222 miles and 19 laps in 75 hours, missing his goal of 260 miles. His performance had pumped additional life into this affair. He proved a favorite with the ladies, many of whom presented him with financial gifts.

At 11:00 p.m. on September 17, LaChapelle finished her last mile in 8:52, the full house cheering the entire way. She completed the event alone, as Von Berg retired one hour earlier, blaming her poor performance on cramps, which she claimed had bothered her since the first day.

In five months since coming to San Francisco, Cotton's dream had not transpired. Cotton was still recovering from his beating. Fannie Edwards fled San Francisco for New York. Von Berg failed miserably after her one California race. However, LaChapelle, with two victories and one tie, had become the darling of the city, extracted revenge on her number one rival, and won $6,000. In less than one year, she had gone from an obscure walker earning a few dollars in poorly lit halls in Wisconsin to making headlines on both coasts and Chicago.

By all accounts, she was enjoying a successful career.

Unfortunately, she still sought that elusive satisfying personal life.

*   *   *

The presence of the East Coast pedestriennes in San Francisco sent walking's popularity skyrocketing. In one neighborhood, 40 boys disappeared. They were found in an abandoned building two days later conducting an endurance walking contest, and charging the public ten cents to watch.

The women's popularity, and especially LaChapelle's, had necessitated a refurbishing of Platt's. According to the *Chronicle*, "Seating accommodations for several thousand more spectators have been added."

But LaChapelle's success came at a price. From late May to mid-September, she had logged more than 1,300 racing miles, all adding to her severe sleep deprivation. Rumors spread that she had contracted malaria as the group crossed Panama on their trip from New York. Regardless of the reason, she needed a lengthy respite from the track. She went to Chicago for recuperation, refusing all offers to walk.

With Edwards also gone, that left only Bertha Von Berg to carry the East Coast mantle, and she had little time to put on a credible performance.

Her next and likely last chance at redemption would come in early October, at a six-day walk at Platt's.

Von Berg, the overwhelming pre-race favorite, would join a huge field of 16 amateur and professional competitors, including Sadie Donley, her 19-year-old sister Alice, Carrie Maynard, and Madame Tourtilotte, Von Berg's foil in Nevada. Perhaps sensing her tenuous position as a top walker, she'd lost 19 pounds since her pathetic performance against LaChapelle. One of her trainers, probably her husband Russ, predicted she would break her six-day record of 372 miles.

On October 9, people began arriving at Platt's around 7:00 p.m. Shorter competitions were scheduled before the main event, including a race between 20 telegraph operators for $20 followed by members of the Yuma tribe, billed as the "Fiery, untamed Indians."

Just before 11:00 p.m., the women jammed the start line. They all wore stylish outfits, many of which would become the rage in San Francisco in subsequent days. The Donley sisters dressed like twins in matching pinafore suits. Von Berg's mauve dress and white sash drew attention, but most focused on the championship belt that adorned her waist.

Some contestants rocked, marched in place, and others looked down. Few talked. They already faced at least two problems. One, the track couldn't hold the field. It measured 24 laps to the mile, approximately 73 yards per lap and two yards wide. Worse, many of the women simply weren't athletes. San Francisco just didn't have the talent to justify so many calling themselves pedestriennes. Organizers now potentially faced the spectacular failures that turned the public against them so strongly in New York.

Predictably, they got off to a rough start. Within hours, two women left the track. One was banished for hitting officials with flowers. Another, claiming the turns irritated her feet, left in tears when judges rejected her request to straighten the track.

The remaining 14 walkers continued. Alice Donley led her sister Sadie by just under a mile, with May Bell Sherman another mile behind, and Von Berg five back.

The *Chronicle* commented on the preferred atmosphere to the recently completed men's race, "They compete better, complain less, they keep neater tents, receive more flowers and wash their kitchen utensils."

Crowds grew the second night, with heavy betting on Von Berg, even though the Donley sisters and May Bell Sherman all battled for the lead. After three days only two miles separated leader Sherman and Sadie Donley, with Carrie Maynard, Von Berg and Alice Donley still in the hunt.

Two more dropped out, one saying she had a dream that she couldn't make any money. However, 12 were still in, with most projected to finish.

Sherman had been labeled a "dark horse," and hadn't said much. She claimed her hometown as Bodie, a California gold-mining town near the Nevada border, and she hid her successful endurance walks while living in Boston, where she once walked 50 miles inside of 11 hours. That encouraged her friends to bet on her. As they began the second half, she pulled away from the Donleys and Maynard. As predicted by her support team, Von Berg had made a move, passing all three with her eyes on first. Alice Donley claimed she was suffering from "sawdust colic" in her hip, a condition many said didn't exist.

At 5:00 p.m. on October 12, shortly after moving into second, a struggling Von Berg fell back again, leaving the track with 231 miles.

Doctors said she was suffering from pneumonia.

She wouldn't return.

Until now, San Francisco had mostly supported her. Somehow, she had escaped public condemnation in Cotton's beating. But on the track she claimed but one victory, in Nevada. In San Francisco her name was more closely associated with quitting races. When she retired she trailed Sadie Donley and Sherman, both amateurs.

In the stands her backers cursed and yelled at feeling duped. The *Chronicle* noted she needed help to her carriage, but later someone later reported seeing her skipping up stairs.

Those without a stake in Von Berg stayed focused on the track, where an exciting finish was unfolding.

While Sherman had built a lead, she could never comfortably pull away from Sadie Donley or Maynard. With just under 24 hours remaining, only 11 miles separated the top three walkers.

The close race packed Platt's for the last three days. Abandoned privacy tents were pulled down and spaces were replaced with chairs to accommodate the growing crowd. A full house cheered Sherman to victory with 337 miles, beating LaChapelle's total by 30 miles. All eight finishers were presented with bouquets. Sadie Donley covered her last mile in 9:09. Sherman asked the band to stop playing, "The Girl I Left Behind Me," since Von Berg had left the building.

Sherman earned a diamond belt. Sadie Donley received a "Medal of the Championship of the West Coast." The top four finishers earned a percentage of gate receipts. Sherman collected $1,234, Sadie Donley $780, Maynard, $358, and Alice Donley, $234. All other finishers received $50.

In spite of the absence of big-name walkers, the performances were credible, the newspaper coverage mostly positive, and no spectacular failures so common in large fields back East. The biggest negative: Von Berg's credibility took a big and permanent hit.

But again, the pedestriennes' faced growing internal struggles. A recovering Cotton used what he learned in San Francisco to try another international pedestrienne six-day championship in New York. Maybe he could convince Gilmore's, now called Madison Square Garden, that New York should give the pedestriennes another shot. Only this time he would set the field and make sure all contestants were established walkers with resumes worthy of a major walking event. Unlike the match in March, which set the sport back when only five of 18 starters finished, he would land a mix of national stars and top locals.

On September 29, 1879, he left for New York to organize another East Coast women's championship race.

Exactly how and why he lost control of that race and his interests in San Francisco remains a mystery.

With Edwards and Von Berg out of the spotlight, Cotton's attentions focused in New York, and LaChapelle recuperating in Chicago, no one stayed in San Francisco to oversee the operation.

That left the door open for DE Rose.

Little is known about Rose, but he organized large men's international events. He had a reputation for taking care of the athletes, which might have been why the men got more positive press and heftier paydays than did the women. Somehow, Rose got control of the international race. He renamed the Diamond Belt, dubbing it the Rose Belt.

He would manage the International Six-Day Championship, then with LaChapelle's blessing, take control over all the West Coast events.

The January 24, 1880 issue of the *New York Clipper* reported that LaChapelle, who hadn't raced or probably even been in San Francisco more than six months, would return west and walk again, but only if "Cotton relinquishes all claim to management which rules governing the trophy give him." She said that Cotton wouldn't pay a challenger enough when she would probably lose to LaChapelle. Cotton generally paid walkers a salary. The walkers preferred a percentage of gate-money. The rules stated the holder of the belt in this case LaChapelle, had to win three consecutive races within a stated timeframe in order to keep it. However, LaChapelle feared she would lose the belt only because no one would take her on.

In some ways, LaChapelle's logic made sense. Increased payouts would make challenging the Frenchwoman more attractive. But maybe she just needed to look harder. Although Madame Anderson preferred solo efforts, she might have accepted a lucrative offer to walk against

LaChapelle. Marshall, who never backed down from a challenge, still walked well, and likely would have relished the opportunity to knock the Frenchwoman down a notch or two. And Sherman had made public her desire to take on LaChapelle.

On the other hand, they might have actually feared losing to her. If such was the case, LaChapelle needed to make a dramatic move, if only to advance her own career. Ousting Cotton must have been a difficult decision. He had brought the women west, had taken all the risks, and afforded them another chance to become successful pedestriennes. He'd even taken a beating because he wouldn't give in to Von Berg's ridiculous demands.

But maybe he had taken them as far as he could.

The betrayal and failures devastated him.

Throughout the latter part of 1879, Cotton had hoped to capitalize on women's athletic events that expanded from walking to the new and exciting sport of bicycle racing. When those didn't work out, he returned to theatre management, specifically working with a local troupe planning a trip east.

On March 3, 1880, he met with the group and a dispute broke about whether or not he had the financial resources to meet his promised obligations. The next afternoon he took his wife to a San Francisco hotel and bid her good-bye, telling her he had to raise some money. That evening he met with the troupe again, and they reached a resolution. After the meeting he did not meet his wife at the hotel, and she went home alone. When he hadn't returned the next morning, she grew concerned.

About five o'clock on March 5, Mr. Locke received a telegram from Oakland:

"Cotton shot himself. Please come over immediately. Mrs. Cotton."

A gardener in the employ of A. A. Cohen at Alameda discovered the body of a man lying on his back under a tree on the vacant lot nearby. The coroner determined he had shot himself in the back of the right ear. Near the body lay a small, six-chamber revolver about nine inches from the right side of his head, two chambers of which were empty. His pockets contained fifteen cents, along with a letter to his wife. The note said he couldn't collect any money owed him, and without it he would default on his loans.

"My pride will not allow me to be a defaulter," he wrote.

Mr. Cotton's plan included taking his wife to stay with some friends at the hotel. Upon leaving the hotel, he took the ferry to either Oakland or Alameda, where he wrote the letter. Despite his assurances to the theatrical company, he had nothing with which to pay expenses.

187

He said that Locke would send Mrs. Cotton back east, and the local Elks Lodge (of which Cotton was a member) would bury him and pay her his insurance policy.

He closed with, "God bless and protect the best wife in the world is the heartfelt wish of your unfortunate husband." Someone reported hearing a pistol shot between 4:40 and 5:00 p.m. on March 4. There were no signs of a struggle.

Edward Cotton was 33 years old.

CHAPTER 28

Queen Amy

hether assembled by DeRose, Cotton or both, a stellar field took to the track just after midnight on Monday, December 15, 1879, for the International Championship Six-Day Tournament.

The fiasco at the March event seemed all but forgotten as the 1,200 who sat in Madison Square Garden looked at the impressive list of competitors. In addition to stars Madame Anderson, Fannie Edwards, and Exilda LaChapelle, the field included two other finishers from the March International Championship: runner-up Bela Kilbury and Baltimore PE teacher Sarah Tobias. In June, a vastly improved Tobias earned $1,000 when she defeated May Marshall in a six-day contest in Feltman's Pavilion. Other accomplished pedestriennes filled out the field, including Amy Howard, a newcomer, but already considered a potential star. That group headlined the 25 who would start.

Cash awards of $1,000, $750, $500 and $250 would go to first through fourth place, with the winner claiming the Rose Belt valued at $500. Rose also promised an additional $100 if any walker completed 100 miles in the first 24 hours.

The Garden roof under construction meant a constant stream of cold air would dampen the spirit of the crowd and the walkers. Several stoves were placed throughout the venue, but they would offer little comfort if a strong front blew through. Daniel O'Leary, in his first association with any pedestrienne event since the Von Hillern-Marshall match almost four years earlier, oversaw the race. The track measured one-eighth of a mile. The scorers' stand sat on the track's north end, the clock and scoreboards hung on the opposite wall.

Beneath the north side seats sat 17 apartments. Under the gallery nine additional smaller structures had been erected.

In a move likely required by O'Leary, the pedestriennes agreed to abide with "rules of conduct" to avoid, or at least minimize, the negative

189

headlines of controversy that frequently superseded pedestrienne races. They promised not to argue, talk loud or use profane language, either on the track or in tents. They were to hold no conversations with spectators, and to keep themselves neat and clean and their hair combed. While on the track, dresses must cover tights. Each walker must hire at least one female or nurse, and each was limited to one male attendant. A top finisher forfeited her position if she left before the race closed at 10:00 p.m. Saturday night.

At 12:01 a.m. the starter shouted, "Go!" Simultaneously, the band played, the crowd cheered and the women took off.

However, down the street the race's first distraction was already taking shape.

Since that afternoon, John Dermody, a 45-year-old unemployed lemon peddler, sat in a bar and bragged to nearly equally inebriated cohorts about his remarkable pedestrian skills. "If I had a backer," he boasted, "I would be a champion."

His friends vowed to back him and to enter him in the six-day walk going on right then at Madison Square Garden, apparently neglecting to mention all the other contestants were women.

Dermody's "backers" got a barber to shave his red beard. They outfitted him in a dress, sash and wig. They adorned him with white walking leggings and slipped his feet into a non-matching pair of balmoral shoes. They pinned a handmade number 32 to his dress and topping off the ensemble, they covered his face with a veil. They hid the costume under a coat and the group then staggered to Madison Square Garden where they paid the admission fee.

Strategically hiding under the stands, they waited for the right moment. When the police were distracted, they removed Dermody's coat and slipped him under the railing and onto the track. He sped away, "arms going like windmills and his raiment flying out behind him like a comet." A roar greeted his bizarre appearance and the laughter continued as he made several zigzagging efforts to catch some of his "rivals." Then he passed near a sergeant who, ran down and grabbed Dermody and led him through another lap before taking him into custody. Dermody spent the night in jail, was arraigned the next morning, sentenced to time served, "still wearing the habiliments of the night before."

Back on the track, the race claimed its first casualty. From the start May Marshall looked worn and haggard, and walked with a shawl pulled over her shoulders.

"She was surly all day," said one official. "She repeatedly interfered with all the other walkers. She had a way of sticking out her elbows spread-eagle fashion whenever anybody tried to pass her." She refused numerous attempts at removal, and only left the track when scorers quit counting her laps.

She claimed that officials gave Mme. Anderson credit for extra laps, but like so many similar charges, it couldn't be verified.

For three days, Howard, Tobias and May Massicot maintained a torrid, record-setting pace, with only a handful of miles separating them.

Crowds were decent in size, but lacked enthusiasm. Mostly they sat trying to stay warm. On top of the cold, the walkers fought cigarette smoke and pollutants from the inefficient stoves.

The pedestriennes left that behind them; they put all their skills on display. New York was witnessing exactly what O'Leary and DeRose had hoped. The pedestriennes apparently understood the results of this race would help determine their athletic futures and that of the sport.

At 10:45 p.m. on December 20, Amy Howard finished in front of 5,000 patrons, but the enthusiasm failed to match the walkers' efforts. The record-braking performances couldn't overcome six days of what the papers described as "torture," and "a joyless walk."

However, the incredible performances couldn't be ignored, and gave racers and organizers hope. The top three walkers beat Von Berg's record of 372, and they didn't get an off day. Howard's 393 miles just topped Tobias' 387. Still, the Baltimore native logged almost 100 more miles than in March. May Massicot took third with 384, Maggie Rowell, 368.

A total of eight walkers completed 300 miles, and six recorded 350. Like Tobias, Kilbury with 354 beat her mark at the first International Championship. The pre-race favorites fared poorly. Madame Anderson left nearly six hours early, turning in a disappointing but respectable 351. Few noticed or cared that Edwards beat LaChapelle. They only placed 10th and 11th out of 18 official finishers.

At 10:45, the referee declared the race closed. He called the top finishers to the awards stand and gave Miss Howard $1,000 and the Rose Belt. Madame Tobias earned $750, Miss Massicot $500, Miss Rowell $250. Fannie Edwards received a gold medal for neatest appearance.

After the awards presentation, the band played, as the prize winners, along with some other finishers, smiled and waved at patrons as they marched a lap around the track, Howard wearing the belt. The women showed great unity and it left the contest on a high note. The event should have proven a great moment for the competitors and the sport. However, O'Leary's name, a top field with strong performances, no public infighting and positive PR did little to connect with the public.

In spite of everyone's best efforts, the International Championship Race flopped.

It marked the death of big-time women's walking on the East Coast.

However, West Coast walking still had life, and still had Exilda LaChapelle. And now the performances of Amy Howard and Sarah Tobias couldn't be ignored.

To continue as pedestriennes now meant moving to San Francisco. But doing so relegated it to a regional sport. While walks would still be conducted in the East for several years, they would garner less attention, dwindling crowds, and smaller purses.

The pedestrienne stars would call the West Coast home.

* * *

Since the pedestriennes appeared on the scene in January 1876, the sport experienced several ups and downs. Popularity dropped after Von Hillern's retirement in June 1878, then skyrocketed when Madame Anderson debuted six months later, followed closely by Exilda LaChapelle. After the March 1879 fiasco, Cotton relocated the pedestrienne hub to San Francisco in April 1879, but that December the sport took another disappointment on the East Coast.

Now solidly based on the West Coast, the pedestriennes needed a new hero to keep the sport alive.

They found one in Amy Howard.

Like many pedestriennes, she had a performing background and she turned to pedestrianism, apparently caught up in the Mme. Anderson madness in March, 1879.

She enjoyed immediate success.

According to Ed Sears, author of *Running Through the Ages*, she defeated Peter van Ness, the speed walker who lost to May Marshall and another man in a quarter-mile race.

Like Fannie Edwards, Cora Cushing and so many others, she walked in the Brewster Building, completing 1,300 quarter miles in a similar number of quarter hours. She went on a tear the next few months. She won a match by walking 50 miles in 10 hours for five consecutive days; she completed a contest of walking 12 hours a day for 14 days. She finished with 588 miles, won by 30 miles, and didn't even walk the last two days. She defeated Ohio pedestrian Champion William Murray three times in 25 and 50 mile matches.

All that and she had not yet turned 18.

Amy Howard had clearly positioned herself as the new pedestrienne star. And she might be the best anyone had ever seen.

CHAPTER 29

Record Setting Pedestriennes

San Francisco's new pedestriennes debuted on May 5, 1880, with Rose as manager, and in a different venue, Mechanics' Pavilion.

Again Rose had assembled a strong field. In spite of reportedly suffering from what was called "Panama Fever" or malaria, LaChapelle, along with Tobias, Alice Donley and even Bertha von Berg, would battle to wrestle the belt from Howard who, if she won that race, got to keep it. The only notable absent walkers were Madame Anderson, who scheduled it but then backed out when she and Rose couldn't reach an agreement, and May Bell Sherman, who was holding out for a race with a purse of $2,000 or more against LaChapelle, Howard and Tobias.

The day before the race commenced about 10 walkers came to Platts' and walked and jogged on the seven laps to the mile track and meet the curious. Exilda LaChapelle told a reporter, "I never felt better in my life. I think it is between Amy Howard and myself."

Platts' doors opened at 8:00 p m., three hours before the women's race started.

Hundreds of excited spectators filled the arena. It was the first women's race in San Francisco since Sherman's October victory, and pedestrienne-mad San Franciscans were ready to see both the new and established walkers.

Rose got out lots of publicity and decorated Platts' with Chinese paper lanterns and red, white and blue bunting hanging under the gallery and on the redwood pillars that surrounded the structure. Multi-colored flags hung from the rafters. Maybe the most attractive additions were the white, cloth-covered bouquet stands which already displayed the symbol of love and admiration toward the pedestriennes. A seemingly endless variety of floral gifts ranging from the ten-cent "bonbonnieres" to the "four-bit combination of roses and gilly-flowers, awaited the complimentary and florally-inclined visitor."

The pedestriennes' privacy tents were arranged along the west and north walls; the scorer's table sat in the center of the west side.

In the billiards area, the sound of cue sticks cracking against balls could be heard throughout the venue, and the pop, pop, pop of the shooting gallery at five shots for a quarter created an excitement that brought long-time followers of the sport back to the hey-day of pedestrianism. Adding to the festive atmosphere, a band played a stream of upbeat tunes.

Other attractions designed to "interest their minds and deplete their purses" included a gambling wheel of race horses; on the east side above the apothecary's shop attracted two-bit gamblers and a new game called "the Babies on Our Block." In one corner, people stood in line to see a minstrel show. From a booth in the opposite corner, patrons could purchase snacks, including a rare treat of ice cream. Candy, fruit and peanut stands dotted the interior.

In and near the privacy tents, men and women walkers and their attendants made last-minute preparations. They double-checked everyone's roles, took inventory of their numerous outfit changes, and checked off their supply of supplements.

At 8:30 a field of nine men led by Frank Edwards began a 10-mile contest for a $100 purse. The pedestrians were instructed to follow heel-and-toe rules, which forbade running and skipping .

Edwards ignored three official warnings about him running, the referee disqualified him in the first mile. The winner came home in one-hour, thirty four minutes.

As the women's start neared, the walkers settled down and prepared mentally and physically for the arduous task ahead. Madame LaChapelle, at least a co-favorite, silently sat on her cot waiting for the call. In her tent the confident looking Amy Howard, "in a suit of blue, reposed at length in her canvas boudoir, her muscular limbs encased in blazing flannel, and covered with leggings of a milder hue...." Her trainer massaged and treated her feet before covering them with a pair of oversized kid shoes. A red, white and blue cap covered her dark hair. A silk handkerchief was tied around her neck.

They seemed oblivious to the noise throughout the arena.

After the men's race the crowd of 1,200 left for the target galleries, snack stands and floral tables. By 10:30, many congregated outside the women's tents. The chattering quieted to polite talking, and then to almost stage whispers. A few minutes before 11:00, eyes turned to the athletes' apartments.

At 10:55, a bell signaled the women to approach the start. As the walkers appeared, patrons cheered. The noise grew deafening when the two favorites, Amy Howard and Exilda LaChapelle, emerged. Respective attendants led and pushed the crush of fans to clear a path across the tanbark track to the start in front of the judges' stand.

The 20 starters packed four across, five rows deep.

As usual, the outfits garnered a large share of women's attention. Alice Donley wore an outfit of black cashmere and light blue satin; Kitty Mason, a black and rose colored satin, and Belle Walton, crème colored brocade and white leggings. For their first race, sisters May and Lodie Grafton, age 16 and 19 respectively, each wore pink and blue cashmere.

The referee called for quiet, then explained the rules, which included that the athletes' official race numbers were visible at all times. Most women stood still as though they were digesting every word. A few first-timers, such as the teenage Grafton sisters, looked everywhere but in the packed stands.

When the referee finished, he turned to the timers, who held up their stopwatches and sent an approving nod. Then he glanced at the lap counters, who gave a like sign of readiness.

This competition with such a strong field came with high expectations, and maybe carried more importance than the International Championship. A failed race here would kill the sport on both coasts. The pedestriennes would no longer have a home.

And just like in New York, they were ready.

The pack took off, some running-they followed a different set of rules than the men's race. A surprisingly strong Millie Young led, but Howard and Tobias soon moved ahead. Alice Donley and Young struggled to keep up. An ill Exilda LaChapelle looked sluggish, but her backers remained hopeful she could cover 65 miles in a day.

The lead walkers maintained their torrid pace. After 26 hours of racing, the *San Francisco Chronicle* gave the scores: Howard, 98; Tobias, 93. Just three hours later, Tobias built a two-mile cushion, but by the following afternoon Howard reclaimed the lead. While early in the contest, the pedestriennes were putting on a marvelous show, maybe even better than New York, when both Howard and Tobias shattered Von Berg's record.

Could they possibly do it again?

With Howard appearing "absolutely fresher than when she started," many speculated that just two days into the race she walked with such ease and strength that picking someone else to win seemed pointless. But she only had a seven-mile lead on Tobias. And while the former PE teacher appeared the weaker of the two, she continued shadowing her rival.

Publicly at least, Howard's husband expressed concern with regards to his wife's lead, saying, "Oh, she is ahead, but not as much as she ought to be, and the only reason I can account for her not having more of a lead is that yesterday she was taken very ill and was obliged to retire for more than four hours." But later he predicted her lead would grow to 10 miles the next night, and when asked if she would win he replied, "Oh, by all means, and not half try."

But she couldn't drop the relentless Tobias.

After three full days, Howard's lead over Tobias shrank to four miles. Both were well ahead of Howard's record in New York, as were two others, including Alice Donley. Crowds grew large and boisterous with everyone cheering for a favorite. The *California Alta* reported, "It's a toss of a penny who wins."

Each day the *Chronicle* published results on the front page directly under its mast head, along with the sub-head, "The Most Exciting Contest Ever Witnessed! See the Struggle Tonight!"

The women's newspaper quotes reflected a competitive edge, but didn't fall into the personal attacks of the three East Coast walkers. Tobias said she would beat Howard if she had to walk 450 miles. Howard said she would keep the championship belt if she had to "run her feet off."

Day three and four saw the departure of six walkers, including both Grafton sisters and Bertha von Berg, whose miserable failure likely ended her career as a pedestrienne. She quit after three days with only 151 miles. Another poor performance made everyone wonder how she ever won the International Championship, and beat Tobias in the process. The *Chronicle* quoted a reporter who said of the fallen athlete, "She had a sad and careworn look that there was no mistaking. Her heart evidently was not in her occupation."

After four days Rose was already confident of a Howard victory. He announced he would put Howard on a San Francisco track against any pedestrienne in the country for between $2,000 and $10,000 a side.

As the second half progressed, the remaining pedestriennes paid for an early blistering pace. In 12 hours the leaders put 14 miles on a spent LaChapelle. She became the latest to drop out. Howard and Tobias continued to press.

Their heightened conflict sometimes overshadowed their dominance. The two leaders each spent 20 of the previous 24 hours on the track. After four days Howard led Tobias by six miles with Donley doing well, but far off the pace in third.

Throughout day five, they battled for the lead with Howard not only winning the race, but the psychological games as well. When Howard dogged her rival, Tobias who must have felt victory slipping from her, turned and raised a hand to strike Howard. The former actress ran crying to an official, who quickly stopped the tensions from breaking into a fight.

Later, Howard entered her tent for a planned long rest. Shortly after, Tobias broke for some treatment. At that point Howard bolted back on the track, increasing her precarious lead by four or five laps. Later, when Tobias tried that tactic, Howard immediately sprang from her tent and walked three feet behind her.

Barring a complete breakdown, both would crush the old record. But with only eight miles separating them, Tobias still had a slim chance on day six.

As the last day progressed, Platts' filled with spectators who cheered almost all day. By the early evening, 4,000 jammed the seats, aisles, promenades, and some even found small open spaces in the gallery. No one could move.

The *Chronicle* wrote, "Along the great circle and a thick fringe of humanity bent over the railing and stared unwearied at the slow movements of the throng below, through which, on their narrow path, the bright dresses of the pedestriennes slowly made their way."

To keep the festive atmosphere throughout the night, Rose hired a second band. When one finished, the other commenced.

With the finish just minutes away, the cheering continued. At 10:10, with 50 minutes remaining, Amy Howard retired to her privacy room with 409 miles. Flowers rained down on her tent.

With the winner decided, the throngs still had reason to watch. Tobias had 398 miles, beating her personal record and even Howard's old mark. Until she finished, the jammed arena of frenzied fans cheered her, pushing her to the end. She stopped immediately after crossing the finish line at the 400 mile mark. Soon, her feet almost disappeared in colorful flower petals. She stood and turned, waving to the adoring fans as they continued shouting and showering her with flowers. Then she entered her tent. With only 15 minutes remaining and the top two positions settled and new records secure, the masses turned their attention to Donley, who would win a hard-fought battle against Young for third.

At 10:50, Howard emerged from her tent. Tobias joined her and in what had become a pedestrienne tradition, all the walkers gathered in front of the scorer's stand. Rose wrapped the belt around Howard's waist. The pedestriennes had put on another remarkable show. The referee made a brief speech then on behalf of the scorers, presented a basket of flowers to the first five finishers. The band struck up a tune and a little girl led Howard and the other walkers around the track to the endless cheers of thousands of patrons who had witnessed the greatest pedestrienne performance ever.

The group walked a lap together, then returned to the scorer's stand when the bell that warned them at 10:55 p.m. six days earlier sounded again, this time officially ending the six-day walk.

Then the award ceremony began. In addition to the belt, Howard collected a small bag of coins totaling $1,000. Tobias picked up $750, Alice Donley $500, and Millie Young, who finished just 10 miles out of third, earned $350.

Howard's record topped her previous best by 16 miles, and Tobias' 400 had beaten the old record by nearly seven miles. Teen Alice Donley's totaled 360 miles, one of the best-ever. She beat her October mark by 74 miles, and even topped Sherman's record of 337. For Sarah Tobias, the only walker to finish both international contests and this one, the race marked another disappointment. In March, 1879, she finished last of five finishers with 292 miles. She had the second and fourth best-ever marks in six-day contests, but could claim no victory. Her only consolation: she'd pushed Howard to two records.

Incredibly, the San Francisco race bested the New York race in virtually every way. Rose recruited a stellar field that included the top two from the earlier race, and 13 of the 20 starters finished. The crowds were large and enthusiastic, and the festive atmosphere, so critical to successful walking events, kept entertainment options high and helped greatly by keeping music going the last 24 hours.

But Rose had more to do. The next night he scheduled the "Grand Carnival Masked Ball," which had been announced on the front page of the May 12 issue of the *Chronicle*. The party would begin at 10:00, with Howard leading a procession an hour earlier.

Rose wasted no time in preparing for the gala.

He decorated the ceiling with bunting, streamers and flags. Assistants wrapped red, white and blue garland around the track railing. Partiers arrived early, but management kept the track and main floor clear until after the Grand March. At 9:00 Amy Howard, with escort Frank Edwards, entered the arena wearing a short sky-blue walking suit, the championship belt around her waist. Sarah Tobias, in a dark silk suit with red trim, followed the couple. Then the other two prize winners, each wearing brightly colored walking costumes, made their entrance. Then in marched approximately a dozen "best costume" prize winners who won a variety of gifts, including a gold watch, a golden cake basket, opera glasses and a box of silk handkerchiefs.

Not since Madame Anderson's triumph in Brooklyn more than a year earlier had the pedestriennes generated such excitement. As a manager, Rose had proven a stunning upgrade from the capable but inexperienced Cotton. Outside of the minor flare-ups between Howard and Tobias, no controversies took place. The dropouts drew little unwanted attention. Crowds and enthusiasm exceeded expectations. This race proved that some life still existed for the professional walkers. And maybe, with Amy Howard's ability to draw big crowds and Rose's marketing and promotional skills, the women could continue walking professionally.

When the pedestriennes took their victory walk around the small track, ears ringing from the endless cheering, the failures seemed far away.

But one had to wonder about the next step. Each time the sport faded, a new star appeared that reignited enthusaism. They now had someone who looked almost unbeatable. She beat Tobias twice, but far from dominating fashion. Could the Howard-Tobias rivalry sustain the sport? Alice Donley and May Bell Sherman had also earned consideration as a top professional. Could one or both become a major force? What about Exilda LaChapelle's recovery? Could she respond?

For now, the pedestriennes enjoyed the adulation. But its brief history showed the sport's fragile foundation could degenerate into a quick fall.

Right now, they had momentum. But could they keep it?

CHAPTER 30

Rapid Decline

The next race represented a departure from previous contests. In an attempt to diffuse some criticism at the sport's brutality and also encourage more walkers to participate, Rose set up a six-day race with a different format, one that had been tried in other markets.

Seheduled for Mechanics', he advertised it as a 100-hour, six-day race.

The women would walk twelve and a half hours a day, with the starting time at 12:30 p.m. on July 11, and stop at 1:30 a.m. on July 18. The walkers would rest the remaining next eleven and a half hours. The reduced total purse of $1,200 included other official prizes, such as a casket containing a diamond ring, pin earrings and a bracelet.

The star-studded field would include Howard, Tobias, the Donley sisters, and Millie Young. Exilda LaChapelle's name appeared in published ads, but she failed to start, still suffering from "Panama Fever."

In front of a surprisingly large crowd more used to an after-midnight start, the athletes approached the judge's stand in even more colorful outfits than usual. Howard donned a blue and red outfit with a matching hat that had "Amy" embroidered on it, and red and white striped stockings. Tobias wore blue and pink cashmere; Alice Donley pink and black.

Early on, Howard again asserted her dominance early, leading after day one. However, Alice Donley dropped out after but 37 miles. She, like many, complained of the sawdust residue.

Although the women quit at 1:00 a.m., Rose scheduled several other activities to encourage late-night festivities. Shorter races of man vs. man and even man vs. horse would help fill the long void. Also, the first night featured a family-friendly carnival with prizes going to the best-costumed child.

After two days Amy Howard led Millie Young by two miles. Alice Donley had dropped out, and a struggling Sadie continued but couldn't maintain top pace. With the Donley sisters out of contention, no one else could challenge, so the top three spots were virtually assured. No one could make up ground on Tobias in third behind Young.

The front page of the July 17, 1880 issue of the *San Francisco Chronicle* stated that with one day remaining, the three leaders were only six miles apart, and the race's conclusion would coincide with the close of a 24-hour walk that included seven mostly known San Francisco area men walkers plus one surprise late addition, Exilda LaChapelle.

But the finale of both races proved a disappointment, both on and off the track. As the 24-hour race started, officials held another late-night children's carnival. They promised each attendee a prize, but they brought only 50 for a group that swelled to 100. The empty-handed kids all cried and rushed referee Aulbach, hoping for some new gift they could take home.

The next night only four of the original nine starters completed the 24-hour event, and two almost came to blows, over one using "annoying language" against the other. LaChapelle experienced another discouraging outing, dropping out five hours early with only 50 miles to her credit.

By then, however, almost everyone recognized what had happened in the women's race. The familiar "go as you please" turned into, "go as I please, won't hurry up and don't care a cent." Places settled, the women strolled until the end. Complaints flew at officials, especially Aulbach. Betting on the women's race declined, the gamblers preferring to take their chances on the more exciting men's races.

Post-race, a furious referee, Aulbach, called the pedestriennes to the judges' stand and admonished them, saying,

> You have made this an exhibition walk, having a tacit understanding among yourselves as the positions to be held at the close. You perhaps are not so much to blame as your trainers, particularly (Frank) Edwards, Young's trainer, who held her back and compelled her to keep behind Howard. There undoubtedly was a conspiracy, although I do not know for mercenary motives or not. It was my intention yesterday afternoon to declare the race off and divide the prize money equally, but considering all circumstances, I have changed my mind and will award you your prizes.

He then gave Howard $500, Young $300, and Tobias, $200. Sadie Donley took fifth and collected $60.

The pedestriennes now faced another threat: their livelihood. Until now their more serious conflicts had been off-track. The ousting of Cotton and his suicide had shocked and angered many, but Rose's masterful managing and promotional skills, and the remarkable performances at Mechanics' in May, had made everyone forgive the popular LaChapelle for replacing him.

Now the public and even officials challenged the women's athletic integrity, a first on such a large scale. Race-fixing and cries of short loops had always threatened to undermine pedestrianism, but to everyone's knowledge, the big-time races always featured accurately measured tracks and impartial judges. Some accusations of fraud were made in the previous walk, the *Examiner* saying Howard's victory had been "arranged," however seemed unlikely in a record-setting performance. Occasionally, a suspicious walker would hire her own assistant to count an opponents' laps for accuracy sake, and few official problems arose.

But Aulbach's official admonishment of the pedestriennes had the potential to subvert the sport. And the timing couldn't have been worse. Just eight weeks earlier the women had shown the nation that they could compete at a high level. They had infused life into the sport and the personalities, especially of Howard and LaChapelle, and was requiting popularity.

But now suspicions grew. If they had "bagged" this race, and few denied they had, then maybe conspiracies surrounded the other competitions.

They had other problems. Even before Aulbach's rebuke, newspaper coverage had decreased and editorials grown more critical. Reporters' curiosity about the athletes had declined. They no longer filled their pages with athletes' quotes and inspirational stories. The writers limited content to race results, injuries and their outfits.

After a brief surge in popularity, the pedestriennes found themselves involved in another scandal, this one self-inflicted and potentially devastating.

But the pedestriennes still had stars who could fill seats and excite a crowd.

The next race would be a bold attempt to capitalize on that.

*   *   *

In early 1881, the pedestriennes stood at another crossroad.

Battered from the press, a once adoring public and even their own race officials, the pedestriennes probably only had one more chance to quell rising criticism and suspicions that now defined them. They needed a top walk, with the best athletes to put on a great contest. And they needed a substantial payoff.

Reverting to a smaller field with familiar names and strong walking resumes, Rose hoped that they could push themselves to another strong performance.

Scheduled for Horticultural Hall in late January 1881, promoters labeled the race the "Championship of the West Coast," and "A Match at Last" in a *Chronicle* ad on January 26.

The payout included gate receipts. The manager received the first 50% and the walkers would split the remaining 50%, provided they covered 325 miles.

The four selected contestants had dominated the sport since the move west 18 months earlier. Three women had won all the San Francisco walks: Exilda LaChapelle, May Bell Sherman, and, of course, Amy Howard. Millie Young's youth and impressive record earned her an invitation. Sarah Tobias, an obvious selection for this elite field, had headed back east.

As usual, each walker sounded confident of victory. "My record is 337 miles in six days. I've never lost a race in my life," says Sherman in a *Chronicle* interview, "and I never felt better in my life than I do tonight."

Sherman said she didn't consider LaChapelle and Young fit enough to be called six-day walkers so long as she and Howard were well enough to fit into shoes. As to Howard, "I don't know if I can beat her." Sherman, just back from a 25-mile race in Oregon, had put on 15 pounds, making her "better to look at, but the race is to the lean."

Without ever seeing her walk, Howard said of Sherman, "They do say she is great, but my record is 409 miles in six days." LaChapelle also claimed to have walked 400 miles in Chicago, in spite of being sick. And although she said she had done no training, she said she never felt better. Teen Millie Young claimed 350 miles in six days.

The doors opened at 8:00 p.m., and seats filled almost immediately. Early arrivals enjoyed a trick bicycle show. Just before 11:00, a drum roll started and LaChapelle led the field to the start. All four entrants wore blue as approximately 1,500 watched the quartet line up on the 20 laps to the mile, six-foot wide track surrounded by a three-foot high rail. At 11:00 p.m. on January 26, the starter shouted "Go!" and the large crowd, quiet until now, cheered; the eight-piece band played, and the champions took off, Howard leading.

They settled into a solid pace. One paper said LaChapelle walked "as if her sole end and aim for her and everyone else's existence was to accomplish laps."

From the outset, Young struggled to keep up; Sherman stayed off the track for long periods of time, blaming her early and untimely respite on cramps. LaChapelle continued pushing, and after two days she led the suddenly gimpy kneed Howard by one mile and Young by seven. Sherman, still complaining of stomach problems, fell behind by 29 miles, closed to 18, only three behind Young, then back to 40. In spite of her swelling knees, Howard retook the lead and maintained a small advantage over LaChapelle with Young just a bit farther behind.

The crowd sat subdued, partially due to rainy weather. The band attempted to "wake" them with "Marching Through Georgia," and "Six Months in the County Jail," and "Pattering Footsteps on the Sawdust."

After three days muscular problems caused Howard to lose ground, and LaChapelle retook the lead. Sherman's persistant pain brought her to tears.

That night while she slept, LaChapelle's husband woke her and told her that Howard was running on the track, and had recaptured the top position.

LaChapelle bolted from her tent, but Howard kept running, making the Frenchwoman think "she was chasing a locomotive." This ended rumors that Howard suffered from stiff joints, a story circulated by "someone," said her husband Frank.

Sherman stayed off the track for most of January 30. LaChapelle and Howard backed off the pace, resulting in Young's support team hissing every time they passed her tent. After several attempts, the race manager finally convinced them to stop.

LaChapelle kept up by alternating between fast walking and running. With one day remaining, Howard led LaChapelle 308 miles to 306.

Again the women had responded. Because of the names and solid performances, crowds grew larger every night. The women were obviously battling, and at this point even Millie Young, whom Howard supposedly feared more than LaChapelle, had an outside shot at winning. But LaChapelle appeared used up, and on the last day she made no attempt to pass Howard.

At 11:00 p.m. on February 1, the race closed with Howard recording 356 miles, LaChapelle 350, Young, 327 and Sherman 228.

Howard won and received the gold and silver slipper, and split the appropriate gate receipts with LaChapelle and Young, the latter making the minimum 325 mile cutoff by two miles.

Howard again proved she was the queen of pedestriennes. By beating Sherman, she had now defeated all the major West Coast walkers. While few had been easy victories, she had won.

Howard predicted a rapid recovery. She said to a *Chronicle* reporter, "It has been a loafing match for me from the start, since no one has pushed me."

Those comments, added to her husband's coy response when talking about her reported stiff joints, made one wonder if she had "bagged" it to avoid taxing herself, and to ensure the public and management got what they wanted: a good race. And if she did hold back, could that have been with management's blessing, or at least their suggestion?

Either way, what should have been a comeback for the pedestriennes proved only a mild improvement over the July disaster.

While the athletes were well-received, the expected excitement for them never materialized. The rain depressed crowd sizes and spirits, and the band's efforts to elevate the enthusiasm never worked.

A San Francisco writer echoed the questions that had plagued the women almost from the beginning, not understanding the purpose, "The only reason Romans threw Christians to lions is because that's what the people wanted. We've evolved from bull fights to prize fights, now dog fights and 'go-as-you-please' walking matches."

*   *   *

The final pedestrienne race in San Francisco took place in May, 1881. Officials again dubbed it "Championship of the Pacific Coast."

Held at Mechanics' it featured Howard, Sherman, Young, LaChapelle and local walkers. Notably missing were Sarah Tobias and the Donley sisters. In an attempt to make the race more competitive, Howard gave all contestants a 20-mile handicap, except LaChapelle, who got 10. It didn't matter. By the end of the first day, the dominant Howard recorded 100 miles, tying her for the lead with Kitty Mason, who started with 20.

As the week wore on, the aura in Mechanics' grew more surreal. The periphery entertainment, once considered a sideshow, now shined in the spotlight. A variety of activities, including boxing, dancing, Greco-Roman wrestling matches, collar-and-elbow wrestling contests, and the usual entertainment gave attendees many options to spend their money and time. On top of that, a ball closed out each evening.

The athletes were again accused of conducting a hippodrome, as the top three appeared to lock their positions instead of challenging each other.

Mason, in third after the first day, walked laden with extra embroidery on her frock. When asked to remove it, she said, "I'd rather die than win a race without looking stylish."

Post-race, the situation worsened. Either through oversight or crookedness, most of the walkers' payouts vanished. All that remained was $450, held by Mrs. EG Cotton, all earmarked for Howard, who won with 364 miles.

The referee made what someone called a "touching little speech of condolence to the other winners," but it did little to appease them and their support team and backers.

Race manager Samuel Shear was arrested May 26, based on a complaint filed by Frank Edwards. Shear embezzled almost $400. When the race ended two days later, pedestrienne Carrie Maynard told her husband Harry, a race official, that she had seen Shear sprinting out of the box office taking the sum of $153 with him. Harry tracked him down and demanded the cash. Shear initially refused, but gave in when Maynard threatened to turn the matter over to the police. When they returned to the venue, a host of race employees had congregated to greet them, all demanding to be paid. A contract proved that that responsibility also fell to Shear, who presumably did the best he could, but his solution did little to make satisfactory compensation.

While the race could claim decent attendance, the "Championship of the Pacific Coast" Six-Day Race proved an uninspiring event that, according to the *Examiner*, "was a miserable failure in every respect."

With women's endurance walking already played out on the East Coast, the walkers and the public losing interest on the West Coast completed the pedestriennes' demise.

Races and endurance walks would continue for years, but the pedestriennes' glory days had ended. From now on walking for money would mean playing in less prestigious venues and taking home pennies instead of dollars. The large enthusiastic crowds who once raised the rafters with deafening cheers, diminished to small gatherings offering polite applause.

Some pedestriennes vanished and returned to lives of obscurity.

Others just couldn't leave the sport that had given them so much.

Epilogue

ven after Cotton took the top pedestriennes to San Francisco, 1879, some walkers stayed East and many contests took place in the Midwest.

New York's Brewster Building, site of the early success of Amy Howard, Bertha von Berg and others, still hosted races, and some drew big crowds and saw remarkable performances. Just after the Howard-Tobias duel in San Francisco, Cora Cushing recoded 401 miles in a walk at Baltimore's Kernan's Summer Garden.

Madame Anderson continued walking throughout 1879. In her first performance after her March 1879 failure in Chicago, she walked in Cincinnati, Louisville, Detroit, Buffalo, and at Tivoli Theatre in New York before competing at Madison Square Garden in December.

She got only a mediocre result at the December 1879 International Championship in New York. Her last known walk took place in Baltimore in May 1880, when she walked to kick off the city's introduction of the electric light.

The odds are good that, having successfully achieved her childhood goal of 'making a name,' she and her husband returned to England, where she either retired or possibly revived her stage career.

Her mercurial one-time manager, Alexander Samuells, lived a life that teetered between tragedy and disappointment. In 1883, Amelia, his alcoholic wife, caught her clothes on fire while working near their stove. She died the next day, leaving her husband to care for their five children, who ranged in age from 14 months to 14 years. At one point, Samuells headed west to try his hand at silver mining. He returned to New York and managed men's endurance walks with mixed results. The Civil War veteran died penniless in 1911.

Fannie and Frank Edwards walked for a few more years, and then disappeared. After 1879, Bertha von Berg apparently returned to working as a seamstress.

After many years of retirement, Daniel O'Leary continued his long-distance walking exploits and maintained his high profile until well into the 20th century. In 1907 in Norwood, Ohio, he equaled Barclay's record by walking 1,000 miles in 1,000 hours, earning $5,000 for the effort. O'Leary was 61. The *Cincinnati Enquirer* called it, "the crowning effort of his long career." Later, he set up some walking clubs throughout Chicago. He died in 1933 at the age of 87.

Exilda LaChapelle, the successful pedestrienne who wanted nothing more than to be a mom, kept walking at least until the late 1880s, still commonly called the "Champion Pedestrienne of the World." It's unknown if she ever reached the happiness she sought her entire life.

By late 1880, she and her husband, William DeRose, opened a bar in San Francisco. While she managed the business, DeRose drank and had affairs. Finally tired of his philandering, she divorced him. He apparently kept the bar, and took up company with a young lady 15 years his junior who "lived the life of a chorus girl." Wanting to straighten herself out, she got little help from the 40-year-old DeRose. While she worked his bar during the day, he kept up his usual extracurricular activities. Numerous reports said he often beat her and she frequently sought refuge at neighbor's homes, sometimes staying for days.

On the night of April 6, 1891, a drunk DeRose came home and pulled a pistol on his lover. She wrestled it from him, shooting him once in the chest and once in the abdomen. Police investigated and charged her with murder, but found no neighbor who took his side.

"She was more sinned against than sinner," said one friend.

Mike Henry, Madame Anderson's coach during her epic walk in 1879, began suffering from what is now called being "punch drunk." Toward the end of his life, the one-time boxer, brain likely damaged from years of cranial beatings, couldn't feed himself. He died in 1886 at the age of 59.

After her string of pedestrienne victories, Amy Howard moved back to New York and returned to the stage with her sister. She died during childbirth in 1885 at the age of 23. It's not known if the child survived.

Like Exilda LaChapelle, May Marshall kept walking well into the late 1880s. Unfortunately, she could only book obscure venues for purses as small as $5. According to her 1911 obituary, she and her husband, one-time pedestrian Henry Hager, retired to the Michigan peninsula, where she spent time with her four grandchildren.

After retirement, Bertha von Hillern spent more than 40 years as a landscape artist, mostly in the Shenandoah Valley area. She showed her work in many cities, including Pittsburgh and Boston. Even in advanced age, she made her mark. In 1923, she won three ribbons at the Winchester (VA) fair for baking bread. She died in Richmond, VA in 1939.

William Gale followed Madame Anderson to America and put on several successful walking exhibitions, including 1,000 quarter miles in 1,000 quarter hours, but he never matched the popularity of Weston and O'Leary. In 1888, he lived in a small apartment in a fourth-story apartment in Cincinnati, the city where he would die in 1905.

He told a reporter with the *Cincinnati Commercial Tribune* that beating Captain Barclay's record 1,500 miles in 1,000 hours at Lillibridge in 1877 was "the greatest moment of my life." Sir John Astley, the British politician and endurance walking aficionado who created the Astley Belt, presented him with the championship belt, which Gale said weighed 102 ounces.

"Where is the belt now?" asked the reporter.

The champion turned red in color and then answered hesitatingly, "I pawned it in New York shortly after my arrival. I was quite short of funds. Later, I wrote to the pawn dealer and he lamented that he had disposed of it."

Afterward

Although the pedestriennes' endurance contests all but died out in the early 1880s, they laid some valuable groundwork as America moved into the 20th century.

For the next several years, women expanded their influence in the world of athletics. They participated in and set high standards in many sports, including swimming and archery. In tennis, Britain's Maud Watson won Wimbledon singles titles in both 1884 and 1885; in 1887, Ellen Hansell captured the first women's singles winner at the US Open. That same year, the Women's French Tennis Championship was held.

The popularity of bicycling also exploded among women, and six-day bicycle races supplanted the six-day walking matches.

Just 20 years after the first women's six-day race in Chicago, Frenchman Pierre de Coubertin organized a revival of the Olympic Games, which were held in Athens, Greece. The Games ran for nine days, and featured 14 nations competing in 43 events in nine sports, and no women competitors. The next Olympics was held in Paris in 1900, with 19 women participating. Since then the Olympics have been held every four years (except for the war years of 1916, 1940 and 1944) until today, when the 2012 Olympic Games held in London saw more than 10,500 athletes compete, including 4,676 women.

The pedestriennes' successes and high profile also contributed to the women's suffrage movement.

The women's rights movement actually began in 1848 in New York, with the Women's Rights Convention. Held in Seneca Falls, the group issued the Seneca Falls Declaration of Sentiments. But 30 years would pass before the "Anthony Amendment" was introduced to Congress. Named for Susan B. Anthony, the amendment would give women the right to vote.

As a territory, Wyoming gave women the right to vote in 1869, and that carried over when it was admitted to the union in 1890. From there, the movement grew until August 1920, when Tennessee ratified the Anthony Amendment by a single vote, giving women the Constitutional right to vote.

Among the pedestriennes, Bertha von Hillern was the only pedestrienne known to be alive when that momentous event took place.

And while we know virtually nothing of the pedestriennes' view on what was then a controversial idea, their accomplishments helped advancements for women. The pedestriennes changed society's traditional thoughts on women's capabilities. Thanks in part to the pedestriennes, women took on new roles and embraced opportunities unavailable to them just a few years earlier.

End Notes

Page 1

i "At a quarter before eight…", *Brooklyn Daily Eagle*, Dec 18, 1878, "The Commencement of the Great Feat at Mozart Garden last Evening—the Appearance of the Pedestrian…"

"At 10 minutes to eight…" *NY Sun* Dec. 17, 1878, "Madame Anderson, Pedestrian" p 2

Page 2

"At five minutes to eight" *NY Sun*, Dec. 17, 1878, "Mme. Anderson, Pedestrienne"
"In no way could Mozart compete…", *Brooklyn Daily Eagle*, July 11, 1877, "The Mozart…" p 4
"Vanderbilt turned down…" Dahn Shaulis, "Pedestriennes: Newsworthy but Controversial Women in Sporting Entertainment,": Spring 1999, page 35
"AR's wealth had peaked…" *Brooklyn Daily Eagle*, July 11, 1877, "The Mozart…" page 4
Ethiopia passenger list from National Archives , 1820-1957, Roll M237_415-0621

Page 3

"she stood five foot-one…" *NY Herald*, Dec. 17, 1878, "On the Track…" p 5
Her womanly appearance, *NY Herald*, Dec 26, 1878, "Mme. Anderson, The Plucky Woman…"
Samuells announces her walking accomplishment, *NY Herald*, Dec 17, 1878, "On the Track…" p 5
Samuells stated she would subsist on rare…" *Brooklyn Daily Eagle*, December 18, 1878, "A Long Walk."

Page 4

Credited laps *NY Clipper*, Nov. 30, 1878
12 x 28 ft. tent *NY Herald*, Dec. 17, 1878 "On the Track," page 5

Mike Henry info found in obituary, May 10, 1889, *Brooklyn Daily Eagle*, "The Death of a Well-known Sporting Man

Officials listed, *NY Sun*, May 10, 1889, "Mme. Anderson, Pedestrian"

"Honest work," and timers from other papers recording times, *NY Herald*, Dec. 17, 1878, "On the Track," page 5

Madame Anderson's pre-walk speech, *NY Times*, Dec 17, 1878, "Woman of Endurance"

Page 5

"Family entry..." *Brooklyn Daily Eagle*, Dec. 18, 1878, "A Long Walk"

"If I fall dead on the track..." *NY Times*, Dec. 17, 1878, "Woman of Endurance"

Page 6

"Even babies don't..." *NY Times*, editorial, Dec. 18, 1878, "Tests of Endurance"

Chapter 2

Page 7

"Church socials..." Peter Radford, *Canadian History Journal of Sport*, May 1994, Vol. 25 Issue 1 , "Women's Foot Races in the 18th and 19th Centuries: A Common and Widespread Practice" page 50

"Winners earned..." Ibid, page 51

Smock races Ibid, page 50

"50 miles in 8.5 hours..." Ibid page 54

Page 8

"attempted 50 miles..." Ibid p. 54

Age of female walkers Ibid page 54

Born 1777, JK Gillon "Robert Barclay Allardice: The Celebrated Pedestrian"

Walter Thom reference 1813 book, "Pedestrianism," from Gillon's "The Celebrated Pedestrian"

Page 9

"wagered 1,000 guineas he could walk," Gillon

"He marked off..." Peter Radford the Guardian.co.uk, August 23, 2011, "Newmarket's Greatest Stayer"

"To wake him..." Ibid, Radford

"times dropped.." Gillon

"all beds were filled," Gillon

"church bells rang..." Radford, "Stayer"

Page 10

He earned "100,000 pounds." Robert Barclay Allardice, Wikipedia, The thousand hour walk
"He sponsored boxer Tom Crib," Gillon
"He died of paralysis…" Gillon
"In 1815, six years…" *Swanseas Cambrian*, Emma Lile, "Professional Pedestrainism in South Wales During the 19th Century
"Due to his job…" TD Dutton, *The Strand Magazine*, July 1903, "Famous Walkers of the Past," pp. 74-75
Josiah Eaton, Ibid. p.78

Page 11

"In 1838, a pedestrian named Harriss…" The *Times*, Dec. 4, 1838 p.2 "Extraordinary Pedestrian Feat,"
"Mary Callinack," Dutton, *The Strand Magazine*, July 1903, "Famous Walkers of the Past," p. 79
"Emma Sharp" by David Barnett thetelegraph&argus.co.uk, May 29, 2009, Remember When? "Long Walk Put Women on the Map"

Chapter 3

Page 12

Ada's birthdate Vegas Quixote, *Marathon and Beyond*, Nov/Dec 2000, "The Untimely Disappearance of Madame Anderson," p. 88
Ibid, p. 88
Family earnings, Victorian Occupations- 1876 Victorian England Revisited. Logicmngmt.com/1876/living/occupations.html
Father's name and occupation on Anderson's marriage certificate to William Paley, April 22, 1878 ref. p67/9

Page 13

She leaves home for the stage…Quixote page 89
Irving knighted, Sir henry Irving, Wikipedia.org
Actress and prostitute, Kerry Powell, Women in Victorian Theatre, e-book location 492
"…Advertise any other way…" Kerry Powell, Women in Victorian Theatre, e-book location 477
"Is not a theatre…" Kerry Powell, Women in Victorian Theatre e-book location 492

Page 14

Irene Vanbrugh, "...one long fight..." Kerry Powell, <u>Women in Victorian The-atre</u>, e-book location 798
"...war without bloodshed..." ibid, location 806
"...I am starving." John Russell Stephens, <u>The Profession of the Playwright: British Theatre, 1800-1900</u> p. 31
"Pull a house down," *NY Herald*, Dec 26, 1878, "Madame Anderson, The Plucky Woman..."
Penny gaffs, Michael Booth, <u>Theatre in the Victorian Age</u>, p. 100
16 hour workdays, Booth, p. 104
Unpaid and penniless, Booth, p. 109
"opportunities to perform..." Michael Booth, <u>Theatre in the Victorian Age</u>, p. 109

Page 15

Anderson marriage, Quixote, *Marathon and Beyond*, Nov/Dec 2000, "Untimely Disappearance," p.89

Page 16

Husband death, Ibid, p. 89

Chapter 4

Page 17

O'Leary birth and early years, Matthew Algeo, <u>Pedestrainism: When Watching People Walk was America's Favorite Spectator Sport</u>, p. 27
Ibid p. 28
Weston walked from Portland (ME) to Chicago, Algeo p. 12

Page 18

Weston turned pro <u>www.walkapedia.org</u>; walking the world on foot and online
O'Leary's first competitive walk, Alego, p. 28
Track lengths, Algeo p. 34
O'Leary defeated Weston, Algeo p. 40

Page 19

Von Hillern defeated a woman in Peoria, *NY Times*, Nov. 6, 1876, "Female Pedestrianism"

Page 21

Marshall birthplace Dover, NH from paper, July 9-10(?) 1877. From Curtis
 family scrapbook
Family sources say she was born in Soperton, ON; obituary from 1911 Detroit
 News lists it as Delta, MI
Marriage from family history

Page 23

"O'Leary looks after both women, *Chicago Times*, Feb 1, 1876

Page 24

Sleep recommendations from Ed James; <u>Practical Training for Running, Walk-
 ing, Rowing Wrestling, Boxing, Jumping, and All Kinds of Athletic Feats,</u>
 1877, p. 14
Diet information from John Goulding; <u>The Amateur's Guide: or, Training Made
 Easy, For Modern Outdoor Amusements</u>, 1877, p 11
Walking form, Goulding p.5
American Pedometer ad section from James, no page number
Shoes advertised in James, no page number
Injuries, James p. 60

Chapter 6

Page 28

"…It was much talked-about…", *Chicago Times*, Jan 30, 1876, "Here's Fun"
Address of Second Regiment Armory, Jan. 31, 1876, *Chicago Evening Journal*,
 "Walking Women"
Address of Second Regiment Armory, *NY Times*, July 26, 1915, "Stricken
 Chicago Identifying Dead" p. 1
Track measurement, *Chicago Evening Journal*, Jan 31, 1876
Capacity *Chicago Inter-Ocean*, Feb 7, 1876, "The Lady Pedestrians Finish Their
 Long Walk, But Are Half-killed with the Effort"
Admission fee *Chicago Tribune*, Jan. 30, 1876, "Pedestrianism, The Female
 Walkers"

Page 29

Pedestrienne's attire, *Chicago Tribune*, Feb 1, 1876, "Pedestrianism: Von Hillern-
 Marshall"
O'Leary starts race, ibid
First laps, *Chicago Times*, Feb 1, 1876, "Pull Back Pedestriennes"

Tribune blasts smokers, *Chicago Tribune*, Feb 1, 1876, "Pedestrianism; Von HIllern-Marshall"

Page 30

Marshall predicts victory, *Chicago Evening Journal*, Feb 3, 1876, "The Girls are Marching"
Fraulein stories lack spark, *Chicago Evening Journal*, Feb 2, 1876, "Feat of Feet" p. 4
Slowing pace, *Chicago Evening Journal*, Feb 2, 1876, "Feat of Feet" p. 4
They walked together, *Chicago Evening Journal*, Feb 3, 1876, "The Girls Are Marching"

Page 31

Reporter visits Marshall in her tent, *Chicago Inter-Ocean*, Feb 4, 1876, "Nony A Weary Foot"
Chicago walking mania, *Chicago Tribune*, Feb 4, 1876, "Pedestrianism"
Rise at 4:15, *Chicago Evening Journal*, Feb 4, 1876, "Local Affairs, Three Miles Ahead"
Marshall predicts she will overtake her rival, *Chicago Inter-Ocean*, Feb 5, 1876, "Nearing the Goal"

Page 32

Dr. Dunne, *Chicago Inter-Ocean*, Feb 7, 1876, "Tired Out Trampers"
Marshall wears O'Leary's shoes, *Chicago Journal*, Feb. 5, 1876, "Feminine Feet; "Germania" Still Ahead, but 'Americanus' Gaining Ground"
Von Hillern's isolation, ibid
Von Hillern will win, *Chicago Daily News*, Feb 4, 1876; "The Petticoat Pedestrians," p 1; (Von Hillern) victory is almost certain, *Chicago Inter-Ocean*, Feb 5, 1876
Von Hillern leads, 191-186, Feb 5, 1876, *Chicago Inter-Ocean*, Feb 5, 1876, p 12

Page 33

Beginning of day six, *Chicago Inter-Ocean*, Feb 7, 1876, "Tired Out Trampers"
Chicago Times, Feb 7, 1876, "Pedestrianism: Close on the Women's Walking Match"
Marshall collapses and is carried to her tent, *Chicago Times*, Feb 7,1876, ibid

Page 34

End of Race scores given, *Chicago Times* Feb 7, 1876 "Pedestrianism: Close on Women's Walking Match"
Von Hillern condition given, Ibid; *Chicago Evening Journal*, Feb 7, 1876

Fixed race? *Chicago Times*, Feb 7, 1876 "Pedestrianism: Close on the Women's
Walking Match"
No more women's walking matches, ibid

Chapter 7

Page 36

Second walking match, Nov 6, 1876, *NY Times*, "Female Pedestrianism"
Marshall-Van Ness Match, Gipe George, *Sports Illustrated*, Oct 24, 1977, "Mary
Marshall was Strides Ahead of the Times When She Beat a Man"

Page 37

Marshall walks Spring/Summer 1877:
Boston 50 miles 10:47 *Boston Globe* April 12, 1877
Boston Herald walked 100 miles in Boston, April 11-12
Worcester Gazette walked 50 miles 11:48 Worcester, MA
Boston Globe, May 30, 1877, 50 miles in 12 hours, failed, "Other Sports"
The Detroit News 1911 (her obituary) walked 50 miles 11:51 in New Bedford,
MA
The Detroit News 1911 (her obituary) walked 25 miles in under six hours, New
Bedford, MA
Providence failure 50 miles in 12 hours May 30
Daily Mercury successful 100 miles in under 28 hours (no exact time given) June
22-23
New Bedford from the *Daily Mercury* 100 miles (fails) June 29-30
New Bedford Mercury 100 miles under 28 hours New Bedford, MA July 8-9
Taunton 50 miles under 12 hours July 23
Marshall challenges Von Hillern to a rematch, *NY Graphic*, Dec 30, 1876

Page 38

Marshall has feet problems, Boston Post, April 13, 1877

Page 39

Thomas was Barnum's press agent *Lowell (MA) Citizen and News*, July 12, 1877,
"Bertha von Hillern's Walk—A Great Feat Handsomely Accomplished
"Chiropodin for strong feet" ad in *Jersey Journal*, Jan 22, 1878
Letters on building, *The Boston Journal*, Feb 15, 1877, "Local Briefs"
"Giles Liniment Iodide Ammonia" ad *Cincinnati Daily Gazette*, April 30, 1878
p. 5
Music Hall packed *Women's Journal* Dec. 30, 1876
Visits an insane asylum *Worcester Gazette*, May 10, 1877, "Local Notes"
Walks Through Clinton, *Worcester Gazette*, May 14, 1877, The Long Walk

City bulletin boards update her progress, *Providence Press*, April 27, 1877;
  "Physical Culture: Miss Von Hillern's 145 mile walk
Gives lecture on physical culture with Leroy Cherrington, *Lowell Daily Citizen*,
  Oct 27, 1877, "Popular Scientific Lecture"
"The Little Wonder" *Worcester Gazette*, May 5, 1877
Crowd goes wild over Von Hillern, *Worcester Gazette*, May 16, 1877, "Her Level
  Best..."
Ad for "Von Hillern Walking Hats" *Worcester Gazette*, May 5, 1877
New Orleans Times-Picayune Dec 30, 1877 denigrates Von Hillern achievements p 12
Parody called Birdie von Killem, *Philadelphia Ledger*, Nov 20, 1877

Page 40
Millie Rose quit after 37 miles, *Chicago Evening Journal*, Feb 3, 1876

Chapter 8

Page 41

Description of Gale's persona, *NY Herald*, Oct 28, 1877 Gale's Great Walk
Height and weight, *Preston Guardian*, Sept 17, 1853
Herald, Ibid

Page 42

Started walking in 1850, *Preston Guardian*, ibid

Page 43

Early performances recorded in *Liverpool Local Intelligence* June 6, 1853
Prize money, *Western Mail* (Cardiff); September 5, 1870
Congratulatory dinner *Western Mail* (Cardiff), Sept 16, 1870
How Weston and O'Leary wowed the Brits with their walking exploits in 1876
  is chronicled in chapters four and five of Matthew Algeo's <u>Pedestrianism:</u>
  <u>When Watching People Walk Was America's Favorite Spectator Sport</u>
Gale's walking goal and track description in June 30, 1877 issue of *Bristol Eng-
  lish Mercury*
Start of walk, *Western Mail* (Cardiff) July 26, 1877
Three collapses, *Western Mail* (Cardiff), Ibid
Finish of race, ibid.

Chapter 9

Page 47

Madame Anderson's British walking records are listed in Dahn Shaulis' "Pedestriennes: Newsworthy but Controversial Women in Sporting Entertainment" via

219

the original source in the May 16, 1880 *Baltimore American and Commercial Advertiser.*

Sleep deprivation info from e-mail interview with Dr. Philip Baker, Dec 13, 2005

Page 48

"Who is this…"*The Era*, Jan 20, 1878
"Styling Herself…" *Lincolnshire Chronicle*, Feb 15, 1878
"Not so-called…" *The Era*, March 3, 1878

Page 49

Fails at 100 mile walk in Plymouth, *NY Sun*, Dec 17, 1878, "Mme. Anderson. Pedestrian"
Madame Anderson, *Leeds Times*, May 4, 1878, Champion Lady Walker of the World

Page 50

Walks at Corn Exchange in Boston (Lincolnshire) *The Era*, Feb 24, 1878
"She should get respect…" *Lincolnshire Herald*, March 3, 1878
"Greatest sensation…" , *The Era*, March 3, 1878
Elizabeth Sparrow quote *NY Sun*, Dec 27, 1878, "Madam Anderson Pluckily Continuing on her Walk."
Completes 1,500 miles in 1,000 at Leeds, *The Portsmith Evening News*, May 21, 1878

Page 51

Ibid, marriage license
Ibid, Shaulis listing of Anderson's victories in England

Page 52

Departed from Glasgow Oct 13, 1878, *Bristol Mercury and Daily Post*, Oct 14, 1878
Arrived New York Oct 22, 1878, NY passenger list, National Archives

Page 53

Von Hillern's walking victories:

89 miles in 26 hours Baltimore Dec 27, 1877 reported in *NY Herald* Dec 28, 1877, "Miss Von Hillern's Walk," p 5
100/28 Baltimore Jan 8, 1877 reported in *NY Herald*, Jan 9, 1878 "Miss Von Hillern's Walk," p 7
89/26 Washington Jan 21, 1877 reported in *Critic Record* (Washington) Jan 21, 1878 p 4

100/28 Washington Jan 28-29, 1877, reported in *NY Herald* Jan 30, 1878 p 7
89/26 Pittsburgh Feb 11-12, 1877 reported in the *Wheeling Register*, Feb 13, 1878 p 1
100/28 Pittsburgh Feb 26-27, 1877 reported in *NY Herald* Feb 27, 1878 p 7
89/26 Cincinnati March 8-9 reported in *Cincinnati Enquirer* March 10, 1878, "Pedalistic, Miss Von Hillern's Feat"
100/28 Cincinnati March 19-20 reported in *Cincinnati Enquirer* March 21, 1878, "Bertha von HIllern"
89/26 Louisville, KY, April 6-7 reported *in Louisville Courier-Journal* April 7, 1878, "Amusements: Miss Von Hillern"
100/28 Louisville, KY April 11-12 reported in *Louisville Courier Journal* April 13, 1878, "Von Hillern Victory"

Ibid, victory in Louisville April 13, 1877
Mrs. Hayes wants to see the walker *NO Times-Picayune*, Feb 1, 1878
Von HIllern has paralysis *Times Picayune* (sourced from *Boston Post*) Nov 30, 1878 p 4
Paralysis rumors not true, Feb 13, 1879 *New Philadelphia (OH) Democrat*
Von Hillern turns to art, *Newport (RI) Daily News*, May 14, 1878
Accompanied by Miss Beckett, *Portland (ME) Daily Press*, July 26, 1877, "The Von Hillern Walk," p 3
Boston exhibits virtualology.com Virtual American Biographies
Von HIllern and Beckett show works, *Shenandoah (VA) Herald*, April 13, 1881, "The Return of the Artists"
Marshall leaves manager in "arrearages." *NY Clipper*, June 29, 1878
Accounts of Marshall's bout with yellow fever were found in a family scrapbook, and exact dates and newspaper names weren't always available
Accounts of other pedestriennes found in *NY Clipper* March 16, 1878; Nov 30, 1878; Dec 7, 1878;

Page 57

Early accounts of Exilda LaChapelle's life found online at the Liz Library Women of Achievement and Herstory.
Hit while trying to pass male competitor, *Wisconsin Oshkosh Daily Northwest* Dec 12, 1878, "The Walking Match"
Pay for Wisconsin races, ibid
100 miles in under 25 hours, *The Madison Democrat*, June 13, 1868

Chapter 11

Page 58

Barnum schedule www.circushistory.org , "PT Barnum's New and Greatest Show on Earth, 1878 Route"

221

Page 59

Samuells' early life chronicled Oct 22, 1913 edition of *Brooklyn Daily Eagle*
Claimed war record, ibid
Ancestry.com lists war record 10,442

Page 60

Samuells' professional history, *Brooklyn Daily Eagle*, July 11, 1877, "The Mozart:
 A New and Important Enterprise in Brooklyn"
Park Theatre, ibid

Page 61

Injured men, *NY Herald*, July 28, 1877, "Brooklyn"
Description of Mozart Garden, *Brooklyn Daily Eagle*, August 12, 1877, "Mozart
 Garden Opening"
Opening night, ibid

Page 63

Samuells and Seifert fallout, *Brooklyn Daily Eagle*, August 28, 1877, "Discordant
 Samuells and Seifert Have a Falling Out"
Atlantic Baseball Club meets at Samuells' Billiards House, *Brooklyn Daily Eagle*,
 Jan 10, 1872

Page 64

Description of Henry in obit *Brooklyn Daily Eagle*, May 10, 1889
Shot by John Downey, *Brooklyn Daily Eagle*, April 17, 1865
Stabbing described, *Brooklyn Daily Eagle*, May 29, 1877
Third shooting described in *Brooklyn Daily Eagle*, Jan 8, 1881

Page 65

Mozart Garden attractions listed daily in *Brooklyn Daily Eagle* throughout last
 half of 1877; most listed on page 1.
Mozart Garden to remain open through summer *Brooklyn Daily Eagle*, May 26,
 1878, "Mozart Garden"
Positive review of Mozart summer attractions, *Brooklyn Daily Eagle* July 26,
 1877, "Mozart Garden"
Praise for Samuells, *Brooklyn Daily Eagle*, Aug 16, 1877, "Amusements"

Page 66

O'Leary said he wouldn't attempt it, *Brooklyn Daily Eagle*, Jan 12, 1879,
  "Madame Anderson How Interest Grew"
Refurbishing of Mozart Garden, *Brooklyn Daily Eagle*, Dec 18, 1878, "A Long
  Walk"
Track distance certified, ibid
Privacy room described, ibid

Page 68

Man jumps on track to walk w/her quarter six, *Brooklyn Daily Eagle*, Dec 18,
  1878, "Commencement of Great Feat," p 4

Page 69

Editorial critical of women walking events, *NY Times* Dec 18, 1878, "Tests of
  Endurance"

Page 70

Interview with reporter in tent, *Brooklyn Daily Eagle*, Dec 18, 1878, "A Long
  Walk"
First song, *NY Sun*, Dec 20, 1878, "Walking and Singing"
Boxer Bill Tovec walks with her, ibid, "A Long Walk"
Doctors check her out, *Brooklyn Daily Eagle*, Dec 21, 1878, "Female Pedestrians"
Surgeon General attends, *NY Sun*, Dec 21, 1878, "The Woman of Endurance"

Chapter 14

Page 72

Doctors assessment, *Brooklyn Daily Eagle*, Dec 21, 1878, "Female Pedestrians"
Interview in tent, *Brooklyn Daily Eagle*, Dec 22, 1878, "A Woman's Pluck"
Sleep deprivation info from e-mail interview with Dr. Philip Baker, Dec 13,
  2005
"A Woman's Pluck," ibid

Page 73

Receives a gift of cut glass, *NY Herald*, Dec 22, 1878,   "The Lady Pedestrian" p 8

Page 74

Obstructions on track, *NY Herald*, Dec 23, 1878, "Madame Anderson's Walk,"
Shoes on wrong feet, ibid

Page 75

Man pays off bet, ibid
Walked while eating a sandwich, *NY Herald*, Dec 23, 1878, "Madame Anderson's Walk," p 8
Tugs on right ear, *NY Sun*, Dec 25, 1878, "Madame Anderson Compared With Champion Walker"
Knocks out Sparrow's tooth, *NY Herald*, Dec 24, 1878, "Mme Anderson's Task," p 8

Page 76

Sparrow quote, "kicked by a mule," ibid

Page 77

General Tom Thumb walks with her, *NY Sun*, Dec 25, 1878, "Madame Anderson compared with the Champion Walker"
Info on Tom Thumb from www.answers.com

Page 78

Dialogue from *NY Herald*, Dec 26, 1878, "Mme. Anderson, The Plucky Woman Still Trudging…"
"…staring at you in the next life…" ibid

Page 79
Treatment of blisters, *NY Herald*, Dec 26, 1878, "The Plucky Woman Still Trudging Along…"
Walking style, Dec 25, 1878, *NY Sun*, "Madame Anderson Compared with the Champion Walker"
Quarter miles times, ibid
Pedestrienne hopeful in brown dress, *NY Herald*, Dec 27, 1878, "The Lady Pedestrian," p 9
People join her on the track, *NY Herald*, Dec 26, ibid; Dec 27, *NY Sun*, "Madam Anderson Pluckily Continuing on her Tramp," *Brooklyn Daily Eagle*, Dec 28, 1878, "Madame Anderson Plodding Along With Tireless Strides"
"Where's the other woman?" *NY Sun*, Dec 26, 1878, "Not Yet Too Tired to Sing."

Page 80

Horseman asks for track certification, ibid
"…keeping up her shake…" ibid
Prominent visitors listed, *NY Sun*, Dec 26, 1878, "Not Yet Too Tired to Sing
Mutton Christmas present, *NY Herald*, Dec 27, 1878, "The Lady Pedestrian" p 9

Problem with boards, *NY Sun*, Dec 26, 1878, "Not Yet too Tired to Sing"

Page 81

Number 873 in 4:49, ibid
Jack's Comanche yell, *NY Sun*, Dec 27, 1878, "Madam Anderson Pluckily Continuing on her Tramp"
Life of "Texas Jack" Omohundro found at www.bbhc.org (Buffalo Bill Historical Center)
Out shopping, *NY Sun*, Dec 27, 1878, "Madam Anderson Pluckily Continuing Her Tramp"
Shoes inspected, ibid
Critical of male walker at Gilmore's ibid

Chapter 16

Page 83

Rumor of a double, *NY Herald*, Dec 28, 1878, "Mme Anderson's Plucky Undertaking"

Page 84

Reporters on hand, *NY Herald*, Dec. 28, "Madame Anderson's Plucky Undertaking..."
"All amusements..." *SF Wasp*, July 26, 1879, "Prevention of Cruelty"
Henry Bergh, *Brooklyn Daily Eagle*, Dec 28, 1878, "Madame Anderson Plodding Along..."
"Thank you for your patronage..." *New York Herald*, Dec 28, 1878, under subhead, "She Makes a Speech"

Page 85

"She delivered the speech..." ibid
Admonishes reporter, *New York Herald*, Dec 27, 1878, "The Lady Pedestrian"

Page 86

Campana earned $500 for his Bridgeport victory, *NY Times*, Dec 23, 1878, "The big Walking Match"
Vanderbilt sets up match between O'Leary-Campana, *Brooklyn Daily Eagle*, Dec 27, 1878, "Pedestrian Efforts" p 2
O'Leary assessment of Hughes, *Brooklyn Daily Eagle*, Dec 30, 1878, "O'Leary" p 4
"...completing his stent seems to ..." *NY Times*, Nov 16, 1878, Determined to Outdo O'Leary

Page 87

Walker's appearance described, *NY Times*, Dec 23, 1878, "The Big Walking Match"
O'Leary big early lead, *Brooklyn Daily Eagle*, Dec 27, 1878, "Pedestrian Efforts," p 2
Campana's outfit described, *Brooklyn Daily Eagle*, Dec 30, 1878, "O'Leary, The Easy Way in Which He Won," p 4
Prediction of race end, *Brooklyn Daily Eagle*, Dec 24, 1878, p 2
Looks fagged, *Brooklyn Daily Eagle*, Dec 26, 1878, "O'Leary and Campana" p 4
O'Leary walks with daughter, ibid
O'Leary coasts to victory, *Brooklyn Daily Eagle*, Dec 30, 1878, "O'Leary…" p 4
Praise for Campana, ibid

Page 88

Anderson style vs. O'Leary, *NY Sun*, Dec 25, 1878, "Madame Anderson compared with the Champion Walker"
A number arrived after O'Leary-Campana, *NY Herald*, Dec 28, 1878, "Mme. Anderson's Plucky Undertaking"
Many celebrities came, ibid
Receives gifts, *Brooklyn Daily Eagle*, Dec 30, 1878, "Madame Anderson"
Girl walks with her, ibid
Inside the tent, *NY Sun*, Dec 29, 1878, "The woman on the Track"

Page 89

Mozart Modifications, *Brooklyn Daily Eagle*, Dec 30, 1878, "Madame Anderson"
Will she hold out? *NY Sun*, Dec 29, 1878, "The Woman on the Track"
Finest coaches, ibid
Henry corrects lap counts, *NY Herald*, Dec 28, 1878, "Mme. Anderson's plucky Undertaking"

Page 90

Sunday attendance, *NY Sun*, Dec 30, 1878, "Madame Anderson's Sunday Walk"

Chapter 17

Page 91

Dumps tan-bark on sleeping patron, *NY Herald*, Dec 30, 1878, "Walking After Midnight,"
Sleeping pianist, *NY Sun*, Dec 30, 1878, "Singing While She Walks,"

Page 92

Prank involving mannequin, *NY Herald*, Dec 31, 1878, "Mme. Anderson,"

Page 93

attire described, *NY Sun*, Dec 31, 1878, "Singing While She Walks,"
"few man can keep up with her..." ibid
"Sing a song.." ibid
Brooklyn Fire Dec 5, 1876, Wikipedia
Fire breaks out in Mozart, *NY Sun*, Dec 31, 1878, "Singing While She Walks,"
Ban smoking, ibid
Samuells and Anderson speak, ibid
Sings, "Nil Derperandum," ibid

Chapter 19

Page 111

"I did not think...." *NY Sun*, Jan 2, 1879, "Hard Lines on the Track"
Arrives late on track, ibid
O'Leary's cousin, *NY Sun*, Jan 1, 1879, "Mrs. Anderson's Walk"

Page 112

Looks at Astley Belt, ibid
Astley Belt history, Lucas, John Apostal "Pedestrianism and the Struggle for the
    Astley Belt" www.ultralegends.com
Waiting for 1879, "Mrs. Anderson's Walk," ibid

Page 113

New Year, *NY Sun*, Jan 1, 1879, "Mme. Anderson's Walk"

Page 114

Creeping laps, *NY Sun*, Jan 2, 1879, "Hard Lines on the Track"
Description inside tent, ibid

Chapter 19

Page 116

Anderson's new manager, *Brooklyn Daily Eagle*, Jan 2, 1879, "Madame Anderson
    The Pedestrienne Passing..."

Large numbers of callers, ibid

Page 117

Quartet sang, *NY Sun*, Jan 3, 1879, "Interesting Incidents from the Eighteenth Day…"
Conquering Hero, *NY Sun*, Jan 3, 1879, "Mrs. Anderson's Endurance"
Ladies' Walking Club, *NY Herald*, Jan 4, 1879, "Mme. Anderson," p 6
Commodore Nutt appearance, *NY Sun*, Jan 3, 1879, "Interesting Incidents of 18th Day…"
Mike Henry's sufferings, *Brooklyn Daily Eagle*, Jan 4, 1879, "Madame Anderson, The Pedestrienne Still on the Track…"

Page 118

Henry's days, *Brooklyn Daily Eagle*, Jan 3, 1879, "Mme. Anderson, The Pedestrienne Steadily Toiling…"
Henry ordered home, *NY Herald*, Jan 4, 1879, "Lady Pedestrian…"
Hazelton replaces Henry, ibid
No end to endurance, *Brooklyn Daily Eagle*, Jan 5, 1879, "The Plucky Pedestrienne…"
Go until 1880, ibid

Page 119

Nutrition information from *NY Herald*, Jan 6, 1879 "Madame Anderson's Fare' p 9
Nutrition evaluation courtesy of Jennifer Neily, Registered Dietician
Only 900 more from *NY Sun*, Jan 5, 1879, "Brooklyn's Walking Wonder"

Page 120

Anderson challenge, Mme. Anderson's Fare, ibid
Walked like 7th Regiment, *NY Sun*, Jan 3, 1879, "Interesting Incidents of the Eighteenth Day…"

Page 121

"During the past three weeks…" *Brooklyn Daily Eagle*, Jan 6, 1879, "Weary Hounds…." p 4
"Indian blood in her…" *NY Sun*, Jan 5, 1879, "Brooklyn's Walking Wonder" p 5
Bell lap, *Brooklyn Daily Eagle*, Jan 6, 1879, ibid
Doubts about performance, *NY Tribune*, Jan 7, 1879, "Madame Anderson's Endurance," p 8

Page 122

Mike Henry brief return, *NY Herald,* Jan 8, 1879, "Mme. Anderson," p 10
Admission price cut, *NY Herald,* Jan 9, 1879, "Plucky Pedestrian..."
Cuts laps short, ibid

Page 123

Gifts received, *Brooklyn Daily Eagle,* Jan 10, 1879, "Madame Anderson, The
    Pedestrian Continuing..." p 4
Henry receives cane, *NY Sun,* Jan 6, 1879, "Madame Anderson's Endurance"

Page 124
Col Sinn's Troupe *NY Sun,* Jan 10, 1879, "Yet on the Track"

Chapter 20

Page 126

Eagle slams doubting paper, *Brooklyn Daily Eagle* editorial, Jan 12, 1879
She won't come out again, *NY Sun,* Jan 13, 1879, Mrs. Anderson's Progress
Woman looking for double, ibid

Page 127

"Don't Get Weary," *Brooklyn Daily Eagle,* Jan 13, 1879, "Plucky Pedestrienne
    Near End of Task"
Barnum performer sings 50 verses, ibid
Child burns, *Brooklyn Daily Eagle,* Jan 11, 1879, "Mrs. Nurse's Mistake" p 4;
    death reported Jan 22, 1879, *Brooklyn Daily Eagle,* "Mrs. Nurse's Folly"
Listens to child sing, *Brooklyn Daily Eagle,* Jan 13, 1879, "Plucky Pedestrian Near
    End of Task,"
"Sea of heads," *NY Herald,* Jan 14, 1879, "Mme. Anderson's Success,"
Dresses as Goddess of Liberty, *NY Sun,* Jan 14, 1878, "Mrs. Anderson's Victory"

Page 128

Anderson finishes the race, *NY Herald,* Jan 14, 1879, "Mme. Anderson's Suc-
    cess," p 8; Jan 14, 1879, *NY Sun,* Mrs. Anderson's Victory, *Brooklyn Daily
    Eagle,* Jan 14, 1879, "Testimonial to Pluck and Endurance," "Victorious"

Page 131

Anderson recovery, *Brooklyn Daily Eagle,* Jan 14, 1879, "Recuperating"

Chapter 21

Page 133

Crawford badly beats Marshall, *Washington Post*, Jan 10, 1879, "Crawford the Champion"
Marshall walking history, *Washington Post*, Jan 21, 1879, "Madame Anderson's Rival," p 1

Page 135

Reporter interview with May Marshall, *Washington Post*, Jan 23, 1879, "Sure of Success," p 1
Folly Theatre track, *Chicago Daily News*, Jan 25, 1879, "Sporting Matters" p 1
Dr. Mary Walker and visitors, *Washington Post*, Jan 27, 1879, "Still on the Sawdust," p 1

Page 136

LaChapelle visitors, *Chicago Daily News*, Jan 30, 1879, "Sporting Matters," p 1
Marshall reaches halfway, *Washington Post*, Feb 4, 1879, "Her Task Half Done," p 1
Marshall interview, ibid

Page 137

LaChapelle reaches 900 quarters, *Chicago Daily News*, Feb 4, 1879, "Sporting Matters," p 1
Marshall weary, *Washington Post*, Feb 6, 1879, "Tug of War in Miss May Marshall's Walk," p 1
LaChapelle completes number 1,000, *Chicago Daily News*, Feb 5, 1879, "Sporting Matters," p 4
Marshall completes 1,467 *Washington Post*, Feb 6, 1879, "Tug of War..." ibid
LaChapelle 1,261/Marshall 1,741 *Chicago Inter-Ocean*, Feb 8, 1879, "Pedestrianism" p 4
Watchers arrive, *Chicago Tribune*, Feb 8, 1879, "Pedestrianism"
Marshall reaches 2,000, *Washington Post*, Feb 11, 1879, "Two Thousand Quarters," p 1

Page 138

Reduced admittance fees, ibid
LaChapelle totals 1,500, *Chicago Daily News*, Feb 10, 1879, "Sporting Matters"
Marshall totals 2,042, *Washington Post*, Feb 11, 1879, "Two Thousand Quarters" p 1

Watchers remain, *Chicago Tribune*, Feb 12, 1879, "Pedestrianism"

Page 139

LaChapelle wakes up patron, *Chicago Inter-Ocean*, Feb 12, 1879, "Exilda
    LaChapelle," p 2
LaChapelle weakens, *Chicago Daily News*, Feb 13, 1879, "Sporting Matters"
Anderson appears, *Chicago Daily News*, Feb 14, 1879, "Sporting Matters"
LaChapelle birthday, *Chicago Inter-Ocean*, Feb 15, 1879, "Pedestrianism,
    Madame Anderson," p 2
Marshall finishes walk, *Washington Post*, Feb 18, 1879, "May Marshall's Great
    Walk"

Page 140

Post-walk, *Washington Post*, Feb 19, 1879, "May Marshall's Feat"
Performance beats Anderson's ibid

Page 141

Marshall performance certified, ibid
2,800 quarter miles, ibid
LaChapelle interview, *Chicago Inter-Ocean*, Feb 20, 1879, "Exilda LaChapelle," p
    8
Undercard races, ibid

Page 142

Trouble walking *Chicago Inter-Ocean*, Feb 21, 1879, "Sporting Matters," p 1
Completes 2,509, *Chicago Tribune*, Feb 21, 1879, "Sporting; Pedestrianism"
2,656; *Chicago Tribune*, Feb 23, 1879, "Mme. LaChapelle Successfully Com-
    pleted Her Walk
Finishes race, ibid

Page 143

Will go 300 more quarters, ibid
Receives gifts and a medal, ibid

Chapter 22

Page 145

"Bartell's off," *NY Herald*, Feb 3, 1879, "Coming Walking Matches
Bartell's failure, ibid

Page 146

Sell copies, "Aug 1885, "A Profane View of the Sanctum ; North America
   Review"
Bartell replaced, *NY Herald*, Feb 4, 1879, "Pedestrianism, Why Did Miss Bartell
   Fail?" p 5
Abbott walks, *NY Herald*, Feb 6, 1879, "Pedestrianism, Miss Reynolds off the
   track" p 6
Bartell returns, *NY Herald*, Feb13, 1879, "Miss Bartell's Walk" p 5
More tracks at Brewster, *NY Times*, Feb 16, 1879, "Walking in Six Cities"
NY Times, Feb 14, 1879, "Pedestrianism Gone Mad"
NY Times, Feb 16, 1879, "Walking in Six Cities"
Burns and Franklin, ibid
Women arrested, *NY Herald*, March 1, 1879, "Pedestrian Feats," p 10

Page 147

Franklin moves to Brewster, ibid
May Bell Sherman, *NY Times*, Feb 24, 1879, "Female Pedestrian Fever"
Fannie Edwards, *NY Clipper*, March 1, 1879, "the Female Pedalists," p 387
Women Fail at Sulzer Park, *NY Herald*, March 11, "An Interesting Match..." p 3
Miss Sinclair, *Brooklyn Daily Eagle*, Feb 25, 1879, "Failed. Miss Jennie Sinclair
   Faints on the Track," p 4; March 27, 1879, *Brooklyn Daily Eagle*, "Miss Sin-
   clair's Failure"

Page 148

Ad for walk, *Brooklyn Daily Eagle*, March 2, 1879, p 3
Sermon by Steele, *Brooklyn Daily Eagle*, March 17, 1879, "Abuse of Pedestrian-
   ism," p 2;
Thompson sermon, *NY Herald*, March 17, 1879, "Lessons of the Great Walk"
Brooklyn Sunday walks, *Brooklyn Daily Eagle*, March 22, 1879, "Municipal. Is
   Sunday Pedestrianism Unlawful?" p 4
Legality of Sunday walking, *NY Times*, March 24, 1879, "Stopping Sunday
   Walks," p 8

Page 149

Anderson in Pittsburgh, *Pittsburgh Gazette*, Feb 11, 1879, "Madame Anderson"
Dragging her feet, *Chicago Inter-Ocean*, March 10, 1879, "Mme. Anderson," p 5
She should leave profession, *Chicago Inter-Ocean*, March 13, 1879, "Mme.
   Anderson's Walk," p 5
Officials try and remove her, *Chicago Inter-Ocean*, March 14, 1879, "Madame
   Anderson," p 8

Page 150

Doctor examines her, ibid
Webb alleges LaChapelle fraud, ibid
24,000 tickets sold, *Chicago Inter-Ocean*, March 15, 1879, "Madame Anderson,
   yesterday at the Exposition," p 3
Anderson leaves track, *Chicago Inter-Ocean*, March 17, 1879, "Mme. Anderson,"
   p 3
Anderson completes walk, *Chicago Inter-Ocean*, March 18, 1879, "Madame
   Anderson, Her Long Walk..." p 3
Other walks, *Chicago Inter-Ocean*, March 19, 1879, "The Pedestrian Craze"

Page 151

Breaks up with manager, *Chicago Inter-Ocean*, March 24, 1879, "Pedestrianism"

Chapter 23

Page 152

Program in May Marshall scrapbook courtesy of her great-granddaughters,
   Gerry and Charlotte Curtis
Money deposited, *National Police Gazette*, April 12, 1879, "The Pretty Pedestri-
   ans"

Page 153

Walton Belt value, *NY Herald*, March 23, 1879, "Another Six-Day Tournament,"
   p 8
Nothing extraordinary, *NY Herald*, March 27, 1879, "The Women's Walk at
   Gilmore's," p 8
Contestants described, *National Police Gazette*, April 12, 1879, "Pretty Pedestrians"
Cameron withdraws, *NY Herald*, March 28, 1879, "The Walk at Gilmore's," p 8

Page 154

LaChapelle leads, ibid
Four others drop out, *National Police Gazette*, April 12, 1879, "Pretty Pedestri-
   ans"
LaChapelle husband flirts, *NY Times*, April 1, 1879, "The Women's Walking
   Match"
LaChepelle withdraws, *NY Herald*, April 1, 1879, "The Walking Women," p 5

Page 155

Second half of walk, *NY Herald*, March 31, 1879, "The Walk at Gilmore's"

Would take $1,000, *NY Herald*, April 1, 1879, "The Walking Women," p 5

Page 157

Von Berg lead, *NY Herald*, March 31, 1879, "Pedestrianism," p 7
Von Klamach story, *NY Times*, , April 1, 1879, "The Women's Walking Match"
Farrand and Rich withdraw, *NY Herald*, April 1, 1879, "The Walking Women," p
    5

Page 158

Rich story, ibid
Clair story, *NY Herald*, April 2, 1879, "The Walking Women, Two More With-
    drawals..." p 5

Page 159

Edwards/Leonardson, *NY Herald*, March 31, 1879, "Cheap Enough..."
Cushing leaves track, *NY Herald*, April 2, 1879, "The Walking Women..." p 5

Page 160

Wallace/Kilbury battle, ibid
Wallace abuse, *NY Times*, April 3, 1879, "The Cruel Tramp Ended"
Walkers finish together, ibid
Controversy w/Von Berg entry fee, ibid

Chapter 24

Page 162

Dr. Benjamin Lee, *NY Times*, May 14, 1879, "The Women's Walk"
Philadelphia Med. Society, ibid.
NYT April 3, 1879, ibid
NYT, May 4, 1879, "The Walking Torture"
LaChapelle divorce, *Oshkosh Daily Northwestern*, April 28, 1879, "Persons and
    Things"
Anderson lawsuit, *NY Clipper*, May 24, 1878

Women's walking can only go so far, *NY Times*, May 4, 1879, "The Walking Tor-
    ture"
Medical community questions walking, *NY Herald*, March 30, 1879, "Athleti-
    cism and Cruelty"

Page 163

Poem, *New York Sportsman*, March 29, 1879, "The Walking Mania"
Boy walks 24 miles, *NY Herald*, March 31, 1879, "Juvenile Pedestrians"
Banning of dangerous entertainment, *NY Times*, May 14, 1879, "The Women's
    Walk"

Page 164

Mme. Andrews, *NY Clipper*, April 12, 1879

Rockwell, *Brooklyn Daily Eagle*, April 14, 1879, Miss Rockwell's Feat
Marshall, *Brooklyn Daily Eagle*, April 16, 1879, Miss Marshall at Last Stops Walking

Page 165

San Francisco history, Wikipedia.org
From Curtis family scrapbook, Marshall earned $25,000 before 1879, when she
    picked up $5,000 for the 4,047/4,047 walk in Brooklyn

Page 167

Cotton quote, *San Francisco Chronicle*, May 27, 1879, "The Walking Match," p 3
Track described, *SF Chronicle*, May 24, 1879, "The Walking Match," p 3
First race, ibid

Page 168

6,000 candles, *CA Alta*, May 24, 1879, "The Great Walking Match"
Ad for admission, *CA Alta*, May 27, 1879
Armstrong to walk, *SF Chronicle*, May 27, 1879, "The Walking Match," p 3
Women pay, ibid
Women appearance, *SF Chronicle*, May 25, 1879, "The Pedestriennes" p 4
Von Berg appearance, *SF Chronicle*, May 26, 1879, "The "Walking Match," p 3

Page 169

Prima donnas, *SF Chronicle*, May 27, 1879, "The Walking Match," p 3
LaChapelle shoes, *SF Chronicle*, July 21, 1879, "Twinkling Heels,"
LaChapelle jokes, *SF Chronicle*, June 2, 1879, "The Four Walkers," p 3
Gifts received, *SF Chronicle*, June 4, 1879, "The Walkers," p 4
Mt. Etna, *SF Chronicle*, June 11, 1879, "The Walking Women,"
Obstructions found on track, *CA Alta*, May 28, 1879, "Persevering Pedestri-
    ennes" p 4; *SF Chronicle*, May 28, 1879, "Three Lady Walkers" *SF Chronicle*,
    June 8, 1879, "the Walking Match," p 3; *SF Examiner*, May 28, 1879,
    "Women Walkers…"

Edwards assisted, *SF Chronicle*, May 31, 1879, "The Ladies' Laps," p 3

Page 170

LaChapelle rips rival, *SF Chronicle*, June 8, 1879, "Three Lady Walkers," p 1
Schooners, *SF Chronicle*, July 11, 1879, "The "Walking Women," p 4
Edwards scandal revealed, *SF Chronicle*, June 15, 1879, "Platt's Hall Pacers"
Exilderated, June 13, 1879, *SF Chronicle*, "The Pedestrians," p 3
Armstrong weight loss. June 23, 1879, *SF Chronicle*, "Plodding Away," p 3
Runs into LaChapelle, June 17, 1879, *SF Chronicle*, "Accident to Exilda," p 3
LaChapelle breaks two min. *SF Chronicle*, June 20, 1879, "The Four Footers," p
  1

Page 171

Emperor Norton, *SF Examiner*, June 13, 1879, "The Lady Walkers"
Norton bio, www.zpub.com/sf/history/nort.html
Piano destruction, *SF Chronicle*, June 15, 1879, "Platt's Hall Racers,"
Flower showers, *SF Chronicle*, June 16, 1879, "The Walking Match," p 3

Page 172

Packed house, *CA Alta*, June 25, 1879, "3,000 quarters," p 1
LaChapelle fast time, ibid

Page 173

Armstrong victory, *CA Alta*, June 26, 1879, "1,200 miles," p 1-5
Women finish, *SF Chronicle*, June 27, 1879, "The Agony Over," p 2
Race format, *NY Clipper*, June 14, 1879, p 93

Walkers introduced, *CA Alta*, July 17, 1879 "Pavilion Belles," p 1
Donley record, ibid
Bet LaChapelle beats Frank, *SF Chronicle*, July 18, 1879, "Pretty Tramps,"
Ibid, "Foiled Blackmailers"

Page 176

Shouts of Von Berg, *CA Alta*, July 17, 1879, "Pavilion Belles," p 1
Start of race, *CA Alta*, July 17, 1879, ibid; *SF Chronicle*, July 18, 1879, "Pretty
  Tramps," *SF Examiner*, July 17, 1879, "The Diamond Belt"
Locke Letter, *SF Chronicle*, July 19, 1879, "The Blackmailers"
Cotton Attacked, *SF Examiner*, July 19, 1879, "…Attack on Manager Cotton";
  July 19, 1879, *CA Alta*, "Brutal Attack on Manager Cotton," p 1-3; , *CA Alta*,
  July 20, 1879, "Arrests for Pavilion Affair"

Page 178

Wordless War, *SF Chronicle*, July 19, 1879, "The Pavilion Path"
Edwards crying, *SF Examiner*, July 21, 1879, "The Ladies' Laps…Unfair Charge
    from the Fair Fannie…"
LaChapelle interview, *SF Chronicle*, July 20, 1879, "Pretty Pilgrims"

Page 179

Von Berg afraid, ibid
Race ends, *CA Alta*, July 23, 1879, "The Ladies Rest…" p 1-4; *SF Chronicle*, July
    23, 1879, The Ladies Rest,"; *SF Examiner*, July 23, 1879, "The Ladies Belt"
400 miles, *SF Chronicle*, July 24, 1879, "After the Battle"
Von Berg victory, *CA Alta*, Aug 8, 1879, "Von Berg and Tourtellott," p 1-4
16 miles in one hour, *SF Newsletter* and *CA Advertiser*, Aug 16, 1879, "Pedestri-
    anism," p 19

Page 180

The Edwards' leave CA, *NY Clipper*, Sept 20, 1879

Page 181

LaChapelle interview, *SF Chronicle*, , Sept 10, 1879, "Before the Battle," p 2
Von Berg interview, ibid

Page 182

Race start, *SF Chronicle*, Sept 11, 1879, "The Women's Walk"; Sept 11, 1879, *SF
    Examiner*, "The Six-Day Match…"; *CA Alta*, Sept 11, 1879, "The Walking
    Mania," p 1-3
La Chapelle builds lead, *SF Chronicle*, Sept 12, 1879, "The Pedestrians
    Progress…"

Page 183

New York Newsboy, *SF Chronicle*, Sept 13, 1879, "The Pedestriennes" Sept 14,
    1879, *SF Chronicle*, "Petticoat Pedestrianism," *SF Chronicle*, Sept 16, 1879,
    "The Walkers"
LaChapelle Victory, *CA Alta*, Sept 17, 1879, "Ladies' Walking Match," p 1-5;
    Sept 17, 1879, *SF Chronicle*; "LaChapelle Wins" *SF Examiner*, July 18, 1879,
    "The Walking Match"
LaChapelle winnings, *Oshkosh Daily Northwestern*, Nov 11, 1879, "LaChapelle"
Boys vanish, *SF Newsletter and CA Advertiser*, July 19, 1879, "Neighborhood
    Boys Catch Pedestrian Fever"
LaChapelle not walking, *Oshkosh Daily Northwestern*, Nov 11, 1879 "LaChapelle"

Page 184

Beginning of race, *CA Alta*, Oct 8, 1879, "Ladies' Walking Match"; *SF Examiner*, Oct 9, 1879, "Place Aux Dames,"; *SF Chronicle*, Oct 9, 1879, "Sawdust Satellites"
Early departures, *SF Chronicle*, Oct 10, 1879, "Cinder Sparks"
Better than men, *SF Chronicle*, Oct 11, 1879, "Pedal Performers"

Page 185

Further withdrawals, *SF Chronicle*, Oct 12, 1879, "The Jealous Joust"
Sherman background, *SF Chronicle*, Oct 13, 1879, "The Clever Sherman's Artfulness Unfolds Itself"
Von Berg leaves, *SF Chronicle*, Oct 14, 1879, "Striding to Success…"
Duped backers, ibid
Sherman victory, *CA Alta*, Oct 15, 1879, "Boston Bodie…" p 1-3; Oct 15, 1879, *SF Chronicle*, "Sherman's March Scores 337 Miles," *SF Examiner*, Oct 15, 1879, "Finishing Touches…"

Page 186

Cotton leaves for New York, *NY Clipper*, Oct 4, 1879
Rose reputation, *CA Alta*, May 2, 1880, "The Ladies' Walk…" p 1
Rose takes over, *NY Clipper*, Jan 24, 1880, "Madame LaChapelle
Cotton suicide, (SF) *Daily Evening Bulletin*, March 6, 1880, "Melancholy Self-Destruction"

Chapter 28

Page 189

Attendance, *NY Daily Tribune*, Dec 15, 1879, "A Six Days' Walk for Women"
Field described, ibid; *NY Sun*, Dec 16, 1879, "Already Tired and Worn"
Accommodations, ibid
Start of race, ibid
John Dermody story, *NY Herald*, Dec 12, 1879, "A Phenomenal Pedestrian…"; *National Police Gazette*, Dec 12, 1879, "Bound to be a Walkist"
Marshall kicked out, *NY Sun*, Dec 17, 1879, "The Women's Footrace"

Page 191

Marshall claims Anderson given laps, ibid
Howard Wins, *NY Daily Tribune*, Dec 21, 1879, "Miss Howard Wins the Belt"; *NY Sun*, Dec 21, 1879, "Tired Women at Rest,"

Page 192

<u>Running Through the Ages</u>, Sears, Ed

Chapter 29

Page 193

Race day, *CA Alta*, May 5, 1880, "The Great Race..." *SF Chronicle*, May 6, 1880, "A Six-Day Contest..."

Page 194

Men's race, *CA Alta*, ibid
Other attractions at Mechanics' *CA Alta*, May 7, 1880, "Excellent Walking..."
Women prepare, *SF Chronicle*, May 6, 1880, "A Six-Day Contest..."

Page 195

Scores after 24 hours, *SF Chronicle*, May 7, 1880, "Belles of the Belt..."
65 miles a day, *SF Chronicle*, May 8, 1880, "Track Trotters..."
Scores after two days, ibid

Page 196

Howard's small lead, *SF Chronicle*, May 9, 1880, "The Walkers..."
"Toss of a penny," *CA Alta*, May 9, 1880, "An Exciting Race" p 1
"Exciting Struggle," *SF Chronicle*, May 10, 1880, Headline
450 miles, *SF Chronicle*, May 10, 1880, "Pavilion Pilgrims"
"run feet off," ibid
Von Berg and others leave, ibid
Von Berg heart not in it, *SF Chronicle*, May 9, 1880, "The Walkers..."
Rose challenge for Howard, ibid

Page 197

Howard cries to official, *SF Chronicle*, May 10, 1880, "Straining and Striving..."
Howard's faux rest, *CA Alta*, May 11, 1880, "Remarkable Records," p 1
Attendance, *CA Alta*, May 12, 1880, "Howard's Belt," p 1-5
Race finish, *CA Alta*, May 12, 1880; ibid; *SF Chronicle*, May 12, 1880, "The Finish; Howard Still Carries..."

Page 198

Awards, *SF Chronicle*, May 12, 1880, ibid
Masked Ball, *SF Chronicle*, May 13, 1880, "The Masked Ball,"

Chapter 30

Page 200

100- hour race, *SF Chronicle*, July 11, 1880, "Mechanics' Pavilion," p 1; *CA Alta*,
    July 11, 1880, "100 Hours." P 1-4
Shorter races, *CA Alta*, ibid

Page 201

Children's Carnival, *SF Chronicle*, July 17, 1880, "Puny Pedestrians"
Go As I Please, *CA Alta*, July 18, 1880 "Women's Wily Ways"
Annoying Language, *SF Chronicle*, July 18, 1880, "Pedestrian Final"
Only four of nine finished, ibid
Aulbach reprimands, ibid
Pedestriennes awards, ibid

Page 202

Howard's victory arranged, *SF Examiner*, May 12, 1880, "The Walking Match…"

Page 203

Announcement, *SF Chronicle*, Jan 26, 1881, p 4
Payouts, *CA Alta*, Jan 27, 1881, "Go As You Please…"
Walkers comments, *SF Chronicle*, Jan 27, 1881, "A Sawdust Quartet" p 3
The start, *CA Alta*, Jan 27, 1881, ibid; *SF Chronicle*, Jan 27, 1881, ibid; *SF Examiner*, Jan 27, 1881, "The Walking Match"
Sherman stomach, *SF Examiner*, Jan 31, 1881, "Sherman's Stomach…"

Page 204

Songs played, *SF Examiner*, Jan 29, 1881, "Sherman Spurred by the Rain…"
Howard retakes lead, *SF Examiner*, Jan 30, 1881, "Willing Walkers"
Scores after five days, *SF Chronicle*, Feb 1, 1881, "The Walking Match…"
Race finish, *CA Alta*, Feb 2, 1881, "Pedestriennes' Match Ended"; *SF Chronicle*,
    Feb 2, 1881, "Amy Wins" p 2; *SF Examiner*, Feb 2, 1881, "Close of the Match"

Page 205

Howard handicap, *SF Chronicle*, May 22, 1881, "the Female Walkers,"; *SF Examiner*, May 23, 1881, "Amiable Amblers"
Other attractions, *SF Chronicle*, May 24, 1881, "The Pavilion Pedestriennes"; *SF Chronicle*, May 25, 1881, "The Female Walkers"; *SF Chronicle*, May 27, 1881, "Pavilion Pastimes"

Money gone, *SF Examiner*, May 27, 1881, "Walking Match Troubles,"; *SF Examiner*, May 28, 1881, "Close of the Walk"

Epilogue
Page 207

Cushing race, *NY Clipper*, May 29, 1880
Anderson races:
April 20-May 12, 23 day walk in Cincinnati, *Cincinnati Enquirer*
June 6, 1879 Louisville, KY June 7, 1879 *Louisville Courier*
2,028 quarter miles in 2,028 quarter miles in Detroit, August 12, 1879, *Detroit Evening News*
August, 1879, Buffalo, NY 2,052 quarter miles in 2,052 quarter hours, "Pedestriennes: Newsworthy but Controversial Women in Sporting Entertainment," Dahn Shaulis, page 50
Completes 4,236 quarter miles in 4,236 quarter hours Tivoli (NY), *NY Clipper*, Oct 25, 1879
Last appearance, May 2, 1880 in Baltimore, *NY Clipper*, May 1, 1880

Amelia Samuells' committed, *NY Sun*, March 12, 1879, "Mrs. Samuells Released"
Death of Amelia Samuells, *NY Times*, Feb 3, 1883
Samuells manages men's race, *NY Times*, June 13, 1899, "Walking Match End"
Samuells' death, *Brooklyn Daily Eagle*, Oct 22, 1913, "Capt Samuells, of Show Fame, Buried"

Page 208

O'Leary, Matthew Algeo, <u>Pedestrianism, When Watching People Walk was America's Favorite Spectator</u> Sport, pp 234-236; 242
Death of DeRose, *The Call*, April 7, 1891, "LaChapelle Killed," front page
Mike Henry obituary, *Brooklyn Daily Eagle*, May 10, 1889, "Mike Henry, Death of the Well-Known Sporting Man"
Howard back on stage, *Logansport (IN) Chronicle*, March 8, 1884, "Athletic"
Howard death, *NY Clipper*, Oct 31, 1885, p 521
Marshall obituary, courtesy of Gerry and Charlotte Curtis scrapbook, *Detroit News 1911*

Page 209

Von Hillern wins ribbons, *Winchester (VA) Star*, August 31, 1923, "Miss Von HIllern Wins Three Prizes"
Von Hillern obituary, *Winchester (VA) Star*, Sept 20, 1939, "Death Comes at Age of 86," p 2 col. 7
William Gale Interview, *Cincinnati Commercial Appeal*, April 15, 1888, "William Gale"

Bibliography

Algeo, Matthew. *Pedestrianism: When Watching People Walk was America's Favorite Spectator Sport.* Chicago Review Press, 2014.

Barnett, David. thetelegraph&argus.co.uk. Remember When? "Long Walk Put Women on the Map," May 29, 2009

Booth, Michael. *Theatre in the Victorian Age.* Cambridge University Press, 1991

Cumming, John. *Runners and Walkers: A 19th Century Chronicle.* Chicago: Regnery Gateway, 1981

Dutton, TD. *The Strand Magazine.* "Famous Walkers of the Past," July, 1903

Gillon, JK. "Robert Barclay Allardice: The Celebrated Pedestrian." http://gillonj.tripod.com/thecelebratedpedestrian/.

Gipe George. *Sports Illustrated.* "Mary Marshall was Strides Ahead of the Times When She Beat a Man," Oct. 24, 1977.

Goulding, John. *The Amateur's Guide: or, Training Made Easy, For Modern Outdoor Amusements.* Peck and Snyder. New York, 1879

James, Ed. *Practical Training for Running, Walking, Rowing, Wrestling, Boxing, Jumping, and All Kinds of Athletic Feats.* Ed James, 88 and 90 Centre St. New York, 1877

Lucas, John. www.ultralegends.com. "Pedestrianism and the Struggle for the Astley Belt"

Powell, Kerry. *Women in Victorian Theatre.* Cambridge University Press, 2007.

Quixote, Vegas (Dahn Shaulis). *Marathon and Beyond,* "The Untimely Disappearance of Madame Anderson." Nov/Dec 2000, p. 88

Radford, Peter. *Canadian History Journal of Sport.* Vol. 25 Issue 1, May 1994,

Radford, Peter. theguardian.com. Newmarket's Greatest Stayer," August 23, 2001

Sears, Ed. *Running Through the Ages.* McFarland, Inc. 2002

Shaulis, Dahn, "Pedestriennes: Newsworthy but Controversial Women in Sporting Entertainment." http://library.la84.org/SportsLibrary/JSH/JSH1999/JSH2601/jsh2601c.pdf, 1999

Stephens, John Russell. *The Profession of the Playwright: British Theatre, 1800-1900.* Cambridge University Press, 2006.

Thom, Walter. *Pedestrianism; Or an Account of the Performances of Celebrated Pedestrians During the Last and Present Century.* Aberdeen: D. Chalmers and Company, 1813.

CPSIA information can be obtained at www.ICGtesting.com
Printed in the USA
LVOW12*1355041114

411513LV00001BA/1/P